The Brooklyn Heights Sublet

By Jonah Cohen

Library of Congress Registration Number TXu 1-900-508

ISBN: 978-0-578-12589-3

Preface

It was not at first the intention of this author to write a book. It actually developed over a period of several years as a result of a series of communications by written letter (in the days when people still wrote letters) with a friend and former college roommate from the University of Miami. At first, the letters were really lots of now seemingly mundane stuff - mostly about jobs, politics, career advancement (or regression) - a promotion here, an award there, a job change disaster, a resurrection, more promotions and awards - in retrospect, all pretty boring.

But the letters began to take on whole new character when I found myself in the so called "illegal subletting" business. The letters I wrote to my friend began to take on the shape of chapters in a book - the subletting disaster itself, the arrival of the tenant from Hell, his discovery by a heartless and ruthless landlord - and the cruel and frightening introduction to the world of courts, lawyers, sheriffs and judges. It was also an introduction to the sub-world of my sub-tenant - a world of bars, motorcycles, life on the edge, and cash-off-the-books "jobs." My friend, a practicing attorney, had the good sense not to offer advice for my special problem, but became an avid, yet disinterested reader of my "chapters," which gave the author the *raison d'etre* to continue, and so the chapters kept coming.

The Brooklyn Heights Sublet is the true story of a sublet that went awry, a seven year trek through the streets, sewers, bars, buildings, and courtrooms of the City of New York. What had begun as a quest for the simple restoration of lost rent had evolved into something far more complex - something far nobler. Was it just the money? Or was it revenge? Was it to lay claim to my tenant's only presumed asset - a classic, special edition, high powered motorcycle - to perhaps satisfy the deprivation of a young child, or even a young adult? Or was it the attainment of justice - absolute and complete justice despite the challenges of an unjust system in an unjust world?

I should also mention that it was with the assistance of a special NYC Deputy Sheriff who took a personal interest in my case in order to help bring about the just conclusion that I so desperately sought for myself, and for my book. Also, I would like to offer a special thanks to my friend Joe who gave me the encouragement and support to put my story into print.

Except for certain passages, which have been written in italics, <u>The</u> <u>Brooklyn</u> <u>Heights</u> <u>Sublet</u> is entirely true. Of course, "the names have been changed to protect the innocent," as they say. The italicized passages either represent something in the distant past, the real dreams of the author, or are pure fiction, written to give the story connectivity and to provide entertainment to the reader - they might have happened in some cases, but in others, probably didn't. The author has attempted to take a serious subject, lived and suffered through personal experience, and present it all in a light, humorous, and enjoyable manner. Here then is my story.

The Author

I. IN THE BEGINNING

The decrepit, old elevator screeched, squealed, and rattled past the third floor, then the second, and then, after bouncing once or twice, came to an uncertain stop at the lobby. And after a few long and suspenseful seconds, the automatic gate slowly opened with more squeaks, scrapes, and rattles, and then finally stopped in sudden silence.

The little boy's father pushed the elevator door open, and father and son walked together, hand in hand through the spacious, echoing lobby of the old Brooklyn apartment house, through the wrought iron outside door, and onto the sidewalk.

"Daddy! Daddy! My motorcycle!"

The fourth floor apartment window flew open suddenly. It was the little boy's Aunt Janie.

"I have it. I'll toss it out to you. Catch it!"

She quickly placed the toy motorcycle into a paper bag and tossed it out the window, but the bag caught the end of the fire escape, and its well aimed trajectory was tragically interrupted. The little toy, with both rider and motorcycle, found itself thrust into a dizzying Valkyrian ride until finally crashing onto the sidewalk. The front wheel went rolling off into a nearby sewer. The remaining plastic parts of white, gold, and black lay in a hopeless wreck strewn across the sidewalk. The rider lay on its back with a broken right arm.

The little boy, in tears, cried out.

*"Daddy - my motorcycle! MY MOTORCYCLE! I
WANT MY MOTORCYCLE!!!"*

In the beginning, it was a small Dutch colony across
the East River from New Amsterdam. It was where George
Washington retreated from the British in the Battle of Long
Island. It was New York's first suburb, attracting the super
rich from congested, overcrowded Manhattan. They built
stately three or more story brownstone mansions for
themselves, their families, and their guests and servants. The
area fell on hard times during the Great Depression, and the
stately brownstones were converted into rooming houses.
Dormers or an additional floor were sometimes added.
Later, they were again converted into apartments, and then
the apartments were subdivided into more, but smaller
apartments. A renaissance began to take place in the late
'70's and '80's. Artists, writers, and others moved in and it
again became a trendy, up-and-coming area. It was
Brooklyn's Greenwich Village. It was called Breukleen in
Dutch, broken land; and in English, the place became known
as Brooklyn Heights, or simply, The Heights.

II. THE APARTMENT

I moved to Brooklyn Heights in the spring of '77. I had just accepted a job at the Naval Support Activity on the site of the old and defunct Brooklyn Navy Yard. It was one of those jobs between real jobs - just something to bring in some income, and to accumulate time-in-service, until a real job would come along.

"The Heights" seemed like the perfect place, and it was only a mile or two from the job. It was an exciting neighborhood of brownstones and row houses, older and newer apartment buildings, restaurants and cafes, bars, boutiques, and book stores. The streets had cute sounding names like Orange, Pineapple, and Cranberry. There was also Love Lane, and of course, the main drag - Montague Street. Mine was Clark Street.

Finding an apartment in New York is never easy, but the Heights was especially difficult. There were basically three ways to get a reasonably priced apartment. The first way was through the real estate brokers. The brokers, being intimately connected with the landlords, had The Heights all sewed up. You almost always had to use them, even if you were lucky enough to find the apartment on your own. It was more like a bribe than a fee, but that's the way it was. Get a broker, preferably several, get lucky, and pay the "fee." The second way was to "make friends" with the supers via a $50 or $100 tip, but making friends is hard. The third way was to find a sublet … legal or otherwise.

I used a broker. It was an old apartment building that was constructed maybe in the late '20's. When new, it must have been an architectural marvel with its brilliant white brick and finely patterned metal work at the roof. But now the brick was a rust stained dirty gray; the metal work was an ugly band of rusted sheet metal hanging precariously at the top of the roof and threatening to fall to the sidewalk at any time. Old rusted fire escapes contributed to the hazard. Only by landlord or lawyer luck was nobody ever killed or injured. The original windows had been replaced with slatted type Jalousie windows in an unfortunate modernization attempt during the '50's. But now some of the slats were missing, having already fallen and smashed onto the sidewalk. In all, the building was in a state of serious disrepair, a horror of neglect, and a hazard to anyone who would venture to come near it, let alone live in it. Nor was the building located in the more fashionable parts of the Heights - it was on run-down Clark Street, sharing as its neighbor, the dilapidated St. George Hotel, with its odd assortment of transient residents. And then there were the homeless who made their home on Clark Street, near the St. George.

The apartment itself was a Spartan 400 square foot studio on the first floor. It had a long narrow foyer, a kitchenette, a bathroom, and a living room, which was really an everything room. Two large windows, one with Jalousies, faced the street. It was rent stabilized and went for $225.06 a month. I wasn't overjoyed with it, but it was cheap, it was in The Heights proper, and I had to compare it with what I had already seen. There was that old, musty five floor walk-up, and I wondered how I would carry my couch or even my bicycle up to the fifth floor. There was that broom closet apartment on the top floor of a brownstone on Remsen Street that somehow was mysteriously always for rent. There was that nice, cozy two room on Hicks Street with the sconce lighting and stucco walls for $181.00. That one went to someone else while I foolishly took the extra day to "think about it." There was that rent stabilized apartment on State Street with the cute corner fireplace. The apartment was rent stabilized, but the unmetered electricity furnished by the landlord wasn't. And there was that viewless, dark dungeon apartment on Pineapple, whose only window opened onto a brick wall, so close, you could reach out and touch it. And so, now there was Clark Street.

"I'll take it!"

It wasn't really such a bad apartment compared to some of the others, and I quickly adapted myself to it. It was only a few short blocks from the Promenade with its breathtaking, panoramic views of lower Manhattan, the Statue of Liberty, the World Trade Center, and the Brooklyn Bridge. And it wasn't too far from Montague Street with its shops, restaurants, and cafes.

My neighbors were friendly enough, but kept pretty much to themselves. There was the homosexual school teacher, Jack, with his strange and sometimes violent relationships, and problems with alcohol. (The apartment walls were thin.) But usually, whenever I saw him, he was just a nice, friendly guy. Then there was Steve, opposite him, who played some pretty good Billy Joel tunes on his piano. And lastly, there was sweet, elderly Mrs. O'Malley across the hall. The superintendent of the building had his apartment in the basement. He was a character that I had to learn to deal with - mainly avoid, if at all possible. John Cashman was a black man in his late sixties with graying hair. I'm not sure if that was his real name, or if they called him that because of his fondness for tips. But usually, we just called him "Johnnie." Johnnie was the man in charge. If you needed something, you went to Johnnie.

I remember being awakened early on a Sunday morning by Johnnie's thunderous voice reverberating endlessly throughout the apartment halls. It seems that one hapless young woman, apparently an apartment hunter, had stumbled into the wrong building. I really felt sorry for her, but those were the breaks.

"Hey! I'm de boss o' dis buildin' an' NO! I AIN'T GOT NO STUDIO APARTMENT TO RENT!"

As a precondition for accepting the apartment, the landlord had agreed to refinish the floor and to fix a broken window. The floor was refinished, and the window pane was replaced, but Johnnie cracked it again while cleaning it with his ammonia. Johnnie was almost as fond of his ammonia as he was of his tips. I didn't want to bother him unnecessarily, but the broken window annoyed me, and the repair was in the landlord-tenant agreement, a contract so to speak. And so, as politely as I knew how, I again asked Johnnie to please fix the window. The response was as expected.

"Hey, when it's really busted, den I'll go an' fix it!"

Needless to say, it never got fixed. I always wanted to throw a shoe through it and really "bust" it, but I never did.

Johnnie showed up unexpectedly a day or two later with some Venetian blinds for the windows, but I had already bought two nice, new bamboo shades, and I never asked for the Venetian blinds.

"Hey, I done cleaned all yo' shades wit' dis he'ya ammonia - nice an' clean."

I had to thank him for his effort, and I didn't want to seem ungrateful, but I had to tell him that I didn't need them and that I had already bought new shades. That response, of course, meant a blown tip.

"What? An' I done wasted all dis ammonia? Shew!"

I wasn't prone to tip giving anyway, and certainly not for unwanted, useless deeds. It wasn't an auspicious beginning.

For some reason I wasn't given a mailbox key when I moved in, and so my mail and unread Wall Street Journals frustratingly continued to accumulate in my box. I had to pester Johnnie every day for a key. The key came several days later with a knock at my door, together with the presentation of my Wall Street Journals.

"Hey, is dis what ya wanted?"

I guess it was tip time, but I didn't oblige - the newspapers were too old.

"Oh yes! Thanks Johnnie, thanks a lot."

I soon discovered that I had other neighbors besides those in the other three apartments on my floor - cockroaches, armies of cockroaches - in the walls, in the floors, and in the closets. I complained to Johnnie, who reported it to the landlord, who sent the exterminator. From a tank with a hose and a nozzle, they gave a squirt here, a squirt there, and a squirt behind the sink, and left in less than two minutes.
The roaches were back in less than that, but the poisonous odors would linger on for weeks. Anyway, I found that boric acid worked better (but not as well as a well aimed shoe), and I could avoid another tip confrontation with Johnnie.

In spite of it all, I soon fell in love with my new home and neighborhood, and became absorbed into it and part of its culture. People always seemed to be walking to or from somewhere - their apartment, a job, a café or restaurant, an art exhibit, a shop …or perhaps to or from some legal affair at the nearby courts on Court Street … or perhaps the Civil Court - Small Claims or Landlord-Tenant - on Livingston

Street.

And like most of the people who lived here, while absorbed in the culture, I also became part of my own independent, private little world. I soon learned to ignore, and then became oblivious to Brooklyn's homeless population.

First and foremost among the neighborhood's homeless was Nelson, an old merchant mariner who had lost a hand in some terrible accident. The gaunt figure with long gray hair, white beard, and blazing blue eyes would wave the stump in the air while giving some of the most impassioned and incredible political speeches I had ever heard.

> *"... but the Communists ... yes, the Communists, and the Socialists, they and the People's Workers Party, the United Front for a Democratic America ... and don't forget the Marxist-Leninists, ... and the*

Bolsheviks ... are all united together in this great left wing Anti-American, Anti-Capitalism, Anti-G-d, Communist conspiracy. They, together with the Federal Bureau of Investigation, the Central Intelligence Agency, the Queen of England, the Sultan of Brunei ... and there are others. We must all take action now. It's not too late! ...

He'd go on like that almost without end. The oration would last for hours. He actually did a much better job of this compelling incoherency than I could ever recollect.

Less notable was - I'll call him the "Bible Reader" - because I never knew his name, and that is what he always did. He read it until the pages were frayed and withered, and then he'd read it again. He was another gaunt figure with gray hair, and wore an army fatigue jacket. The greatest living authority on the Bible was right here in Brooklyn, but went unknown to the world. He was clean, quiet, and always reading. He could usually be found at his home at the Clark Street subway station, inside the Saint George.

There were yet others who were still less notable, along with a bag lady or two. I'm sure they all had stories, but I could only guess at what they were. Perhaps a long and serious illness had wiped out their life savings, a mental condition, a gambling problem, or a problem with drugs or alcohol ... or perhaps it was an eviction by a callous and ruthless landlord, ... or perhaps they had been sued into poverty by an aggressive and greedy lawyer ... or perhaps it was a sublet that had gone awry.

My neighborhood and its surroundings had all the ingredients for some great adventure, some great happening - mystery, excitement, international intrigue - but for the most part, there was none of that. My quiet, routine, idyllic kind of lifestyle was interrupted by only a handful of events. There was the great fire at the Hotel Margaret during its renovation on Columbia Heights.

There was also the bicentennial celebration and the tall ships. And there were the two times that I served on jury duty - one a thirty day stint on a medical malpractice case that drove my bosses crazy - and the other, a criminal case involving the theft of Brooklyn Union gas by a slumlord posing as a handyman for some obscure, probably nonexistent, supposedly sick landlord. It was I who single-handedly turned the jury around to the cause for criminal conviction, and convict we did. It's amazing how juries will vote just for the "sake of going home." Anyway, what is even more amazing is that ultimately, the system works.

But here there was no story, or the story wasn't mine. I was the innocent spectator. Indeed, I had spent countless hours on the Promenade, sometimes jogging, but more often just sitting on a bench and gazing in wonder at that magnificent city from the Brooklyn shore, without really being a part of it. Providence would change all that. My idyllic, carefree life would end. A new chapter would begin.

III. TO MOVE, OR NOT TO MOVE?
THAT IS THE QUESTION.

It began when a job opportunity presented itself on eastern Long Island with the U.S. Department of Defense. At last there was hope for a real career! I would not be a Budget Clerk at the Naval Support Activity forever. And so, I accepted the offer and thereby became another of a relatively small but growing cadre of reverse commuters, people who live in the City, but work in the suburbs. Reverse commuters face many problems, but two come to mind. They have the blinding sun on their windshields in the morning, and on their windshields again for the commute home. They also usually arrive home too late to compete with the city people for rare and precious parking space.

The commute was long and difficult, but on a good day (and there were many bad days) I could tear up the BQE, fly over the Kosciusko Bridge, race down the LIE, and usually be at my desk in forty-five minutes flat. On one particular morning, there was an accident and long delays. Miraculously, I managed to make it to work at exactly eight o'clock, but that didn't prevent the now daily tardiness comment from the boss.

"Jon, I got a call from the guard's office. They tell me you turned in here this morning on two wheels!"

Sometimes it's just impossible to please bosses. Actually, they called them Supervisors then, and Team Leaders now, but they're still bosses.

I had to brown-bag it in those days. The trainee spot didn't pay that much. Johnnie, the super, saw me early one morning with my brown bag. I was especially pressed for time that morning and slapped together a tuna fish sandwich in a most unceremonious way. He stared at me with my cheap vinyl Government-issue briefcase and brown paper bag. There was no avoiding him.

"Good morning!" I said.

"Hey! De garbage go down de stairs."

"What?"

"I said take de garbage downstairs."

I hadn't noticed it before, but the bag was badly wrinkled and beginning to ooze mayonnaise oil. It was a little embarrassing, but I had to answer in order to avoid losing my lunch to the garbage.

"This isn't garbage, Johnnie - it's my lunch!"

Johnnie continued to eye me down with doubtful scrutiny. I was already running late for work and didn't have time to debate. I pleaded.

"Really Johnnie, it is my lunch!"

He watched as I made my way out the door to make sure that I didn't dump my "lunch" in front of the building.

Now once out of the building and beyond the sight of Johnnie, the next challenge was to remember where I had parked my car, to hope that it was still there - not stolen or vandalized - and to hope that it would start, thereby depriving the City's parking enforcement triumvirate - Police, Traffic, and Sanitation - from generating badly needed revenue.

I had grown weary of city life, and its daily routine was becoming a drag. The long commute eventually destroyed my Honda Civic with its tiny 1.2 liter engine and twelve inch wheels. The old car was burning oil so badly that I had to drive around with a case of the stuff in the back seat. I think it was when the thieves smashed out a window to steal the oil that I made my decision to leave Brooklyn. I had to drive to work that day with a broken window in a cold wet rain, sitting on broken glass - and no motor oil. I reported the incident to the police, but they acted as though it was my fault.

"Why do you own a car in the City?" I was asked by a police administrative aide.

"Well, excuse me, but I do need it to get to work. Did I do something wrong?"

And the question I had to ask myself was, "Why am I in the City?"

The condo on eastern Long Island represented a new and better life. It was brand new, clean, and pristine. It had the works - swimming pool, tennis courts, club house, central air-conditioning, and best of all, parking in front of my unit with no alternate-side-of-the-street parking regulations.

And yet, it was not without considerable feelings of nostalgia and bitter-sweet memories that I would leave Brooklyn. But the decision had to be made. There was no turning back. There was, however, one small problem that had to be resolved before I made the big move. That was breaking the lease.

It shouldn't have been a problem. The apartment, small and dumpy as it was, was rent stabilized in a hot real estate market, and in Brooklyn Heights, proper. Certainly Mr. Kravitz, my landlord, would be only too happy to get rid of me! He could easily re-rent it and get a higher rent under the vacancy decontrol allowance; or he could inventory it - i.e., add my empty apartment to the other empty apartments in the building and take the building co-op (empty low rent apartments aren't "no" votes); or, perhaps he could take advantage of a hundred other landlord-lawyer tricks! No, breaking the lease would certainly not be a problem. He would want my apartment, and I would simply give it to him. I decided to talk to Mr. Kravitz.

Surprisingly, it was only the second time that I had spoken to him in the past ten years or so that I had lived there. I was generally a non-complainer. The first time was a fruitless attempt to get a paint job. He'd buy the paint, and I'd do the painting, but it never got anywhere.

Kravitz was never an easy person to speak with. He'd say as little as possible, volunteer no information, was always in a rush, and would leave you with a sick, empty and disgusted feeling, so that after the "conversation," you'd ask yourself, "Why did I bother?" But ending the lease was important. It had to be done. I called the landlord.

"Hello, Mr. Kravitz?"

"Yes. Who is it?"

"This is Jonah Cohen."

"Who?"

"Cohen? ... Your tenant in apartment 1C?"

"1C ...?"

"Yes, 1C ... on Clark Street ..."

"1C on Clark Street? Oh, yes ... Cohen. What can I do for you, Mr. Cohen?"

"Well ... uh, I want to talk to you about my lease ..."

"Well?"

"I've been transferred to a job on eastern Long Island, and I want to, ... uh, I mean I have to ... well, I've enjoyed the apartment tremendously over the years, but now ..."

"Excuse me a minute, Mr. Cohen. I have another call."

"Offer them $375,000 cash - top offer. If they don't want

19

it, they can keep it. Harry, they're wasting my time. And the place has to be delivered empty. Got it? No tenants! We want it without tenants, without squatters, without guests. I can't be bothered with these ridiculous, little people ... get back to me on this fast!"

"Now, what were you saying?"

"Well, I was saying that I have been transferred to another job and I..."

"Mr. Cohen, please get to the point. I don't have all day."

"Well, I was saying ..."

"Excuse me Mr. Cohen. I have to take another call."

"... Harry, forget that one. What's happening with the one on Columbia Heights? Raise our offer to $950,000. We can go to contract tonight. Don't let that one go!"

"Mr. Cohen?"

"Ok, I've taken another job and I have to terminate my lease."

"WHAT?!!!!!!!!!!!!!!!!!!!"

"I said that I have to terminate my lease."

"Mr. Cohen, you are responsible for the full term of your lease and for fulfilling all your obligations!"

"I know, but I have to ..."

"Please do what you have to do. I'm really very busy."

The conversation ended abruptly with a rather loud click; and again, I had to ask myself, why did I bother? I had to get rid of this apartment one way or another. I couldn't pay both Kravitz his rent and Brooklyn Federal their mortgage payment. Kravitz was not only difficult to talk to, he was intimidating and dangerous. A direct legal confrontation with the landlord-lawyer simply had to be avoided.

As the weeks and months passed, the condo deal on Long Island progressed. I eventually closed on it and took title, but I continued to pay Kravitz his rent. It was a struggle. Things were tight and my resources were running thin, but if I would stop paying rent, I would incur the terrible and unforgiving wrath of Kravitz and his lawyers. I heard that they hunt down absconding tenants like escaped convicts. Kravitz would find me for sure. I would be very easy to find. He'd sue for all the rent that I would owe him, plus lawyer fees and costs, plus penalties and interest. Surely, he would win a judgment! Then he'd put a lien on my new condo, and surely, I'd become another one of Brooklyn's homeless. Was that what happened to Nelson … or the others? No! Not paying Kravitz his rent was definitely not an option. The only other option was subletting.

I read the rent stabilization lease rider over and over again until I nearly had it memorized. Subletting was not prohibited. There was a step-by-step procedure to be followed. I would need the landlord's permission in writing. The landlord would have to be given a copy of the lease with the subtenant. The landlord would have to approve the subtenant. If, however, the landlord did not give his permission and acted unreasonably in his refusal, then I, the tenant, after following the required steps specified, had the right to sublet without the landlord's permission. The rent stabilization lease rider went on, however, with more about the landlord and the tenant, and the landlord's unwillingness, and unreasonable refusal to allow a sublet, and finally ended with "… however, such action may result in litigation."

Litigation! It was this part that was most confusing and troubling. I tried reading the rent stabilization lease rider again, but my eyes would focus only on one part, and it was this part that was to be forever embedded into my brain as the words of the Ten Commandments were etched into tablets of stone. It almost became the eleventh commandment. The holy words read:

"The tenant shall not sublet without the landlord's permission ..."

I would have to get the landlord's permission. I wasn't looking forward to another ...shall I say ... dialogue? ... with Kravitz, but it had to be done. And so, as repulsive as it was, I called Kravitz again, now with my subletting request, lest I found myself in violation of the sacred commandment.

"Hello, Mr. Kravitz? This is Cohen, your tenant in ..."

"Yes, I know who it is." He wasn't overjoyed to hear from me.

"I ... uh, I would like to ..."

"What, Mr. Cohen? I'm really very busy."

"Well, we spoke about my apartment last time ... I mean your apartment ..."

"Yes ...?"

"Well, I would like to sublet it ..."

"WHAT?!!!!!!!!!!!!!!!!"

The chill ran down my spine like death itself, but somehow I found the strength and courage to continue.

"Now what I need is your written permission, but first, I think I'm supposed to send you a copy of the written lease with the subtenant, and the rent amount ..."

"Mr. Cohen, please go ahead and do whatever it is that you think that you're supposed to do."

"Well, I'll need to know, first of all, the correct rent amount for ..."

During the course of my stay at the Kravitz estate, the

lease termination date had mysteriously changed from June to September, most likely so that the landlord would benefit from an approved rent-stabilization increase; but, I was never sure if this was proper, or what the rent really should have been. The lease should have been renewed in June, but wasn't. Since I had to furnish the landlord with a copy of the sublease with the prospective tenant's rent, which would be at a 10% premium to what I, the prime tenant would pay, I had to know what the legal rent really was. Kravitz offered no help. I tried again.

"Now if the lease expired in June, the rent stabilization increase should have been 3.2%, not 5.8%. How was it increased to 5.8%?"

"Mr. Cohen, I'm not your bookkeeper."

"But I have to ..."

"Mr. Cohen, have you spoken with an attorney? ... Look, Mr. Cohen, just follow all the steps in the rent stabilization laws ... but let me tell you this. I'm not going to be easy on you."

"But I ..."

"I have to go."

And with the ominous words of Kravitz still ringing in my ears, I once again had to ask myself, why did I bother? Following the steps in the landlord-tenant law would mean certain battle in open court. He already so much as told me that point blank. This was his specialty! Suing tenants in court was his living. He thrived on it, quite literally. I had fought a few parking tickets in traffic court, but it was obvious that I was no match for the great real estate lawyer.

The real estate market was still red hot. I couldn't cancel out on the condo deal, but it might have been possible to flip it – sell at a quick, small profit after buying it. That wasn't the plan, or what I wanted, but at least it would avoid certain litigation. Another profitable out was to rent the condo. Images of rolling green lawns, ponds with fountains, tennis courts, and swimming pools were fading fast. I discussed this brilliant plan, the renting option, with a friend at work. We weren't in agreement.

"Man! ARE YOU CRAZY? Rent your new condo? Not a good idea, man … Definitely not a good idea. Don't do it, man … don't do it!"

I didn't heed my friend's advice. Was status quo so bad? I still liked Brooklyn Heights and the City, in spite of it all, and now I could also be a landlord, make some money with the condo, and avoid litigation with Kravitz. I wondered if my decision to rent was not born out of some strange fascination with my landlord adversary, Mr. Kravitz, or with landlords in general, but I dismissed this strange thought. My decision to rent was based on financial necessity and legal prudence. I found a broker and put the condo up for rent. But a month passed, and then another, and as the red hot real estate market began to cool, no suitable tenant was to be found. Kravitz still got his rent, Brooklyn Federal still got their mortgage payment, and Cohen, Inc. was quickly sinking into a financial abyss with a cash-burn rate faster than a new dot-com.

Kravitz told me to discuss my situation with a lawyer, but I didn't know any lawyers and I certainly couldn't afford any lawyers … except maybe Blumfield. Of course! Blumfield! Blumfield was my closing attorney for the condo who, unfortunately for me, blundered big time at the closing. It seems that he had gone on an extended vacation in the Dominican Republic and neglected to make it back in time for the closing. I got hit with delay of closing penalties and additional interest. The closing itself was pretty ugly. I found myself arguing with my own lawyer amidst all the other lawyers who waited patiently in delightful anticipation of devouring the carnage. Blumfield supposedly had a verbal agreement with the builder's lawyers to change the date of the closing, but there was no way to prove it, and I had to ask the stupid question,

"Did you get it in writing?"

I had to get on the phone with the builder, client-to-client as they said, to argue my hopeless case. And so, in a room full of experienced lawyers (except possibly Blumfield), all listening intently to every word, I pleaded my case. Why did I need a lawyer if I had to do all the arguing? It was as if I were defending him for being late! The builder was courteous, but the response was as expected.

"Mr. Cohen, I'm sure you can understand. Your attorney's delay has cost us in additional interest and penalties."

Blumfield did put on quite a good performance though - he wasn't a total waste. He'd jump up and down and yell and scream,

"TYPICAL BUILDER'S BULLSHIT! THAT'S TYPICAL BUILDER'S BULLSHIT!!!"

I was curiously amused with the presentation of this astute legal argument and my lawyer's oratory skills. It made the entire room quake, and the pens roll to the floor. But in the end, I wound up paying the fees, the penalties, and the interest, as well as the builder's lawyer, the bank's lawyer, and the title company's lawyer. I paid Blumfield only two thirds of his agreed upon fee. (During the closing, we had to step outside to, shall we say, discuss things. I should have fired him on the spot, but that would have meant walking back into the closing room alone, green, stupid, unprotected, and friendless - raw meat for the lions, so to speak. And so, we compromised on his fee.) In spite of everything, we did finally close and I was given a set of keys.

Blumfield perhaps wasn't the best one to go to for legal counsel, but he was already my lawyer, and I paid him. Anyway, he was all I had. His advice regarding the present state of affairs concerning the sublet, and for whatever it was worth, came as something of a surprise.

"I don't really see a problem here. Why don't you just go ahead and rent it? You know … on the sly."

"What?! You mean without the landlord's permission?"

"It's done all the time."

I wondered about the lawyer's response. It wasn't the answer that I expected, but it was exactly the answer that I wanted to hear. The answer was simple, beautifully and elegantly simple. It was really the only thing to do. Blumfield finally got something right. Kravitz, an absentee landlord in a run-down building, already pre-occupied with too many other lawsuits and real estate deals, probably really didn't care. Cohen in 1C couldn't be very important. As long as he got his rent, there would be no problem. Anyway, my decision was born out of financial necessity. I decided that I would sublet on my own - permission or no permission. And it would be with the blessing and very sound legal advice of my real estate attorney, Mr. Irving M. Blumfield, Esq. I would move. I would sublet. I would leave Brooklyn.

IV. The Sublet

First, I had to tell Johnnie, the super, what I intended to do. I never trusted him in general, and he was, after all, the landlord's agent, but I had no choice. Johnnie had to know - and I had to trust him. If he went to the landlord, the subletting would end at the start and nothing would be lost.

I caught him early on a Sunday morning while he was mixing water and ammonia to do the lobby floor. The odor was strong enough to keep even the roaches away, but only until the floor dried.

"Good morning, Johnnie. I … uh, have to talk to you. Something's up."

He put down the mop and came into the apartment with an annoyed, but curious look. I figured I'd get right down to it. There was no point in delaying.

"I'm moving, probably soon. I bought a condo on eastern Long Island …"

And then the bombshell …

"… and I'll be subletting this apartment."

Would old Johnnie fly into one of his rages? Would he yell and scream at me? We were never really the best of friends. We sort of existed in a state of mutually peaceful co-existence, like with the roaches. And like I said, I never wanted to trust him, but now I had to. I braced for the worst, but his reaction surprised me. It was amazing. People get used to people, and parting really is "sweet sorrow." His face almost melted. His eyes watered up with tears. And then, in a soft, almost broken voice asked,

"An' does he know?"

"No."

There was no need to identify who the "he" was. But of course he knew! IDIOT! I told him! ... But then, maybe not. We sort of left it hanging, and there was no further discussion or communication between the landlord and his tenant about the subletting or anything else. No, "he" didn't know. Johnnie continued.

"Well, jes' keeps on payin' yo' rent."

"I will, Johnnie. No problem. I will ..."

"You know, I never once went against de people o' dis buildin' ... never ..."

I guess I had misjudged old Johnnie all these years. He really was a good guy. We shook hands, and he started to leave. I called out to him.

"Oh, Johnnie ... thanks for taking care of things here. Thanks for everything."

I slipped old Johnnie a twenty. He took the bill, folded it into thirds, placed it into his shirt pocket, smiled ever so slightly, nodded in thanks, and returned to his morning chores as if the foregoing exchange had never taken place. Johnnie was now working for me - he was now _my_ agent. I had made a friend.

The thing now was to get the place rented - fast. I thought my ad was cute. It read simply:

```
************************************
```

BROOKLYN HEIGHTS

STUDIO APT. FOR RENT - $535

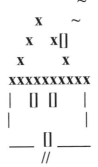

Call Jon   XXX-XXXX

```
************************************
```

I placed copies of the ad on the supermarket bulletin boards, a lamp post or two, and a Citibank cash machine - and the phone went wild! But like most bargains, there just had to be something wrong with it. Most people weren't interested in a sublet, especially one "on-the-sly," as Blumfield so eloquently put it. But the rent stabilization laws did give the tenant the right to sublet. It was written into the Constitution and the Declaration of Independence. It was like freedom of religion, or freedom of speech, or the pursuit of happiness! I had the freedom to sublet! I had the right to sublet, and I decided that I would exercise this right!

There was one very strange call. It came about 6:00 P.M. and there was an odd story with the call. Some young woman said she was calling about my ad in The Voice. She spoke quickly, and somewhat incoherently, but it was something about leaving a job on Long Island, and she wanted to know if the apartment was still available for sublet. What was strange was that I never placed an ad in the Voice, and the story paralleled my own in reverse. This was a Kravitz agent for sure! Come on Kravitz, you can do better than that! Kravitz only came to the building once or twice in the ten years that I was there. It was probably out of morbid fear of contracting some disease from the roaches, or perhaps being hit with falling debris from his building, that he stayed away, so there was actually little danger of being discovered.

"Apartment for rent? No ... I'm sorry, you must have the wrong number."

I had several prospects come - an architect, an accountant, business people ... and various others of uncertain origin or occupation. They all said that they would get back to me, but never did. It wasn't quite what they were looking for. Then I met Peter Southington. Peter seemed to be a clean, quiet, and respectable young man with a pleasant and friendly disposition. He said he was in the food catering and entertainment business. I wasn't sure exactly what he did, but he said he'd take the apartment. He was leery about the sublet part, but the place really was a bargain. Still, certain things needed some explaining.

"... Now, I wasn't able to get the landlord's permission, but I do have the right to sublet. I'll introduce you to the super, Johnnie - he has to know. If you have a problem, go to him, or call me, but ... DON'T GO TO THE LANDLORD!"

I introduced Peter to sweet, elderly Mrs. O'Malley across the hall, and then to Johnnie - with another warning.

" ... Now, he may yell at you a little, but that's just his way. Don't be afraid of him - he takes care of us here."

Peter was getting used to things.

"I'll leave some furniture … The washer works, the freezer doesn't."

We signed a lease before a Notary Public. He gave me a check, and I gave him a key.

"The place is yours. Come and go as you like."

Peter was happy. He had found a home.

I removed the last of my things and made the move eastward. I loaded up Old Faithful (my Dodge Dart), and with Moby Dick (my goldfish) in a bucket, we quickly absconded from Brooklyn in secrecy and under cover of night.

The condo, new, pristine, clean, and perfect, was a radical change from the Brooklyn apartment. To my horror, I noticed that I had transported three roaches to the new condo, but then realized that there was really no danger. They were severely dehydrated and confused in their new environment. The City was seventy miles away, the old hiding places were gone, and the nests of friends, family, and relatives, were forever severed. The overwhelming odors of freshly poured concrete and new gypsum board were the odors of death! I watched curiously as they wandered aimlessly in varied directions, and then in defeat, returned to the box. Survival was impossible, but just to make sure, I scooped them up, and then, without the least bit of remorse, gleefully crushed them with the sole of my shoe. Brooklyn was gone forever.

Peter's references checked out very favorably, and the checks that he gave me were cleared and paid. He did call me a week or so later in my office. A pang of fright shot through my entire being. I feared it was all over. What happened? Did Kravitz decide to make his decennial visit?! Damn!! What luck! Peter began.

"Would you mind ... would it be ok if I set up some bookcases?"

The simple request left me limp.

"Bookcases? That's it? Peter ... do whatever you want. Just do it quietly."

Peter proved himself to be a perfect tenant ... or subtenant actually. The rent was always on time, and he seemed to get along well with Johnnie and the other people in the building. Kravitz, the landlord, received his rent from me in blissful ignorance. I tried not to be too prompt with the rent, lest he become suspicious - a few days to a week late was good. Things went very smoothly, better than smoothly - like clockwork. Sometimes Peter would send a little note with the rent. Things like,

"How are you on this cold January morn'?
I hope you're keeping well and warm."

And the messages on his telephone answering machine were always entertaining and creative - poetry, classical music, literature, or a quotation from the Bible. In July it was simply,

"Went to the beach! Leave a message."

There was only one time that the rent was late. His father had passed away, and he had to be out of town. His mother paid the rent from Texas. Peter was so reliable that I only called him when it was absolutely necessary, or at lease renewal time.

Even so, I made it a point to visit the Brooklyn apartment once a year, before Christmas. The visit was more to keep

32

things right with Johnnie, than it was to inspect the apartment. It was at this time that I would give Johnnie his Christmas bonus - a turkey and twenty dollars cash, that got raised five dollars every year. He accepted the small bribes graciously. Our conversation was minimal.

"How are you, Johnnie?"

"Good. Yourself?"

"Fine, thanks. How's everything here? No problems?"

"No problems."

"Anything happening with the building yet?"

"Na ... everything's the same."

"Well then ... Merry Christmas."

We shook hands and we were set for another year. I went up to Peter's apartment. He was friendly, and happy to see me. The little one room studio, once the place I called home, and once so familiar, now seemed old, decayed, strange, and different. It had been re-painted with a fresh coat of antique white paint. The apartment was neat, clean, and in order. A pleasant, but somewhat less than professional looking painting of a winter forest scene hung over the couch. He told me that his mother had painted it. He had just taken something hot off the stove.

"Would you like some pasta with spaghetti sauce?"

It was a cold day and I really was hungry, but I didn't want to impose upon Peter, nor did I want to stay in that apartment any longer than I had to. (The criminal does re-visit the scene of the "crime.") I thanked Peter and I politely refused, but I was touched by the humble but well intentioned offer. I had to finish up my business here.

"How is everything?"

"Fine. I'm really enjoying your apartment. I took my girlfriend to the Brooklyn Academy of Music and we had a great time …"

"And Johnnie? You get along with him?"

"He's a character. Some girl was here last Sunday apartment hunting. I couldn't hear her well, but I had no trouble hearing Johnnie's voice thundering through the lobby, 'NO! I AIN'T GOT NO STUDIO APARTMENT TO RENT!' The poor thing must have been so embarrassed …"

"Sounds like a familiar story. I wonder if it was the same one. She must know something about the vacant apartments here … But you get along with him?"

"Johnnie? Yeah, sure, he's ok. We get along. We're friends."

I lingered, reminiscing about the old place. Peter caught it.

"Memories, huh?"

"Yeah …"

"Well, then …"

"Right, I really have to be going. Take care, Peter … and Happy Holidays!"

"Thanks, same to you. Happy Holidays."

Things went on like that for three years. I was proud of myself and my real estate management expertise. Of course, the real kicker in keeping the apartment was to get in on the insider's price should Kravitz decide to co-op the building. I could keep it and become a real landlord and charge market rent, or "flip" it, buy it and sell it, and make an instant twenty grand or so, maybe more. Landlords sometimes inventory apartments because empty apartments can't vote against co-op conversions and Kravitz was a master of inventory.

And so, I had accomplished the impossible and made everybody happy besides. Kravitz got his rent, faithfully and always nearly on time, Johnnie got his "tips," Peter got a cheap place to live in a trendy neighborhood, and I got my ten percent rent premium with the co-op kicker. I also managed to avoid a broken lease with its resulting litigation. What I had pulled off was nothing short of genius! I had done it all! Yes! I had become a real estate genius!

V. The Sub-Sublet

The call came on an otherwise quiet afternoon at the office. It was Peter. He was going to move. It was bound to happen sooner or later, and now here it was. Nothing is forever. He was exuberant.

"Jon, you have to see this place - three large rooms, oak floors, huge windows facing the sun ..."
He went on for a while. His present joy was my impending disaster.

"... and it's only $495 a month - in Manhattan!"

"$495 in Manhattan??!!"

"Well, it's through a friend ... and it's on the Lower East Side - Alphabet City, but it is on a good block and ..."

Peter was such an honest and genuinely nice guy that I just couldn't hold him to the lease. Besides, could I sue in what might be regarded as a technically illegal sublet? Sue Peter? No! If he wanted out, I wouldn't try to keep him. I didn't know what I would do with my lease with Kravitz. I'd have to get another subtenant, but there was more, and it got worse.

"... Oh, Johnnie's really sick. He's been in the hospital over three weeks ... I heard he has a brain tumor the size of a grapefruit ... poor guy ... There's a new super here now."

"Oh, SHIT!!!!!!!!!!!! ...."

I felt bad for old Johnnie, and certainly didn't wish it on him, but somehow, all I could think of were the Christmas turkey with the thirty dollar tip, and the sudden loss of a very much needed friend and ally. Things were falling apart fast. Peter wasn't finished. There was yet even more.

"Oh, … and they're working on the building … steam cleaning the outside brick, new stairs, finishing the basement … Kravitz has his son supervising the construction. I think he took over the business. He's here almost every day now."

"Did he see you?!!!"

"Yeah, sure, but he doesn't know who I am, and he doesn't know who lives in this apartment … or any of the other apartments in this building for that matter."

"When are you moving?"

"Well, I don't know … soon, I hope. There are people living there now and they have to move first."

We were in the middle of the lease, and I was back to my original problem.

"What about my lease with the landlord?"

"Can't you get out of it?"

"No …"

There was a moment of silent tension between the tenant and his subtenant. Peter broke it.

"Jon … this other apartment is really nice. I don't want to lose it. It's Manhattan … and the neighborhood …"

"I know, I know … Peter … can you get me someone else?"

Peter recognized my problem, and his own obligation under the lease that I had with him, so he was more than willing to cooperate.

"Ok … let me work on it. I'll get you someone else."

Faced with a problem with no solution, sometimes it is best to let the laws of inertia rule. Peter didn't move for a while. His dream apartment was slow to vacate. We kept in touch during that period. Renovation of the building continued and Kravitz, Jr. made his daily visits. About two months later, I happened to call Peter for an update.

"Hi Peter. How are things?"

"Fine. My apartment is almost ready. I'll be moving soon, hopefully on the first."

"Do you have a tenant for me?"

"No … but I'm trying. I'm running an ad in The Voice. It shouldn't be long now. Don't worry. I'll get you someone."

"How's that new super?"

"Jose? No problems."

"And Kravitz, Jr.?"

"Oh, well …"

"WELL??!!"

"Well, I did something a little stupid. He called out to me with your name, and I must have been dreaming or something, so I didn't answer him. But it's ok. He doesn't suspect anything."

"Are you sure?!"

"Yeah … it's ok. I really don't like this guy though. He's here a lot now, with all the construction and everything. But, yeah, it's ok. His mind is on the construction, not the tenants."

Another week flew by. Peter called me in the office. There was no new subtenant yet, but there was hope.

"Jon, I'm getting some calls for this apartment. They're calling …"

"And …?"

"Well, the women don't want this apartment, and … well, nobody is crazy about this sublet deal, but don't worry. I'll find somebody."

Peter was true to his word. He came through for me. He called me at home in the new condo, very late on a Sunday night.

"Jon, I found a tenant for us."

"Really? Fantastic!!"

"Now, I'll give you all the information I have on him and you can check him out."

"He already looked at the apartment?"

"Yup."

"And you told him about the sublet? And the landlord?"

"Yeah, he doesn't mind. He'll take it."

"And he can afford the rent?"

"He says money is no problem."

"And you met him, of course."

"Yeah, he's ok. He seems like a real nice guy."

"What's his name?"

"Midnite … His name is Midnite."

"MIDNITE?! … Did you say 'Midnite?!'"

VI. The Sub-Subtenant

My initial relief and joy at the prospect of a new tenant quickly dissipated and was replaced by that same sick, hollow, empty feeling as I continued my discussion with Peter.

"Midnite?! Is that a name? What's his real name?"

"Well ... I don't know his real name, but that's the name he uses ..."

"Midnite??"

"Yeah, sure ... I know lots of black people named 'Midnite.'"

I really wanted to believe Peter, but I didn't know any. I tried again.

"But doesn't he have a real name? A last name?"

"Michaels, I think ..., but Midnite is the name that he goes by. It's almost legal. That's his name."

Peter was so honest and upright that I knew that he wasn't putting me on. And yet, I still didn't feel right about this, and if you don't have the right feeling about something, then don't do it.

"The right feeling." "The gut instinct." What are they? They are the sum total of all life's experience, education, and contemplative processes. They are the ultimate focus and confluence of all social, physical, chemical, molecular, and sub-atomic interactions within our very bodies, right down to the most infinitesimal and abstract quark with its own peculiar spin. They are all these culminating at that certain crucial split nanosecond in space and time that we recognize as the instant of decision! *"The right feeling." "The gut*

instinct." Trust in it!

And so, the *"gut instinct"* cried out an emphatic and gut wrenching "NO!" The decision was made. I would go on to the next prospect on Peter's list.

"Peter, who else do you have?"

"That's it. Just him."

"What? What about all those calls … and the ad?"

"Well, this real estate market has cooled a bit … and it's hard renting a sublet, especially one that's … well, illegal … sort of … look, he's ok. Why don't you just check him out? Then decide."

I had no choice. Peter was getting ready to move in a few days. There was no one else, and besides, perhaps I was being a bit prejudiced. Just because he was black and had a black person's nickname didn't mean that I should not rent to him. Peter was right. I'd check him out first. I could always say no.

"What does he do?"

"He's a salesman, sort of, a street vendor."

"A street vendor?! Is that a job?!"

Well, I thought it over. Not everyone can be a doctor, or a lawyer … or have a Government job. I guessed that as long as he had a job, it would be ok. Peter gave me his employer's phone number together with some references. I called the employer, not knowing quite what to expect. A young woman with an Afro-American accent and pleasant manner answered the phone.

"Good afternoon, Trans Hudson Imports."

"Good afternoon. I'm calling for a reference on an employee … uh … do you have someone there named, uh … Midnite Michaels working for you?"

It turned out that yes, he did work there … well, kind of.

The office, warehouse, or whatever it was, was in New Jersey. Midnite would get the merchandise and sell it in the City.

"... and uh ... he's reliable?"

"Oh, yes! He's a manager. He sets up his booth, he deals with customers ... He's one of our best!"

"And, uh ... 'Midnite?' Is that his name?"

"Yup, that's what we call him."

The employment part seemed to check out. I then called the phone number of a previous landlord, but kept getting the same pre-recorded message. Next, I called his prior landlord, a certain Carl Edwards, who turned out to be only a friend. But now I was again being prejudiced. After all, Peter lived with a friend also, and used him as a reference. I had to call Peter back, but I hadn't made up my mind and I didn't know what to do. I had to talk with this Midnite. Peter had forgotten to give me Midnite's number. I'd call Peter, get the number, talk with Midnite, and then make my decision.

"Hi, Peter. You forgot to give me Midnite's phone number."

"Uh ... I don't know what it is. I don't think he has one."

"No phone? Where does he live?"

"I, uh ... uh ... I don't know. I don't think he's living anywhere now."

"NO PHONE?? NO ADDRESS?? WHO IS THIS GUY? ... Peter, I don't know. I really don't know about this."

"Well, should I have him call you?"

"How do you get in touch with him?"

"He calls me."

"Ok, right, have him call me."

I really didn't want to talk with him, but the law of inertia was already in motion. Midnite called me in the office and we talked. Yes, he had that street vendor job, and some other odd jobs. He spoke slowly and politely with a faint accent of the Islands. He seemed ok. Perhaps he was just a regular ok kind of guy, a little down on his luck. I should be objective. I should fight off the negative "feelings." I needed a tenant and he needed a place to live. He gave me his best sales pitch, and I listened.

"Look, I'm quiet. I don' cause no trouble … I pay my rent …"

I continued to listen as Midnite went on with his good-tenant-attributes speech. He tried hard, and he was quite good, but my *"gut instinct"* was making me sick. My mind drifted back to the job, and then to some training I had had with a DIS (Defense Investigative Service) Agent. It never happened, but when faced with a difficult situation, or if ever a defense contractor were to even hint at a bribe, the thing to do was not to refuse, and certainly not to accept, but to buy time. Say, "I never did anything like this before. Let me think about it," and then run and call the special telephone number. Midnite was just about finished talking.

"… and I get along well with everyone."

"Ok, well, let me think about it …"

"Look … I really need your apartment, man."

"Yeah, well, I'll have to talk to Peter. You'll be subletting from him. Oh … by the way, what's your real name?"

He hesitated, but he was desperate for the apartment, maybe literally desperate, so he gave it to me.

"It's Neville."

I felt that I was the recipient of some deep, dark secret,

not to be divulged to anyone. It was as if a bond of trust was formed by the revelation of the name. The secret of the name would be safe.

"Ok, like I said, let me think about it ... We'll be in touch. What's your number? ..."

"Well ..."

"Oh that's right ... you don't have one. Ok, call me tomorrow afternoon."

I called Peter again. He had already begun to move his things.

"Hi Peter. I spoke with this Midnite guy."

"And?"

"Well, I don't know."

"Jon, I have to be out of here in another day or two."

"I know."

"Did you check out his references?"

"Yeah, but ..."

"Well?"

"Well, I don't know. Did anyone else call for the apartment?"

"No ... Come on, Jon ... Just because he's black ..."

"No, it's not that ..."

"So?"

"Well, I don't feel right about this ... What do you think?"

Peter was hardly an impartial party to this deal. I knew that he had his own interests at hand. That was obvious and understandable, but I still needed some assurance, and I trusted Peter.

"I think he's ok ..."

"But ... 'Midnite?'"

"Come on, Jon. Give him a break ..."

"Well … I …"

"Jon … give the guy a break."

The phone fell silent for several long seconds. Compassion would crush reason. Tums would cure the gut. The dams of the floodwaters of mercy - *rachmanot* as they say in the Hebrew - were beginning to break. I was prejudiced. The *"gut instinct"* had to be wrong. Facts, not feelings were important. The decision had to be made. There really was no one else. It would be ok. Of course … it would be ok. The fateful words were spoken.

"Ok, let him in."

VII. Midnite

My new tenant, Midnite, who was technically Peter's subtenant and my sub-subtenant, or something like that, moved in the next day. It was during the last two days of Peter's move, so that I had both of them living there at the same time. With all the packing and unpacking, and traffic in and out of that tiny apartment, I could only imagine and fear the confusion and noise that might have been taking place during the transition of subtenants. I could only hope that they had managed to avoid Kravitz, Jr., who was now there at the building every day managing, inspecting, collecting rent, or doing whatever it is that landlords do. And I could only hope that they managed to "work it out" with the new super, Jose. I was on eastern Long Island, a good seventy-five miles or so away from the scene. I didn't know. I didn't want to know. I just wanted it to be over.

The important thing now was to get a lease signed with Midnite, and get my rent money and some security. I called the apartment to make an appointment with him. Was Peter gone? Did Kravitz, Jr. see Midnite? Was Midnite living there now? Was it all calm and cool? I nervously made the call.

"Hi, Midnite?"

"Yeah!"

He recognized me immediately.

"How's everything?"

"Everything's fine."

Everything was fine!? Really?? They pulled it off?! The keen suspecting eye of Kravitz had been avoided, or perhaps to be more accurate, evaded. Midnite would be off from work on Friday, so we agreed to have the lease signing then. I wasn't happy about going into Brooklyn, and I really didn't want to meet this Midnite, who certainly couldn't have looked anything like Peter or me. It was just that, well … he might be noticed. Nor did I want to risk bumping into the landlord, and maybe having to answer some embarrassing questions. But it had to be done. Business is business as they say.

I got to the apartment at about noon. Construction on the building was continuing at a feverish pace. There were already new stairs and new basement windows. There was parked on the sidewalk, directly under the window of my first floor apartment, an old, black BMW motorcycle from the early '70's that looked like it had seen some use, and was now on its last remaining miles. Its distinctive large headlight was originally clear plastic with a button-like center, but was now badly yellowed. The license plate had been removed to hide the identity of its owner, thereby being protected against the zeal of the parking enforcement agents who routinely blitzed the area. The BMW had been rendered "ticket-proof." Odd looking wires emanating from the motorcycle led up to and disappeared into the window, barely keeping alive a nearly permanently discharged battery. Yet, the old BMW still exuded a feeling of power, respect, image, and a loose, carefree life-style that mirrored that of its most probable owner. Midnite was a biker.

The mission had to be completed. I collected up my courage and ascended the few steps at the front entrance. I rang the buzzer in the lobby. It was the buzzer next to the name "Cohen." Nothing had changed. Officially, I still lived there. Midnite was slow to come to the door. He might have been sleeping. I rang again as my anxiety heightened. And then, in the dim florescent lit lobby, a tall, thin, shadowy figure began to emerge, and as he came to the door, toward the light of day, I could see him more clearly. He was very tall, maybe over 6 feet 2 inches. His skin color was close to carbon black. A large gold earring shined brightly in his left ear. He had very long, straight black hair cropped close to the skull on each side. He wore a long white bandana which was tied to his hair, and trailed down to the floor. He wore torn, faded blue jeans and scuffed up, sockless leather sandals exposing callused feet that might have told of a long, arduous journey from some unknown distant place. But the greeting was friendly, and the smile broad and inviting, exposing a full set of very large white teeth.

"Hi, I'm Midnite."

VIII. The Lease

After my initial shock, I returned the greeting, and trying to hide my emotions, smiled back, pretending that there was nothing at all unusual about this encounter between two people from vastly different worlds. What was done was done, but perhaps one should not judge his fellow man by appearance only. Anyway, it was too late. It was only then that it occurred to me how little I really knew about my new subtenant. Where did he come from? Who was he? Could he be an ex-convict? A drug dealer? Did he belong to a gang? Did he carry a weapon?! What about my neighbors? Were they in danger? What had I done?! Was I responsible for him? Could I be sued? ... And perhaps worst of all, what about poor, dear, sweet, old Mrs. O'Malley across the lobby?

I decided that I wouldn't concern myself with it. Once again, the Law of Inertia would rule. I couldn't do anything about it anyway. I was here to get a lease signed. That was my goal. That was my objective. I didn't know. I didn't want to know.

The apartment was a wreck. Some of Peter's things were still there, piled up in cartons, nearly to the ceiling. Midnite sat down by the desk on the swivel chair that I had salvaged from the Brooklyn Savings Bank's dumpster. He looked silly sitting on it, as it was much too low for him. Midnite did not appear to be the executive type anyway, but what looked even sillier, was Midnite taking out his checkbook and writing out two checks for $535.00 each, one for the first month's rent, the other for a month's security. He asked me if it would be ok to post-date the checks to the 15th, and I agreed. Technically, he was still Peter's subtenant until the 15th, so the request was not unreasonable. He crossed his legs, squinted, and slowly and painstakingly wrote out the checks numbered 002 and 003. Check 001 went to Peter. (The account had just been opened - an obvious fact that I had stupidly realized much later.) Midnite happily completed the difficult fiscal task, and handed me the two checks.

"Well, there you go. That does it."

"No, not quite. We have to sign a lease."

"What?"

It took a little coaxing, but I was eventually able to convince Midnite to sign a lease. I showed him the lease form that I had prepared, printed in the obscure legalese meant only for lawyers and judges. He read it (or pretended to) with squinty eyes and a puzzled look. It checked out. He was ready to sign.

"No! No! Not here. We have to go before a notary."

"A notary?"

"Yes."

I felt resistance. Things were getting too legal and complicated, but he agreed to it. I really wanted to get this over with fast, attracting as little attention as possible, but in a neighborhood of strange and assorted street people, a place where gay and lesbian couples could walk freely, arm in arm without attracting much attention, I'm sure Midnite and I made an especially strange looking couple, and a not unnoticed pair. I was fortunate that the lobby was vacant, and that we were able to slip quietly and quickly through the front doorway, but some of the neighbors and their children happened to be in front of the building. Of course they recognized me, ... but not my strange new "friend" - who was now their as yet unknown new neighbor. I said "Hi," and smiled stupidly while Midnite clutched the tightly rolled up lease in his hand. It was quite possibly the only "real" lease that he had ever had in his life.

We managed to make it past the neighbors, turned the corner on Hicks, passed by his beat up BMW motorcycle (the battery was still being charged), and went on to get the lease signed. The actual lease signing didn't come easy either as we struggled to find a notary. The notary hunt continued as we strolled together through the streets of Brooklyn Heights. Our conversation was sparse, and our shared company was awkward. It was beyond awkward. It was ... surreal, like the paintings at the art exhibits on the promenade in the spring. Surreal - the unlikely or unnatural juxtaposition of abstract images. And yet, here we were, unnaturally juxtaposed in the real, physical world.

I didn't want to pry too much into his background for fear that it would "kill the deal," more from my end than his. (Ignorance is bliss.) I searched aimlessly for a topic of mutual interest other than that of our soon to be landlord-tenant relationship. And then I hit upon it. I would ask him some questions about the moped that I had recently acquired for "free" in a telephone solicitation scam. Of course, motorcycles - well, sort of. This was the connection. It was what we both had in common.

The new "EMEI 500" motorcycle was about to make its debut in the U.S., so the sales pitch went, and the manufacturer, the Chengdu Aviation and Technology Company of Chengdu province of the People's Republic of China (then "Red China") was about to launch a huge mass marketing effort. They went on to say that there were already over a million of them in use in China. Global

Marketing, the importer, was test marketing the product before actual operations began. It seems I had been statistically and demographically selected as one who would be most likely to try and enjoy the new "EMEI 500" motorcycle absolutely free of charge. All I would have to do is ride it for 50 miles, answer a brief questionnaire, and send a certified check for $301.74 to cover ocean freight, dealer preparation and insurance, plus another $75.00 shipping to Long Island. Well, in this world, nothing is really free, but still, $375.00 or so for a motorcycle wasn't a bad deal.

My "EMEI 500" arrived on an icy, cold, dark December night via truck freight. The bold print on the carton read, "MOTORCYCLE - MADE IN CHINA." The lettering was impressive, but the carton looked too small to hold anything that might be as powerful as an "EMEI 500." My supreme ecstasy quickly turned to curiosity as I opened a package from inside the carton that looked like bicycle pedals, and then to disappointment when I realized that I had bought a moped with a 50 cubic inch engine.

Nevertheless, I was determined to assemble it and do the test run and evaluation, pretending that I "wasn't had," but the moped had arrived in damaged condition, the weld at the chromed luggage carrier had broken, the chrome plating at the headlight bracket was peeling, the paint job was shoddy, and the tire air valves leaked. The manual was printed on paper the quality of newsprint in not just poor, but even comical English. An air-cooling fin on the tiny one cylinder engine was broken, and it was always hard to start. The list of defects didn't end there. The Commies still hadn't gotten it right. In spite of it all, I fell in love with the stupid thing and set it up in my living room as a conversation piece. I would gleefully toot the horn and flash the turn signals for any and all visitors as I related to them the unusual story of my acquisition.

"... and it was absolutely free - I was statistically and demographically selected."

Some time after the "test trial," one of the crude, flimsy clutch plates had broken and the importer had gone out of business, making its replacement almost impossible. And now here was Midnite, someone who lived bikes, loved bikes, and knew bikes. While we were heading up Montague Street, I asked Midnite about a clutch plate for the moped. It must have sounded ridiculous to a real biker, but it was important to me, and it was worth a shot. Midnite seemed like a "procurer." The response was a short and cryptic,

"I'll see what I can do."

And after several more minutes of awkward silence suddenly came,

"Man - I really dig this neighborhood."

I thought it was a good sign. I'd have a tenant who would stay. Eventually (and thankfully), we found a newsstand inside a building on Court Street that had a notary. The lease signing itself was awkward, and the notary spoke a poor broken English. The notary neglected to ask for identification, but Midnite offered something anyway. I didn't know what it was and didn't care. Finally, the lease was signed by both parties and notarized. It was now legal, more or less - a contract binding on both parties - signed and executed. The sublet deal was completed - the signing evidenced by the seal and signature of the Notary Public. I gave my new tenant a set of keys, we shook hands, and I wished him good luck. Midnite had a home.

IX. Armageddon

And the sixth [angel] poured out his bowl on the great river, the river Euphrates; and the water thereof was dried up that the way might be made ready for the kings that come from the sunrising. And I saw, coming out of the mouth of the dragon, and out of the mouth of the beast, and out of the mouth of the false prophet ... spirits of demons, working signs, which go forth unto the kings of the whole world, to gather them together unto the war of the great day of G-d the Almighty... And they gathered them together into the place which is called in Hebrew, Har-Magedon.

(Revelation, Chapter 16)

I was proud of myself and my real estate expertise. I had done it all! Now I had a new subtenant and I'd still get the ten percent premium on the rent, but more important, if the building went co-op, I'd get in on the insider's price. Renovations were still going on - the building was steam-cleaned, the basement was refinished with new windows and brickwork, and the broken slate stairs at the building's entrance were re-done. Kravitz was, without a doubt, getting ready to do something with the building, and maybe soon. Midnite, the new subtenant, had a home and a cheap place to live. Perhaps I had rid the city of one more homeless person. And lastly, Mr. Kravitz, my landlord would continue to get his rent. I'd still have to work out a deal with the new super, but that wouldn't be a problem - all supers are corrupt. They are ultimately the agent of whoever pays them. Yes! I had become nothing less than a real estate genius! And so, with my real estate problems finally under control, I could concentrate on my job. It would be a busy month. There would be an audit team coming from Region Headquarters, there was a pre-award survey scheduled at one company, and there would be a First Article Test at another, not to mention the volumes of reports that had to be completed. My supervisor would be coming to the plant, just to make sure it all went smoothly.

It was a sunny, pleasant, late summer day when, upon returning to my office from my first appointment, I was handed an innocent looking slip of paper by the receptionist. I glanced at it quickly and I knew it was trouble. A nauseating and empty feeling set in. The note read,

"Midnight called –

Needs to talk to you today.

Very ..."

Very what? There was no more on the little slip of pink paper. Very bad? Very soon? Very important? Whatever it was, it wasn't "very good." I looked at the note again. He had called the day before, but I was out for the holiday. It was Rosh Hashanah. I guess it had all been "inscribed," as we say. DAMN!! What a lousy way to start the new year! I told myself, "Don't panic. It could be anything. Just keep cool. It's probably nothing. I'm too busy. I'll call later."

But it was Midnite who called later, and the news was not good. It was much worse than not good. The unthinkable had happened. I listened as he related to me the disaster that had befallen upon us. Kravitz, Jr. had spotted Midnite, followed him into the building, wanted to know who he was, and immediately ordered him out. What lousy luck! And it all had to be on the New Year, Rosh Hashanah! If Kravitz had been in *shul* where he belonged, it might never have happened. But it was meant to be - on the first day it was inscribed. My subletting venture was over. My real estate career was ended. Perhaps it was now best to end it all on the landlord's terms, cut my losses, and get out fast. I continued to listen as Midnite went on with his tale of horror.

"An' den he says, 'Well, who are you?' An' den I says, 'Hey, I lives here, mun. Who dee hell are you?' An' den he says, 'I'm dee lan'lode.' An' now dee lan'lode wants me dee hell outta here ASAP!"

What was there to say? Would there be yet another homeless person on the streets of Brooklyn? And would I be the cause of this homelessness? I answered stupidly with feelings of guilt.

"...eh, eh ... well, that was the risk ... and I did tell you before you moved in ... Well ... I'm really, really sorry about this. Those are the breaks ..."

He didn't answer, but perhaps there was a way. It wasn't over yet.

"Look, let me call the landlord. Maybe we can work something out. I'm sure we can work it out. You don't have to move yet. You're still my tenant."

But it was Kravitz who called me. I wasn't in. I called him back, but it was Kravitz, Jr., the son who answered. I had never seen or spoken to him before. The voice was harsh, deep and raspy. It was intimidating and threatening in tone and manner. I could only imagine what my landlord might have looked like - short with wavy black hair, heavily pocked face; yellowed, crooked teeth; and slanted, bushy eyebrows over small, beady, dark brown eyes, slightly crossed. He spoke slowly and directly. Every sentence was an order, and the last word of each seemed to go up one octave. And as he spoke, the chances of Midnite's continued tenancy were dwindling down to zero. The sick, hollow, empty feeling returned, and that too was much worse.

"Hello, Mr. Kravitz?"

"Yes. Who is it?"

"It's … it's your tenant in 1 …"

"Mr. Cohen?"

"Ye … yes."

"I've been wanting to speak to you. Who may I ask is that 'person' living in your apartment?"

"Wha … what?"

"I said who is living in your apartment?"

"Uh … no one, uh … he's just a friend."

"A FRIEND???"

Midnite didn't look like someone who was likely to be my "friend," but I had no other response. I couldn't say that he was my tenant. I certainly couldn't say that he was my brother. I couldn't say anything. My heart skipped two beats, my pulse raced wildly, and I was scared as unholy hell, but somehow, I still managed to answer. I just stayed with the story. Yes, when in trouble, just stay with the story.

"Yes, a friend."

"And where do you live?"

"Where?

"YES! WHERE?!"

"Uh … Clark Street, of course."

"NO YOU DON'T! Your buddy Midnite lives there and I want him out NOW! PRONTO! NOW!"

My voice quivered, my hand shook, and my stomach was turned inside out, and yet I had to find the strength to respond.

"But ... Mr. Kravitz ..."

"I said NOW! UNDERSTAND?"

The Cabbalists say that we are made of two souls, the animal soul, and the G-dly soul - the *Nefesh Elokit* - the soul that is truly a part of G-d. I would appeal to Kravitz's *Nefesh Elokit*. The holy sages couldn't be wrong. It had to be there ... somewhere.

"But Mr. Kravitz ... he, he needs a place to live. Can you ... well ... maybe you can ... maybe you can give him a break?"

"NO!"

I was repeating Peter's own words, but this time they fell on cold, hard, lifeless stone. I tried again for the last time.

"But Mr. Kravitz ..."

"I said NO! GET HIM OUT ... or it's gonna cost! IT'S GONNA COST!!"

"Ok, ok. Let me talk to him. Maybe I can get him to leave. I'll get back to you, Mr. Kravitz."

"WHEN?"

"Tomorrow."

"NO! TODAY! Call me today, before 2:00 P.M."

There was nothing to do except to comply with the landlord's order.

"Ok, before two."

I called Midnite with the bad report.

"What do you want to do? You know, I can fight this. It's my right to sublet and your right to live there. Just pay your rent, and let me take care of Kravitz."

I wasn't sure of anything I was saying, but I thought it

was so, and I would have fought to protect my rights, and even the rights of my subtenant. The prospect of fighting Kravitz in open court was too horrifying to contemplate. I was really hoping that Midnite would avoid the court scene and just go away. He gave me the answer I wanted. Perhaps, it would all be over.

"I guess I'll have to go."

"Can you be out by the fourteenth?"

The lease was from the fifteenth of the month to the fourteenth of the next month. It would be the end of the first month, the fourteenth - a clean break.

"I'll be out sooner, by the first."

"Fine."

I called Kravitz, beating his two o'clock deadline by five minutes, and informed him of our decision to comply with his order to vacate. At his request, I wrote him a letter stating our intention to vacate. It read,

"At the request of the landlord, all persons and belongings will be removed within 30 days."

So now, with the agreement with the landlord, and with the agreement with Midnite, things were beginning to look better for a quick exit. I knew that I was giving up my rights to the apartment, but now the objective was to just get out.

Unfortunately, I had already deposited one of Midnite's rent checks. He called me to tell me that he had placed stop payment orders on both checks, and also that his imminent departure would be somewhat delayed.

"But you can't do that! You already agreed to leave! I already notified the landlord! And the rent! I need it to pay

<u>my</u> rent to the landlord! You said you were leaving!"

"Hey, look mun ... I gotta do what I gotta do, ok?"

"But ... but the rent! I need the money ..."

"Oh, and I'll need more time. My new place ain't ready yet."

"But you have to pay rent, and I already made a deposit. That check will bounce! And I wrote a letter to the landlord ... you said you were leaving ..."

"Hey mun, gotta go."

Things were again spinning wildly out of control. Nothing was solved. The forces of man and nature, and landlord and tenant, were moving on their own momentum. There was nothing to do. Midnite had taken up permanent residence in my apartment, and Kravitz, my landlord-lawyer, had hired a law firm that specialized in landlord-tenant matters. They were in fact eviction specialists. Weissman, Chapman, and Krantz were the best in Brooklyn! But why would a lawyer need to hire a law firm, especially one of the caliber of Weissman, Chapman, and Krantz for an eviction in a simple so called "illegal-sublet?" Was I special? I remembered Kravitz's words, "IT'S GONNA COST!" Or perhaps it was Midnite who was special.

Kravitz didn't wait until the end of our 30 day agreement. It was only a few days later that I received a letter from his lawyers by certified mail. It was a 30 day notice - a notice to vacate the premises within 30 days or face further legal action. It was a "holdover" because I had continued to pay my rent. Kravitz's legal costs (that I would wind up paying according to the lease) were adding up fast. A few days later, I received another letter, this time from Kravitz himself. It was a copy of my own cleverly worded vacate letter with his own handwritten response, written with obvious, excessive pressure, so that the pen nearly tore through the paper. I had chosen my words carefully. Basically, I wrote that he had requested, and that we would comply, leaving out all the gory details. He was obviously pissed. He thought my letter needed some amending.

"The above is <u>inaccurate</u>. You attempted to illegally sublet your apartment without the landlord's permission ...

Your failure to comply with this request will result in additional expense and inconvenience!

MK"

I called Midnite. The call was urgent, but he wasn't in. I had to leave this awkward message on his answering machine: "Midnite ... we could work together ... together ..." I thought it would be worth a try. He would still keep the apartment, and we'd fight Kravitz together in court. Tenants (and their subtenants) have rights! Constitutional rights! Human rights! Civil Rights! Maybe we could even hit Kravitz with a discrimination suit! But how? We would have to hire a lawyer, and who would pay for it? Me? But before any of this fantasy could become a reality, he would have to pay me my rent, and Midnite wasn't paying rent, or anything else for that matter, to anyone. My call to him was not returned, and doubts about Midnite's imminent, or even eventual departure began to set in. I called him again. This time he was in. I pleaded.

"Midnite, please … you must leave … we only have a few more days to comply with the landlord's order. You MUST leave."

"Oh, mun … Say what?"

"I said YOU HAVE TO LEAVE!"

"HEY, MUN - I DON' HAVE TO DO NOTHIN'!"

There were still a few pieces of beat up furniture and other things of mine in the apartment. I told him that I would be reclaiming them. Midnite needed some encouragement to hasten his departure.

"Oh … I'll be coming over to move some of my things out."

"Hey, mun - you can do what you want, but I'm stayin' right here!"

We were at a stalemate. No progress was made. When the thirty day period ended, my office phone went wild - Kravitz Sr., then Midnite, then Kravitz Jr, then Midnite, and again Kravitz, the elder, and finally Kravitz, the younger.

"WELL? IS HE OUT?"

"No."

"IT'S GONNA COST! When is he leaving?"

"I don't know."

"Did I say I want him OUT? O … U … T … OUT! NOW!"

I slouched down on my desk chair. My legs were crossed at the ankle. I took a deep sigh. All was lost. What would be would be.

"Well … he doesn't want to leave."

I braced myself for the explosion of words that were sure to follow, but at the ensuing impasse, a dialogue opened up between the landlord and his tenant, perhaps for the first time. Maybe it was foolish, or maybe it didn't matter anymore, or maybe I had made a conscious decision to cooperate with the evil landlord in a joint effort to remove the non-paying subtenant. It was time to take sides and I had to ask myself, who was really the enemy? Actually it wasn't so much a dialogue as it was a cross examination, but anyway, it was what it was.

"How long has this Midnite been there?"

"Only about a month."

"And before that?"

"Someone else."

"Who?"

"Peter Southington."

"I thought that was you!"

"Well ..."

"How long was he there?"

"Oh, about a year."

He was there much longer, but I couldn't say that. I still had to protect myself or I'd be sued for even more. The landlord's cross examination continued.

"Where did you find this Midnite character?"

"Peter found him."

"Yeah. He found him all right. Probably sleeping in a cardboard box under the Williamsburg Bridge. What does he do?"

"Uh ... I don't really know - a street vendor or something - works for Trans Hudson Imports."

"And what else do you have on him?"

"Not much - prior addresses, references, Social Security number ..."

"Can you fax that over?"

"Sure, no problem."

" ... You know something? I think I saw him somewhere

before … Let's see. Where did I see that guy? … Where was it?"

"You saw him!??"

"Yeah … where was it? … That's right! In the City! He was selling fake jewelry or something on Canal Street … and he looked like he was stoned out of his mind. He was just standing there, gazing up into space, with a joint in one hand and a fake necklace or something in the other. Was that him?"

"Well, eh …??"

"That was him, wasn't it?"

"Well, I don't know."

"Look, Mr. Cohen … Can I call you Jonah?"

"Sure, Jon is ok."

"Look, Jon. I'm not looking to make trouble for you, and I'm really glad that we're having this dialogue. You know, I have responsibilities for the safety of the people in this building. We don't really know who this guy is … a criminal … a drug dealer … Look, just get him to leave. Ok?"

"Ok. Sure, Mike. I'm trying. I'll talk to him, but I'll need a little more time."

"How much?"

"Two weeks."

"Ok, but remember. TWO WEEKS!"

Exactly how I would be able to remove Midnite in two weeks was a mystery, but at least it bought a little time. I called Midnite that afternoon. I tried to explain the urgency of the situation, that he absolutely had to leave, and that if he persisted in staying, things could get very, very expensive, but he was intransigent.

"For you maybe. Not for me!"

"For both of us! Look, Midnite, Kravitz is getting ready to go to court and he's talking to his lawyers."

"Look, mun, I have no fear of courts and lawyers."

The remark stunned me. Everybody is afraid of lawyers! Midnite was truly from another world. When you have nothing, you have nothing to lose, and nothing to fear. I tried again.

"Midnite - YOU HAVE TO LEAVE!! YOU MUST LEAVE!! LOOK!! I'M TELLING YOU ..."

"SHUSH ... Hey, mun, don' tell me what I have to do. I spoke to a lawyer. I don't have to leave."

"But ... but, yes, you do ..."

My last words drifted into absolute silence on deaf ears. Midnite was calm, cool, and collected, and in total control. I had lost it, and I had lost the debate. He was determined to stay. Did he really speak to a lawyer? Did he even have the money for a lawyer? It amazes me that people who have no money always seem to have money for lawyers, airplanes, and cable TV. Anyway, so now there was Midnite's lawyer (if he really had one); Kravitz, my landlord-lawyer; and the Kravitz eviction specialist lawyers. We would be going to court for sure, but where was my lawyer? Blumfield? I tried again.

"Midnite - you have to leave."

"Why?"

I didn't know why. In the depths of desperation, the only thing that I could think of was to put my own physical self in the way of his free tenancy. I would personally take back the apartment!

"Because, because ... I'm moving back. It's my apartment. I'm paying the rent, you're not, and I want it back. Ok? Be out!"

I thought seriously about this ploy, but decided against it. Maybe Kravitz was right. He could be dangerous. He could be a criminal or a drug dealer. I knew nothing about him. It was a bad idea.

Then I hit upon another idea, and I thought that it was simply brilliant. It was that instantaneous flash, the beginning, the birth, the very inception of the idea before it is received, understood, or acted upon. It was what the Cabbalists might have called *Chochma*. I thought that I would invite one or more of the neighborhood's homeless persons into my apartment to share it with Midnite. After all, were Nelson and the others any less deserving of a home than Midnite? That would make him leave for sure! And besides, I'd be sheltering the homeless. That's what Isaiah said to do - it would be a *mitzvah* so to speak!

Fortunately, I regained my senses and returned to the physical world. The idea was killed before it was acted upon. I needed to empty the apartment, not fill it up. This too was a very bad idea, and now I was out of ideas. My two weeks were over. I called Midnite again, but it was useless. He wouldn't budge.

"Look, mun. I'm not movin' and I'm not payin' you any rent 'til I get confirmation from dee lan'lode dat I can stay heeya."

"But … he's not going to do that, and it's not going to happen, and … this is going to court!"

"Hey, mun …"

"Midnite, listen to me. Suppose I helped you find another apartment? You can still be my tenant. We'll find another place, a nicer place. Give Kravitz back his dumpy apartment with his rats and roaches …"

"Oh, mun! Wise up, huh? You don' get it. You really

don' get it. You are what dey call between a rock and a rock. Don' bother me no mo'. I'm stayin', ok? I'm stayin'."

Midnite was right. I didn't get it, and I hadn't yet "wised up." Midnite had found a free place to live, had no intention of ever paying rent, and no intention of ever moving. It was exactly what he was looking for, and he had found it. Perhaps it was he, and not I who had become the "real estate genius!" I tried again for the last time.

"But, but ... this is going to court!"

"Oh, mun! Look, do what you have to do. I like it heeya and I'm stayin' ... Oh, and if you call me again, I'll sue you for harassment. Get it mun? I'll sue you!"

I had barely recovered from my tenant's threat when the phone rang. I thought of letting the receptionist at the switchboard take the call, but I picked it up. It could have been business, but it was Kravitz. He spoke in the same deep, slow, threatening monotone as before.

"Well, he's still there. What's happening?"

"I ... I can't get him to leave ... Mike, I need a little more time."

"No more time. Get him out!"

"But ... but I ... I can't ..."

"Mr. Cohen - It's gonna cost!"

"But ..."

"IT'S GONNA COST!!"

"I ... I know."

"Call him! Keep calling him. Don't stop calling. Then call me back."

I didn't call anybody. I tried to get back to my work, but it was impossible. The phone rang again within minutes. I couldn't deal with yet another call from Kravitz, or Midnite, or maybe Kravitz's lawyers, or maybe even Midnite's lawyer. I let the phone ring this time until the receptionist took it. It was my supervisor. I had to call him back.

"Hi, Ken. What's up?"

"Your phone's been busy all afternoon."

"Well ... It was a busy day."

"What's happening with that First Article Test at Comtronics?"

"What? Oh, uh, well ... I had to take care of some unplanned priorities."

"You had to do what?!"

It was late in the afternoon. I had forgotten all about it, I had already missed two other appointments, and I hadn't prepared for the Region audit.

"Ken, I'm really sorry. I'll take care of it first thing tomorrow."

It was 4:30 P.M., time to go home. It had been a terrible day. I was tired, stressed, and completely obsessed with horrible thoughts of lawyers, and the lawsuits which would surely lie ahead, but the day was finally over. I packed up my briefcase and was about to close the door to my office when the telephone rang yet again. It might have been my supervisor. It might have been important. It might have had something to do with the Region audit or that First Article, but it was my landlord again with his same sickening, threatening, raspy voice.

"Well, is he out?"

"No, but I'll be over at the apartment this weekend to remove the last of my remaining things - some furniture ... shades ... and I'll be vacating ..."

"It's gonna cost! IT'S GONNA COST!"

X. Clark Street Revisited

And so Midnite, far from being homeless, had become a "permanent resident" - a squatter, paying no rent, and with no intention of ever leaving. I kept in close contact with the landlord - something like a Hitler-Stalin Pact with Midnite as Poland. Mr. Kravitz, a *Cohen* - righteous priest that he is - had not yet begun litigation, but my complete cooperation was of the utmost importance. I told Mr. Kravitz that I would be making a trip into Brooklyn to clear out the last few of my remaining things from the apartment, precedent to my returning the apartment to him in a clean and vacant condition. I had also told Midnite that I was coming to remove all my belongings - everything.

It was a cool, crisp October day. When I got there, Midnite was not in. The place was a total mess and now I saw this Midnite character for what he really was. I eyed the tiny apartment in horror and took a deep sigh. There were stacks of unopened cartons and articles of clothing scattered everywhere. There was a table in the center of the room with papers on it and lots of small change, mostly pennies. There was an unpaid parking ticket, a checkbook with no money, and a passport from Trinidad and Tobago with a ten year Visa. So Midnite was an alien, but at least a documented one. Midnite was legal, more or less. There were bank statements, again with no money, but with service charges and stopped payment fees. These were for the two checks that he gave me in order to rent the apartment. There was a letter from a girlfriend, a service check from Vinnie's Pizza, and two cans of Coors Silver Bullet in the refrigerator, and, ... and, ... Yes! The Lease! It was the notarized lease that I had signed with him. It was the only thing that elevated him from the level of squatter, but was it a *contract*? Where was the *consideration*? There was no money paid, therefore there was no contract. What should be done with the worthless piece of paper? I thought it over for a moment, confiscated the lease, and left him the following note, taped to a cardboard box facing the door:

Midnite –
You owe me $535.00. Be out by the 1ˢᵗ of the month. You don't live here anymore!

JC

I proceeded to remove the storm window that I had installed in the bathroom, leaving only Kravitz's broken, drafty jalousies. I tore down my bamboo shades, leaving bare windows facing the street. I destroyed these beyond use and dumped them in the garbage. And lastly, I rolled out my portable washing machine, loaded it up in the trunk of the Dodge Dart, and took off like a thief in the night. Midnite called me late that night. He said that he could have me arrested. He wanted his lease back ... and the window that I took out. It really was quite cold that night.

And so, with obsequious enthusiasm, I had complied as best I could with the landlord's demands. I removed all my belongings and surrendered up the premises.

XI. A New Home for Midnite

It was a hell of a mess. How to get out of it? How to set things straight. How did it all happen? I fell into this so innocently, or perhaps gullibly, greedily, or stupidly. I found myself in the middle of a hostile landlord and a deadbeat, immobile tenant. I was "between a rock and a rock," as Midnite had so ineloquently put it. But what was done was done, and now it had to be undone.

If the problem was simply that, for whatever reason, Midnite was unable to find another place to live, maybe, just maybe, I would be able to find a place for him. Certainly, my credit was better than his, even now. He could still be my tenant, he could pay me his rent, I would have a real estate investment ... and my conscience would be cleared of having contributed to New York's homeless population. And of course the wrath of Kravitz and his lawsuit would be ended. Sometimes the answers to major problems are simple. I discussed my idea with my friends at work.

"Jon, are you crazy?!! Are you completely out of your mind? Get rid of this guy and stop feeling sorry for him."

Well, I knew that it wasn't a good idea, but I thought that maybe it would be the one in a thousand chance that would work. If I could just find him a cheap, dumpy co-op, or a rental somewhere, everybody's problems would be ended. I planned to be in Brooklyn that weekend, and I told my subtenant that I was coming. We were supposed to look for a place for him to live. Enthusiasm was lacking.

"Hey mun, come if ya want ... but don' bother me no mo'! Ok?"

I got there at about 11:30 A.M. and rang the buzzer. He was still sleeping. I rang again, and after a few minutes, he came to the door, sleepy and shirtless. The greeting, if there was one at all, was not as friendly as at first, but he led me in anyway, and then proceeded to crawl back into the floor mattress. It was obvious that I wasn't going to get any cooperation, so I got right to work, but first things first.

"Hey Midnite, can I use your bathroom?"

Can I use *his* bathroom? Of course I can use *his* bathroom! It was my bathroom! I was the one paying the rent here!

"Yeah," he said, and continued to pretend to sleep. I went back to the apartment hunt.

"Let me use your phone."

He handed it to me, pulling it out from under the covers. I embarked on my mission.

"Now, we're going to find you a place to live."

I found a nice, fairly cheap studio on the fifth floor with a courtyard view, overlooking lawns and gardens, really pretty, with lots of sun. I almost would have taken it for myself. If I could just have gotten him to look at it, maybe he'd move. He didn't want to look, but expressed some detached interest. But then I remembered! I called the sponsor again and asked this very important question.

"Is subletting allowed?"

"Yes, but the subtenant must pass the board."

My heart sank. It was hopeless. How could this deadbeat alien from the gutters of Trinidad possibly pass the board? But, perhaps there was yet a way. We would try.

"Hey, Midnite," I called out. "Think you can pass the board? You know, fake them out?"

Midnite was confident. I wasn't.

"Maybe you can wear a suit and a tie?"

"I don't own one."

"Rent one!"

It was obvious that we weren't getting anywhere. Midnite never wore a suit in his life. But then he told me that he had to leave for a job interview. Yes! A JOB INTERVIEW! Perhaps there was some small glowing ember of hope after all.

"If I'm going to be paying you all this rent, I'd better get goin'."

I remained in the apartment, and surprisingly, he gave me the key to the front door, and took off on the motorcycle. I could only imagine what the job was, or if even there was a job at all. Nevertheless, I persevered with undeterred enthusiasm.

I looked at Concord Village, and then some rentals, and somehow ended up at a real estate broker on Montague Street, opposite Capulet's. I filled out an application, and sat down at a desk with an agent.

"... and what kind of apartment are you looking for?"

"A studio or one bedroom ... nothing fancy ..."

"And when will you be needing it?"

"Uh ... well, I don't know exactly. You see, the lease is up, but I don't know exactly when he'll ... I mean I'll be moving ..."

"This isn't going to be a sublet, is it?"

"Oh, of course not. Actually, I'm looking for a friend."

"Well, why can't your friend look for himself?"

"Uh ... because he's out of town."

"Well, when he gets back, we'll be happy to show him what we have."

"Well, actually, he needs the apartment as soon as possible ... a little trouble with the landlord ... and he just started a new job, and ..."

"Mr. Cohen ... just have him come in here. We'll be happy to find him a nice place."

We weren't getting anywhere. Midnite could never get a real apartment on his own and no one else could possibly be as stupid as I was. I had no more excuses. I could only think of the black man from Trinidad and Tobago now living rent-free in my apartment. Brooklyn Heights, the cradle of Liberalism, wasn't exactly Mississippi in the '50's or '60's. I was desperate and so I continued on.

"He can't come!"

"Why not?"

"Well ... he's black."

"Sir! We do not discriminate here! Just have your friend come in."

It was no use. Midnite could not possibly be explained and I was already as red as the rose in her blouse. I had to give up. The whole scheme wouldn't have worked anyway.

"Right ... sure ... we'll do that. Thanks for your help."

I went back to the apartment. Midnite was still gone. I made a few more calls, and then gave up on this silly, futile search. I still had the key, the only key to the main entrance to the building. Should I take it with me? No. He could still buzz his way in. I placed the key next to an opened letter that I happened to see lying on the desk top. It looked like a woman's handwriting. I picked it up with curiosity and read:

My Dearest Midnite,

It's been so long, much too long, and I really do hope we can get together soon. Things here have been hectic with the job and all, but I'll be flying into New York in a few days.

And I really do look forward to seeing you again and spending some time together. Let's put the past behind us and start anew. Perhaps it could be like it was and perhaps, just perhaps ...

XII. The Alien's Woman

She pressed the button next to apartment 1C. Printed next to it was the name of the prime tenant, "Cohen." Nothing had changed. She didn't have to wait long. Midnite came right out to greet her. So she had come after all, and he was surprised, even overjoyed to see her again.

"Come! Come in, sweet lady. Please do come in!"

She was a young woman in her twenties, thin, but well proportioned, and quite good looking. She worked as a legal secretary at a downtown Manhattan law firm. She had happened to stop at the Hudson Grill after work one day, and that is where they met.

The apartment was still upset from the move, even though he had done his best to tidy it up. But still she looked it over with disgust.

"Midnite, Midnite honey. Is this it?"

She looked at the broken window that Johnnie the super had never gotten around to re-fixing, the two or three slats in the other window that had fallen out, the tiny kitchenette, the cracking plaster at the ceiling, and the humble little room with its very Spartan surroundings. A strange, unidentified odor seemed to emanate from the basement.

"Midnite, this place! How could you live here?"   "It's not so bad, really. Ya jes' have to get used to it. I like it here. An' dee best part is dee rent."

"The rent? What are you paying here for this dump?"

"Nothin'. It's free!"

The young woman was educated and came from an upper middle class background, but she had slipped back into the vernacular in her concern and excitement. Trouble was in the wind.

"Midnite honey - What da hell yo' talkin' 'bout? Deeya ain't nothin' in dis world fo' free."

"Sha, sha - Yo' Midnite, he knows what he's doin'. Dis heeya is an illegal sublet. Ya see, dis guy, dee tenant, he has to pay dee rent, but I don' have to pay no rent. He went an' rented widout dee permission o' dee lan'lode. An' now dey's a goin' to dee court. I spoke to a lawyer. It'll be a year befo' I'm outta heeya."

"Midnite, I don't like it. It's, it's ... well, it's just plain wrong. It's dishonest."

"Sha! It's survival. You do what you have to do to survive ..."

"Besides, they could sue you!"

"Oh, sweet lady. Sweet, dear, beautiful, innocent lady ... You don' get it. To be sued, you have to have somethin' an' I have nothin'! Dey can go an' sue each other, but dey can't sue me."

"Well, maybe. I don't know ... But Midnite, what about your future, a job, money, a better place to live, a better life? Midnite, what about a better life for us? I can't live like this. I can't live like you do. I need more. I need security. I need a supporter. I, I ... I need somebody who can take care of me! And ... and ... It's not you!"

"SHUSH WOMAN! NO MO'! Yo' heeya 'cause yo' loves me - an' I loves yo' - and we'll work it out. Trust me! We'll work it out."

"Midnite, I really have to be going."

"Oh, pretty lady - please stay, please ..."

The conversation had become heavy, and he hadn't intended it to be that way - not tonight, especially not tonight. He went to the refrigerator and took out two cans of Coors Silver Bullet and opened them. She refused at first, but soon relented at his gentle persuasion and took a sip of his. And after a few more sips, she began to feel more relaxed and comfortable in his presence.

"Hey, I ordered a pizza from Vinnie's, an' dey's a couple of great movies on dee cable ... Please? Please stay?"

"Well ..."

She had decided to stay after all. The first movie was "Blues Brothers," a movie about a couple of second rate musicians putting the band back together. The second was "Pacific Heights," about a con artist tenant and his victimized landlord-couple. The evening went quickly, and they enjoyed the company of each other. But now with the movies watched, the pizza devoured, and the beer drunk, it was time for her to go. She thanked him for the evening and was getting ready to leave.

"Wo, wo pretty lady - Don' go an' run out on me now!"

"But I have to go to work tomorrow."

"Oh, pretty lady, stay tonight. Please stay. I need you. Please, please stay."

"No, Midnite, we ... we're just not right for each other ... but we'll talk again some other time."

"NO! Now! Let's talk now!"

The earlier argument had resumed, but now with even more intensity than before, until finally, he put an end to it. He would be the victor. He would dictate the terms. He would conquer. He would possess.

"We are right fo' each other. You know it, woman. Why else would you be here?"

It was true. Why was she there? She cared for him. She loved him in spite of everything.

"Oh, Midnite, I don't know. I don't know. My head is all frazzled - I'm confused. I don't know what to do."

She began to cry. They embraced.

"Oh, my pretty lady, my sweet, beautiful lady ... Look, I have plans, real plans. We're doin' it. We're puttin' dee band back together. It's gonna work dis time. I spoke to a couple uh new guys - one from Queens, one from the City - they're good. An' I got dee connections. We're gonna do it! We're gonna hit it big! I know it. Trust me. Deeya is real talent heeya - just trust me, pretty lady ... just trust me."

She wanted to trust him, more than anything. Her heart said yes, but her head said no.

"But Midnite, the life of a musician ... bars, cafes ... always on the move ... never settling down ... and you never know from where your next dollar is coming. That's not a life! That's not a future!"

"SHUSH! Don't worry about the future. There is no future and there is no past - there is only the present. There is only the now! Just live for today - just survive - just live! Think only of the present - the now! Woman - Live for the now! Live for the present! Live for yo' man!"

The room fell silent. There was no further conversation. He drew her closer to him, and ever so gently placed his hands on her shoulders, carefully massaging them, and then he pulled her dress over them, exposing bare, beautiful, perfect skin, and ...

And they were together as one being, together as one individual physical entity. And there was unity on the earth between the man and the woman - total completeness - absolute oneness. And as the Cabbalists say, there was unity between the Sefirot in the World of Yetzirah, the World of Formation - uniting the Sefira Tiferet and the Sefira

Malkhut, both coming together in perfect union, perfect completeness, perfect harmony, and perfect oneness. Tiferet - Beauty, and Malkhut - Majesty uniting together in the World of Asiyah - Action - Completed Creation. And the Sefirot of the supernal world paralleled the physical world below. The male and the female joined together to become one. The male and the female joined together in perfect, harmonious, complete, physical union. And they were one.

The alien and his woman slept a long, deep, and restful sleep, far removed and unaware of the outside world around them. It was in the early morning hours before dawn. A light rain fell outside. A car that was stopped at the corner for a red light blared out a line or two of Billy Joel's "The Piano Man," and then sped away. A passerby with heavy heals clicked his way quickly past the apartment window. A cockroach, unseen, unheard, and unknown, scurried quickly across the apartment floor. The traffic light on the corner of Clark Street lit up alternately in red and green flashing bizarre images of alternating colors on the apartment wall. And the ever omnipresent protector and benefactor of all within, the entity whose name yet embraced the apartment door with its physical presence, was the prime tenant of the apartment. It read:

"COHEN, APT. 1C"

And with it, the invisible, but implied inscription:

> *Give me your tired, your hungry, and your poor,*
> *Your huddled masses yearning to breed for free,*
> *The wretched refuse of your teeming shore,*
> *Send these, the homeless, tempest-tossed to me ...*
> *(The New Colossus, Emma Lazarus (paraphrased))*

81

Dawn gave way to daylight, and it was evening, and it was morning, one day.

XIII. Trick or Treat

"WELL, IS HE OUT?!!"

"No."

It was Monday morning at the job, and it was my first phone call of the day. It was my landlord, Kravitz again and I just couldn't deal with him anymore. The words came out without a plan, but it was obvious that I needed help.

"No. He's not out and from now on, I ask that you talk to my lawyer ..."

"Your lawyer? Who is he? What's his number?"

"Well ... I'll have him call you ... probably today ..."

There was no lawyer, at least, not yet anyway. I'd have to work on it. It was just a short term ploy to ward off the evil landlord.

"Look, Mr. Cohen ... Jon ... It's all right if I call you Jon?"

"Sure."

"Ok, Jon, I'm really not looking to make trouble for you and I'll try to settle this thing as *painfully* as possible." Pain was no doubt Kravitz's domain of expertise. The Freudian slip proved it. It was his specialty.

"Uh ... Mike ... excuse me ... but, I think perhaps you meant to say *painlessly*?"

"Painfully? Did I say painfully? Well, I meant to say painlessly. You see ... I have dealt with so much pain. Do you think it's easy being a landlord? Do you think it's easy dealing with tenants ... the City of New York, the Rent Stabilization Board, code violations, heating, plumbing, building maintenance ...? Do you have any idea how difficult it is to evict? If a tenant isn't paying rent, does that mean that the taxes don't have to get paid, or the mortgage on the building ...?   No! Being a landlord is not easy ... and nobody likes the landlord. We're always the bad guys ... Well ... now you're the landlord ..."

He went on for a while like that until even I began to feel a little sorry for him. It was a lousy business to be in. But I had to agree with him. I was the landlord. He returned to the matter at hand.

"Jon, you're his landlord. This guy is really raking you through the coals, isn't he? You know, there are certain things that a landlord can do to ... say, 'encourage' a tenant to leave. Like, sort of make it ... say, 'inconvenient' for him. I see that Brooklyn Union Gas is doing some work on Clark Street, and there might be ... uh ... say an interruption in gas service ... and Con Ed is also doing some work ..."

"You mean you want me to ..."

"Well ... I don't want you to do anything, but there are ways and ..."

"Right, Mike! I'll see what I can do."

"Good. And be sure to let me know what's going on."

"Sure Mike. I sure will."

I called the gas company and the electric company and told them that I would be moving back to the apartment and that the billing party should be switched back into my own name. This done, it would simply be a matter of turning the power and the gas off. Halloween was approaching. October 31st would be the turn-off date. Lights out and "Trick or Treat."

XIV. A Lawyer for the Prime Tenant

The lights went out at the apartment on Clark Street on Halloween, exactly on schedule. Midnite had little trouble putting them back on, but I'm sure he burned a few candles for a day or so.

I found myself back at my office the next morning, again waiting for the call from the landlord, which was sure to come, and it did.

"HE'S STILL HERE!"

"I know … and I'm still trying to …"

"Mr. Cohen, who is your lawyer?"

"Well, I don't have one quite yet, but …"

"Mr. Cohen, we have a court date coming up. Whether or not you have a lawyer, it's in your best interest to be there. We need your testimony for your tenant's eviction. Ok? I want to move this along as expeditiously, and as quickly as possible. We do expect you to be there. When you get a lawyer, have him call me, but either way … BE THERE!"

I didn't know what to do. I had never been to court before. Except for Blumfield, I had never even spoken to a lawyer before. My friends at work said to ignore it. I'm out of there, and I should just let him have his apartment back. Whatever happens would be between the landlord and Midnite. But I was being sued, and the faster the removal of the subtenant, the less it would cost. And maybe I should present my side of the case to the judge. It was my right to sublet. Shouldn't I protect my interests? Or maybe not. Lawyers are expensive. What to do? What to do …?

My uncle had his office nearby. Whenever anyone in the family ever needed advice (or a dental checkup for that matter), they would seek the wise counsel of my Uncle Larry. Surely he would know what to do. I decided that I would call him.

"... and my tenant moved out and brought in this illegal alien. He's not paying me any rent, and he refuses to leave. I'm paying his rent! And now the landlord found out about him ... and the landlord is suing me! He wants us both out, and he's taking us both to court ... There's a court date coming up ... and ..."

"You know ... you know ... Jonny ... How did you ever get yourself into this? We always thought you were smart."

"Well ..."

"Look, I can get a couple of thugs who'll scare the living crap out of him ... maybe even break his legs. We'll get that son-of-a-bitch out of there. Should we do it? Should we? Should I get them?"

I thought about it for a minute. I had never known my uncle to talk like that before. Certainly these things just weren't done in our family, but at the time the idea had some appeal. He had to be joking, but I wasn't sure. Anyway, I decided that it would be a very bad idea. No. The thugs were out. We'd have to do it the legal way. My uncle went on.

"Do you have a lawyer?"

"Well, I thought that maybe I'd represent myself ..."

"YOU CAN'T GO TO COURT WITHOUT A LAWYER! They'll make mincemeat out of you. Look, let me make some calls. We'll get you a lawyer. We'll get you a good lawyer. We'll get you a bastard! ... You say this guy is an alien? Did you call your Congressman?"

"No."

"Why not? Call him! Call him now! He's on the Foreign Relations Committee. Call him. We'll get that son-of-a-bitch out of the country ... on a boat and out of the country. Call him! Call him today and I'll make some calls. And call me back around noon. Let me get to work on this."

I felt much better after talking with my uncle. I knew things would work out. Things were starting to happen. I called my uncle back at about noon. Yes! He had the name of a lawyer, his own lawyer - a good lawyer. I called the lawyer immediately and spoke with the legal secretary. There was a slight problem.

"Mr. Rosenberg has taken ill and is no longer practicing law ... however, I can refer you to his associate. Would you like me to do that?"

We were drifting into the unknown, but what else was there to do?

"Sure."

"Ok. He's Louis Greenberg and his number is ..."

It turned out that Louis Greenberg was a "Court Street lawyer." I swear he sounded exactly like Walter Mathau with a cigar and scared the crap out of me. Louis Greenberg, Esq. (known to his clients as "Louie the Leach") would do the eviction for $750.00. The consultation over the phone was free. I had a "good lawyer."

"... and where exactly is this apartment?"

"On Clark Street in Brooklyn."

"Huh, huh ... And how many floors are in the building?"

"Oh ... about ten, I think."

"Huh, huh ... And how many tenants are on each floor?"

"Well ... maybe four apartments on the first floor, and

maybe about five on the other floors ..."

"Huh, huh ... That's forty-nine apartments. So ... it's fair to say that there are perhaps about a hundred people in the building?"

"Well, some of the apartments are empty."

"Huh, huh ..."

I had to interrupt the good lawyer. I didn't understand his line of questioning which had nothing at all to do with my special problem. Surely the good lawyer knew more about the fine points of law than his would be client, but we weren't getting anywhere.

"Excuse me, Mr. Greenberg. I don't understand what this has to do with evicting a subtenant."

"SUBTENANT? You mean you're not the landlord?"

"Well, I am, sort of ... You see, I rented without the landlord's permission, and I have to evict the subtenant because he's not paying any rent, and the landlord wants him out, but under the New York City Rent Stabilization Laws, I do have the right to sublet, with or without the landlord's permission."

"Oh, I see. Well like I said, it's $750.00 ... but I can't guarantee results."

Louie left me with very bad feelings. Shouldn't one's own lawyer express confidence? I wouldn't be using Louie. I called my uncle and told him the bad news.

"Ok. We'll find you another lawyer. Did you call your congressman?"

"Well, no. Really, Larry, I don't think that he'd be interested."

"CALL HIM! And I'll find you a lawyer, a good lawyer. Call me back!"

I called him back, and then I called him again, but still no lawyer.

"Jonny, I'm working on it. We'll get you a good lawyer."

It was getting to be late in the afternoon, and still there was no lawyer for the prime tenant, but I trusted in my uncle. Somehow I knew he'd come through. It was almost 4:30 in the afternoon, almost time to go home, and here it was. The call came. Uncle Larry had found a good lawyer.

"Call your mother and ask her to call Leibavitz."

"LEIBAVITZ!? OH ... NOT LEIBAVITZ!!"

Mr. Leibavitz was an old, small town country lawyer in Connecticut. The family had used him from time to time over the years for various tenant problems with limited success. New York was out of his jurisdiction, but he would have been useless anyway. I thanked my uncle for his efforts, but I was on my own again, and unrepresented.

Depressed, nervous, and sick over the upcoming trial, I began my drive home. Then I remembered an ad in the local newspaper. Flanagan and O'Brien will take any case, large or small, and the consultation fee of $25.00 would be waived if you used them. What was there to lose? One lawyer was as incompetent as another. I decided I'd use them, and the consultation would be free. I stopped in at Flanagan and O'Brien, saw the receptionist, and was asked to wait outside. Lawyers are very busy people, but after a short wait, I was invited in for the consultation.

"... and I have this alien from Trinidad and Tobago living in my apartment. He's not paying rent and the landlord is evicting both of us. There's a trial coming up soon, and I need a lawyer."

"You sure do. And, Mr. Cohen, where exactly is this apartment that you sublet?"

"Brooklyn."

"BROOKLYN?! Mr. Cohen ... Mr. Cohen ... Do expect me to travel all the way into Brooklyn?"

I thought to myself, why not? Tens of thousands of people do it every day. But then, lawyers are special people.

"Mr. Cohen, if I have to go to Brooklyn, you would have to pay me for my travel time at $150.00 an hour, plus my travel expenses, plus my standard legal fees, plus court costs, plus all other incidental, as well as all other non-specified expenses. Do yourself a favor and go to the Brooklyn Bar Association and find a lawyer. They will help you. Ok? Please see the receptionist on your way out to pay the fee." Ok? Was that the $25.00 consultation? That's it? What did I expect for $25.00? Obviously I wasn't using them, but now I was obligated to pay $25.00 for this "consultation?" I felt cheap, and he wasn't interested, but I wasn't going to pay $25.00 for nothing. Still, I had to ask the question.

"Do I really have to pay $25.00? You know, I don't think it's fair, after all, it was supposed to be waived and now ..."

"Mr. Cohen, Mr. Cohen ... forget the $25.00."

We talked a little about my special problem and the supposedly "illegal" sublet and what to do about it. The good lawyer leaned back on his executive desk chair, turned to the side so that he faced me in profile apparently staring blankly at the wall, brought the five fingers of his left hand to the five fingers of his right, pressed them both together, drew them away again, repeated the motion four or five times, and finally brought the two hands and ten fingers together. A profound legal opinion was about to be rendered.

"What you have to do here is evict the subtenant, but since you are not technically the landlord, you have to do it in the owner's name. So, what you should do is get the landlord's permission to evict in his name and begin your own legal proceeding ..."

Right! Like old man Kravitz was going to give me his permission now when I couldn't get his permission in the first place.

"And what will be the outcome? Will the subtenant have to pay me his rent?"

"Maybe not. The court might not look favorably upon your wrongdoing ..."

My "wrongdoing!?" "Maybe not!?" Did this mean that I could be Midnite's landlord forever and maybe never collect a dime? I gave a homeless person a place to live, got cheated big time in the process, continued to pay his rent, and now this becomes my "wrongdoing?" Why did I do this stupid thing? Was it the last remaining malignant cell of Liberalism within me that suddenly went wild? I had to find a way. There was a way, my way ... and without lawyers. I thanked the good lawyer for his useless advice and left off where I started, only the happier for not having to pay him his $25.00.

I was on my own ... pro se ... as they say.

XV. The Raid

I was back at the job in my office. Nearly everyday now seemed to start out the same. Kravitz Jr. would call me for an update on Midnite's imminent departure, and so, here was yet another call.

"Mr. Cohen ... I really don't mean to keep bothering you at your job, but ... you did mention your lawyer?"

"Uh ... lawyer, right ... well ... I spoke to a couple and ... well, I'll be representing myself."

"Oh... Well, Mr. Cohen ... I really don't want to be hard on you, but you should really do everything you can to get him out. Do you call him?"

I stopped calling him, maybe under threat of being sued. We really weren't on speaking terms at this point. A long silence passed. It was the landlord who spoke.

"Look ... why don't you try doing this? Go back to the apartment. Take a suitcase with you. Tell him that you have to move back in ... that you're inviting your parents over for Thanksgiving ..."

I told Kravitz that I would think about it. It sounded like another not so good idea, but now I would try almost anything. I added a few of my own improvements to the Kravitz plan. It was a cold, gray November day when I drove into Brooklyn with my empty suitcase. I took my suitcase and walked into Brooklyn's 84th Police Precinct, went up to the desk, and addressed the attending officer.

"Officer! I just got in from out of town and there's a squatter living in my apartment! I don't have a place to live. He doesn't belong there. I don't know what to do and my parents are coming over for Thanksgiving and ..."

"Woe! Stop! You said you have a what in your apartment?"

"A squatter, and he won't leave ..."

"Ok, look. What you have here is a civil case. The Police Department handles criminal cases. What you have to do is run, don't walk, run to the Civil Court and get him out as soon as you can. I see you have a problem, young man, but there is really nothing we can do."

It looked like my plan had failed, but as I turned to walk out, the officer called out to me.

"Wait! If you want, go to the front of your building and call 911."

"What?! You want me to call 911 for this?"

I didn't take 911 calls lightly. After all, this wasn't really an emergency. Well, it was, but not that kind of emergency. The officer explained to me that except for answering the 911 call, nothing further could be done by the police. And so the plan was put into action. I made the call at the corner of Clark Street.

"911 Emergency Operator."

"I need police assistance. There's a squatter in my apartment. He could be dangerous."

I gave them my name and the address, and in less that four minutes, two patrol cars arrived, complete with red lights flashing and sirens screaming. Four police officers jumped out, two from each car. I ran over to them and told them the problem. I went through my story quickly, still holding the suitcase, and with tears in my eyes summed up my allegedly desperate situation.

"... and my parents were supposed to come over for Thanksgiving."

Again they told me that this was a civil case, and that they couldn't do anything, but I was showed considerable sympathy by a certain young female officer, Officer Ortiz. She told me that perhaps they could talk to him, maybe even scare him out and so we gave it a go. And with me personally leading the charge into the building, followed by the four uniformed officers, we came to apartment 1C. They told me to open it, but the key didn't work. The security lock was bolted from the inside and I didn't have the key to it.

"OPEN UP!! POLICE OFFICERS!!"

The order was followed by loud pounding on the door, loud enough so that poor old Mrs. O'Malley across the hall had to open her door a crack to see what all the commotion was about. And again,

"POLICE!! OPEN UP!! OPEN UP!!"

Midnite was surely inside. The door was locked from the inside, and the motorcycle was parked outside by the window on the sidewalk, yet he remained inside, safe, secure and silent as a dead roach. And amidst all the commotion and confusion, I began to think. It was the part of the plan that wasn't thought out. IDIOT! What if he opened the door? He would say that he had a lease. I would say that there is no lease and I don't know who you are, and show me your lease. And he would say that I stole his lease, but then came another shout, now even louder than before.

"POLICE OFFICERS - WE'RE COMING IN!!"

With my heart pounding violently, the inevitable confrontation between Midnite and me was only seconds away. Poor old Mrs. O'Malley closed her door and locked it. In her fifty or so years in this building, there was never anything like this before. We waited outside the apartment, listening for signs of life from inside, or a click of the lock …but there was nothing. The occupant inside remained silent as stone. The police could do nothing else. It was just as well, the confrontation would have been a little embarrassing at best. Officer Ortiz did her best to console me, but the plan was foiled. It was then that I remembered the motorcycle, Midnite's unregistered, uninsured, uninspected, ticket-proof BMW motorcycle illegally parked on the sidewalk. I pointed it out to the kind and compassionate Officer Ortiz.

"Can you get that?"

Never before had I seen four cops write so fast and with so much enthusiasm. Within seconds, the BMW was plastered with tickets. I looked around. I had created a scene and a small crowd began to gather. I had won a tiny victory, but Midnite was still sleeping in my apartment. Officer Ortiz suggested that I go to the Civil Court immediately and wished me good luck. The four police officers returned to their cars and sped away. The crowd dispersed. I stared a minute or two at the BMW and its shroud of tickets blowing in the wind, and then I began my walk to the Civil Court. I was still carrying my empty suitcase.

XVI.   Civil Court

I had never been to Civil Court before. I had never been to any court before. Should I have a lawyer? Where do I go? I found myself at the court on Livingston Street and went up to the Landlord & Tenant Part. Civil Court is a very busy place - crowds of people, long lines, and very stale air. Do I get to see a judge right away? What should I say? I wasn't prepared. I happened to get on the longest line and waited until it was my turn.

"Can I help you?"

"Well, I have this alien living in my apartment, and he's not paying rent, and I can't get him to leave, and now the landlord ..."

"Where are your papers, sir?"

"What?"

"Your court papers - the Petition and Notice of Petition."

"Notice of Petition ...?"

My ignorance must have appeared overwhelming, and now I was holding up the line, and further delaying, and infuriating every other landlord with a non-paying tenant living in his apartment. The clerk continued, but spoke so fast that little could be understood.

"Yes, court papers. You have to file a Petition and a Notice of Petition. Get the forms at the legal stationery store on Court Street, complete it, have it notarized, come back for an index number, pay the $35.00 fee, have a copy served on the tenant five days before the court date, and return service three days before the court date. Next please."

"Notice of Petition ...? What's that? Where?"

"Sir, I suggest you see a lawyer. Next!"

Civil Court wasn't going to be easy. I did manage to get the forms at the legal stationery store. The store clerk knew exactly what I needed. In fact, the forms were already on the counter. Obviously, they sold many Landlord & Tenant forms - eviction papers - the Petition and Notice of Petition. In fact, they could have made a nice living selling these alone.

But the forms were confusing. How do you fill them out? When is the court date? Where is there a Notary Public? I struggled, completed them as best I could, got it notarized, and returned to the court. The line had grown even longer, but again, it was soon my turn to see the clerk. It was the same clerk. Of course, the forms weren't completed right. And I was supposed to have made copies. He had to make the copies. The clerk was clearly annoyed, but he did try to assist in his inimitable and abrupt manner.

"Look! You take this, staple it to the back of the Petition, and you take this, and you staple it to the back of the Notice of Petition. Then you serve the copy of the Petition and the Notice of Petition on the tenant, and then you have to bring back the original, with the Affidavit of Service ..."

The clerk really was trying to be helpful, but he was standing with his back to a large window, and it was already the fall season. The sun was now retreating to the South. It shined brightly through the court building window so that the clerk could be seen by the pro se tenant-landlord only in silhouette, placing the pro se at a distinct disadvantage. The air had also grown more stale, and had thickened in the late afternoon. And as the clerk continued with his tirade of instruction, its reception by the pro se tenant-landlord began to fade. All concentration was lost. I could only focus on the fine spray of saliva emanating from the clerk's mouth, clearly visible in the rays of the afternoon sun. I held my breath lest I come down with some terrible disease, and hoped the ordeal would soon be over, but the fine mist of saliva lasted throughout the session. They floated through the air as tiny, rainbow colored deadly droplets. They sparkled, they floated, and then burst, disbursing their deadly poisons on any unfortunate litigant who happened to breath them in. I had become hopelessly confused, and looked it. I wasn't listening. The clerk continued, and then looked up.

"WHERE'S THE BLOCK?"

"Well, eh ... What about the process service? Who serves the papers?"

"Have a friend do it, or get yourself a professional process server. That'll run you about $75.00."

"$75.00?!"

"Next please."

A professional process server! Do they wear uniforms? Do they carry badges? Do they have guns? Did I need a professional process server? The case was getting big and expensive. I thanked the clerk, and was happy to be out of there and once again in the more or less fresh autumn air. The next step was to get the papers served on Midnite.

XVII. The Eviction

I didn't intend to spend $75.00 on a process server. Anyone over the age of 18, not a police officer, and who is not a party to the action can serve papers. I spoke to my uncle, and he reluctantly agreed to do it.

"Now, it has to be given to him in hand. To get a money judgment, he has to get the papers in hand."

"Well, I don't know. Is he dangerous? You know, one has to be careful these days. He could be dangerous. He may have a gun, or a knife … Who knows?"

"He doesn't know you. Just give him the papers. Really, Larry … I thought that we were going to get a couple of thugs to break his legs, and now you're afraid to just give him the papers?"

"Suppose I just left it under the door. That's good enough. I'll just leave it by the door and go. Ok?"

Well, this was the best service that I was going to get. Maybe he was right. So, that's the way we did it. The affidavit of service was signed, notarized, and filed with the court.

Meanwhile, the calls from my landlord kept coming, now on a daily basis, requesting an update on Midnite's impending eviction. I had been keeping him informed of the interruption of gas and electric, the police raid on the apartment, the letters I had written to my Congressman, the letters to the Consulate of Trinidad and Tobago, the letters to the Immigration and Naturalization Service, and now the Petition and Notice of Petition for his removal. Thus far, nothing worked. This would all have to be settled in court.

But wait! There was yet one more thing we could try. The call came on a Friday afternoon. It was Kravitz with another "suggestion."

"Mr. Cohen, you are the prime tenant. I can't do anything ... but you can. It's your apartment. You have the keys. Now ... if you've been subletting for a while ... let's just suppose this ... then there might be many sets of keys out there somewhere, and you would have a responsibility to protect your subtenant, or his belongings, or the apartment from any unauthorized persons possibly re-entering the apartment ...Get it?"

"You mean you want me to change the locks? A lock-out?"

"Now, I don't want you to do anything, but if that is what you would like to do, then do it. Like I said, it is your apartment and if you want to change the locks, you have my permission to go ahead and do it. I am granting you permission to change the locks."

Well, I wasn't completely stupid. Kravitz was using me and I knew it. He was afraid of being sued by the subtenant - I was all gung-ho. Midnite would be out, I would give the apartment back to Kravitz, and it would all be over. Sunday would be perfect. That was the day he worked. I would have all day to play around with the locks, or if need be, I would be able to go to a locksmith. It was a clear, crisp autumn day, a little on the cool side. I took the long drive into Brooklyn. I got there about 10:30 A.M. I carried with me a shopping bag filled with assorted small tools and locks for the job. I eyed the spot under the window of the apartment where he usually parked his motorcycle. It was gone! All systems go! He wasn't home. I entered the building and I knocked at the apartment door, just to make sure that he was at work at his job, but to my shock and horror, I heard,

"WHO IS IT?"

He was home!?? Oh, damn it! What happened? He wasn't supposed to be home on that day! I was scared out of my wits. I turned, walked out quickly, and kept on walking, daring not to look back, lest I be turned into a pillar of salt. The entrance door slammed shut behind me with a loud bang. I skipped down the five entrance steps, mingling quickly with other passersby on the sidewalk, but then I heard the entrance door slam shut again. I knew it was the alien searching for the unknown source of the knock, and like two darts at my back, I could actually feel his penetrating eyes. Would he recognize me from behind? Would he call or come after me? I continued to walk quickly.

I made it back to my car, and parked about a half a block down Clark Street. What to do? What to do? He wasn't supposed to be there, and now I would have the long drive back home ahead of me. I decided to wait it out. I was hereon a mission, and it would be accomplished. From inside the Dodge, I could see the front entrance of the building as well as the apartment window. His BMW motorcycle was now parked legally on the street. I guess Brooklyn's Finest and Officer Ortiz had really taught him a lesson. Then the thought entered my mind. I should park the Dodge in the empty space in front of the motorcycle, and then, suppose I didn't see the stupid thing while backing up. Do it! Yes! Do it! Bash the Dodge into his damned motorcycle! And then take off. Do it!!

I didn't do it. I waited … and waited, and watched from my point of surveillance on Clark Street, inside the safety and security of Old Faithful. He was near the open window of the apartment, talking on the telephone. The conversation ended, the window was closed, and there was no further activity. It was getting to be late afternoon and nothing was happening. The weather had changed and was getting cold. The motorcycle was still there, and he was still in the apartment, warm and comfortable. I was outside, cold, hungry, and my bladder filling up fiercely. I took a quick break, satisfied my biological needs, and returned to my post. And now, with most of the day gone, and night approaching, I began to wonder if he would ever leave. Perhaps not! Another day wasted. Nothing accomplished. It continued to get colder and darker, but then, suddenly, the lights in the apartment went on, and then at about 7:00 P.M. they went out. Something was finally happening! And now, with acute concentration turned toward the apartment building entrance, I waited anxiously for the appearance of the dark alien. Suddenly the door opened. No! It wasn't him. It was just a neighbor going out for an evening stroll on the promenade. But now, only a half minute later, the door opened again! Yes! It was him, but now almost invisible in the dark, night air. He walked over to the motorcycle, started it up, drove it over to its spot under the apartment window, parked, walked back inside the apartment, and turned on the lights. Crap!! That's it? Is that the whole day? Damn it! Nobody ever goes anywhere on a Sunday night! I continued to wait, but for what, I didn't know. But then, at exactly 7:30 P.M., the lights again went out, the dark alien exited the building entrance again, walked over to the motorcycle, started it up with a deafening roar, and took off to who knows where. In seconds, he was gone. Success! I now had access to the apartment.

The apartment was fairly neat. It was fixed up much better than the first time. There was a full sized bed in the center of the room taking up most of the space in the room, and some small pieces of furniture. Midnite planned on staying. So now, this was my chance. The eviction would begin! I moved a chair out into the hall, and then some cartons, but then I began to think. IDIOT! I was doing it all wrong. Get the locks! First the locks! The locks had to be changed first! I studied the ancient locks. They were too old, too complex. I couldn't get it apart without breaking them. I would need special tools and more time. I couldn't do it, and it was already too late to get a locksmith. I was cold, hungry, tired, and I needed more time. Without much hope, I studied the locks some more, but then I heard the frightening roar of a motorcycle!

"RRRRRRRRRRRRRRRRRRRRRRRRRRR!!!!!!!!!!!!"

OH SHIT!!! HE'S BACK!! I was in trouble, and about to break out in a cold sweat. Quick! Bring back the chair from outside. NO! There's no time! Turn off the lights and lock the door! I can't! I had already started to take out the screws. Wait! Get the dead bolt and lock it from the inside. Lights out! Door bolted from the inside! And like Midnite during the police raid, I remained still and silent, barely daring to even breath, and waited for the inevitable sound of the front entrance door slamming against the frame, announcing the alien's arrival. But the sound didn't come. Instead, the motorcycle seemed to be going away, the roar of its engine becoming more and more faint. It was a false alarm. The room fell completely silent.

I put the lights back on and studied the little apartment

some more. There were court papers on the desk. Kravitz had had him served, as well as me as licensor. The parking ticket I had seen on my first visit had grown to a neatly folded stack of maybe three inches. And on the night table was a twelve inch hunting knife, a blown up glossy black and white picture of him playing the bongo drums in a band, a checkbook with no money, neatly filed personal papers in a cardboard box, and ... United Airlines ticket receipts to San Francisco for Christmas - round trip. He planned on coming back! And then, next to the ticket receipts was a Trinidad and Tobago passport. A PASSPORT! If he's legal, make him illegal! ... The passport! ... GET THE PASSPORT! ...

The original plan couldn't be completed, and now I was still in some danger. Who knew when he would return? I had to get out of there. I had brought along with me an American Flag which I now draped over the apartment window from inside. America for the Americans! America is taking back Brooklyn! I brought back the chair and cartons that I had moved out into the hall, left the lights on, and locked the door. I had thereby reclaimed my share of Brooklyn from the alien invader.

The courts would be better than this. Anything would be better than this. It was time to go ... and fast! I made my way to the Dodge in hasty retreat from enemy territory. Old Faithful started right up, and I began the long trip back home, back to clean, pristine suburbia, back to safe and secure eastern Long Island.

XVIII. Landlord and Tenant Court

Midnite was still living in my apartment, I was still paying his rent, Kravitz kept calling me, and our court date, scheduled for December 5th was fast approaching. I reconciled myself to the fact that we were going to court. There was no stopping it. That's what Midnite wanted, that's what the landlord wanted, and it didn't matter what I wanted.

Preparation and knowledge is always the best defense. I spent nearly every night before the trial at the library reading about landlord-tenant law, immigration, rent stabilization, or anything else that I thought might be useful. There was an interesting pamphlet from the INS about immigration. There was also a book - Getting into America - Deutch, and there were several others.

It would be a sixty-five mile trip into Brooklyn for the trial, during the height of the rush hour traffic. The miles on Old Faithful were piling up fast. I would have to be up at 5:00 A.M. Kravitz called me in the office the day before the trial to make sure I would be there. Perhaps, to protect my own interests, it would be better to show up and testify against the alien squatter. Should I say that he's a squatter and I don't know him? Then he would say that I signed a lease with him. And I would ask him to show it. Then he would say I stole it … Or should I just say that I subletted without the landlord's permission? … It was ugly!

I didn't sleep well that night. I would get to see my landlord for the first time. I guessed that court would be as good of a place as any to meet your landlord. What did he look like?   And what was behind that deep, raspy, threatening voice?   Yes, my landlord!   What did he look like? … What did he look like? …

He could be seen on a clear night with the full moon shining.   The small hunch-backed figure would slide down a rope anchored to the roof of the building, making its way from the top floor apartment windows to the street level windows, his black cape flying wildly in the wind.   He was terrifyingly ugly!   His face was heavily pocked.   He had three badly yellowed and decayed teeth remaining in his mouth.   His small, beady eyes were close together and nearly popped out of his head.   There was a deep scar across his left check, the result of a fight with a tenant who couldn't pay his rent and was about to be evicted.   He would swing on the rope, bouncing from window to window with the agility of a cockroach.   He would make his grand entrance at the apartment of those unfortunate tenants who were in arrears, and would demand, in his deep, threatening, raspy voice,

"Ah ha!   THE RENT!!   It's gonna cost!"

"Welcome to King's County Civil Court!   There is no talking allowed in the courtroom during the calendar call. There is no food, beverages, or smoking allowed.   There will be two calendar calls.   Listen carefully to these instructions. When you hear your case, landlord will answer, 'Landlord ready.'   Tenant will answer, 'Tenant ready.'   If you do not hear your case, listen for the second calendar call …"

The court officer continued on with his instructions in his inimitable, authoritative monotone.

So this was Landlord-Tenant Court. I arrived at the court very early, took a seat in the second row, and waited for the room to fill up. I studied the courtroom. I was amazed at the squalor and cheapness of it all. Landlord-Tenant Court is a low priority item in the City's budget - tenant evictions are discouraged. What do you call the place where the judge sits? Well, it's made of plywood, like something put together for a fourth grade play. That's right; they call it a bench, just like where the homeless people sleep in the park. The judge sits on a bench!

Finally, the room filled up with about 400 people, nearly all minorities - Brooklyn's huddled masses - the poor, the tired, the hungry - the wretched refuse! They were all being thrown out of their apartments! And now, with the calendar call completed, it had to be repeated again - in Spanish. They were wasting my time. I was hoping to get back to the job that afternoon, but the calendar call continued to grind on endlessly. My thoughts: *"Why don't they do it in Hebrew also?"* But eventually, the calendar call ended and the room fell silent, the silence interrupted only by the piercing monotone of the court officer.

"Enter Justice George M. Clancy. PLEASE RISE!"

Judge Clancy was black. He was an older man with graying hair, and a determined, vindictive manner. The good judge had a way of accentuating the last word of each sentence by raising its pitch and volume. His eyes would scan the room like radar locking onto any evil landlord that might be present. The long-winded, self-righteous speech began, his deep resonant voice striking fear into the hearts and souls of these same evil landlords.

"Judge Clancy here. I look around the courtroom here. There are a great many of you facing some enormous difficulties. My purpose here is to ensure that all of you are treated fairly and justly while navigating your ways through these difficulties. It is now December. It's becoming quite a bit cold outside. I looked around while coming to work today. I saw that the puddles of water on the sidewalks have turned to ice. I WILL NOT SIGN any warrants of eviction today! When the temperature outside is below 65 degrees, I do not sign any warrants of eviction! There were two landlords that we found guilty of lock-outs. Those landlords are going to JAIL! And holdovers ... in the case of a holdover, an eviction can be extended for six months, and in certain cases of hardship, additional time is given ..."

My eyes were transfixed on the judge. My heart was racing. I couldn't believe the words entering into my ears. My case was a holdover. Stupid me! I was paying my rent. That made it a holdover. And the lock-out (gulp!), I did that. I could have gone to jail! But the judge wasn't finished. There was more, and he continued on as I listened in confused, horrified amazement.

"Today is the fifth day of Chanukah. The fifth candle is the candle of mercy. It truly is the candle of mercy! It stands for justice, decency, humanity, and above all, MERCY! I will not grant any evictions today! ..."

Well, this was my territory. I never heard of the "candle of mercy." He had to have made it up. It is special in that it never falls on Shabbat and therefore, it does not compete with the Shabbat candles. Also, the fifth night is the first day of the new month of Tevet. But this has nothing to do with mercy. Indeed, Chanukah is not about mercy! It is about the wars against Antiochus Epiphanes and the Syrian Greeks. It is about the victories of the Maccabees and the wholesale slaughter of pagan cities where all males were put to death by the sword. But mercy? No! It is not about mercy. What we need is a team of Maccabees to evict all the deadbeat tenants!

He went on like that for a while longer, but finally, the merciful judge finished and the cases were called. A hundred and fifty were called before mine, but now here it was.

"Kravitz vs. Cohen."

"Landlord present."

"Tenant present."

"Application."

The third response came from a voice from the back of the courtroom, but who was it? The calendar call continued. Rooms were assigned to cases. The calendar call went on. What happened to Kravitz vs. Cohen? There was no assignment. There were no instructions. It was completely ignored. There had to be an omission or a mistake. I got up to inquire of the Court Officer about Kravitz vs. Cohen.

"SIT DOWN! You're out of order!"

Out of order? I sheepishly returned to my seat. I was baffled and confused. Whose voice was this from the back of the courtroom answering "Application?" What did "application" mean? I was the tenant here. I was supposed to be the only tenant here! And as the calendar call continued, I was approached by a young man dressed in a suit and tie. I think we were the only two people dressed in suits and ties. I wasn't hard to find among Brooklyn's wretched refuse, and he wasn't at all what I expected.

"Are you Jonah Cohen?" he asked.

"Yes."

"I'm Mike Kravitz."

We had never seen each other before. It was our first

meeting.   The voice was nothing like the voice on the telephone, but the conversation flowed as if we had known each other for years, which in effect, we did.   Kravitz continued.

"Can you believe that judge? Can you? Look, in case you're wondering, here's what's going on. Your buddy Midnite showed up here, and he just asked for an adjournment. When they finish the calendar call, we'll all approach the bench. Just tell the judge that you're the tenant, he's the subtenant, and whatever happens, happens."

The case was called. I approached the bench with Kravitz. We both faced the judge. And as we faced the judge, I could sense a mysterious presence at my back and over my left shoulder. It was Midnite! The alien spirit in the flesh, towering nearly a foot above me, had come! He wore a silly baseball party hat, much too small for his head, and secured around his chin with a rubber band. He was dressed in blue jeans and boots, and wore an earring in his left ear. He held designer sunglasses in his hand which he had placed on the judge's bench. Midnite obviously didn't take the courts seriously. His entire manner made a mockery of the whole thing, and here I was, dressed in my best suit and tie. I thought one was supposed to show respect for the court. Idiot! Now was not the time to look rich and prosperous! He wasn't supposed to be there, but now it was all three of us facing the judge.

"Who's the landlord here?"

Kravitz responded affirmatively, and then the judge looked at me. I stood erect, faced the judge, and giving the Court its due respect, responded in a loud and clear voice.

"I'm the tenant."

Judge Clancy then looked at Midnite as if his appearance

and attire were perfectly normal.

"I'm the subtenant. I requested the adjournment. I have to get a lawyer."

"Adjourned to December 27th."

That was it? It was all over? I was in a fog, not yet adjusted to what had just happened. It was another wasted day. I walked outside with my landlord and we talked a little. Midnite had postponed the case. We talked some more, and as we talked, Midnite suddenly appeared – remolecularized like an alien from Star Trek. The encounter was unfriendly.

"You're going to jail, mun!"

"Pay your rent!"

Suddenly he was gone. Mike offered to buy me a cup of coffee. I accepted. We took a booth at a nearby luncheonette, and we talked. Mike wound up buying me a complete breakfast. I realized that accepting it might have been a foolish thing to do. After all, he was still the enemy! But anywhere that there is a free meal to be had, especially one from the landlord, take it! I gave him copies of my letters to the INS, to the Trinidad and Tobago Consulate, and a copy of my letter ordering him to vacate. I told Mike of my commuting problems and a little about my job. He told me about the improvements he made to the building. He asked me for a ride back to his building, but I was too cheap or poor (from paying him Midnite's rent) to pay for parking at the court parking lot, so we walked back to the apartment building together. He introduced me to the new superintendent and showed me the work that he had done on the building. He said a little more about how hard it was to be a landlord, and again how nobody likes the landlord. I told him that it was a nice job that he did on the building, but

I barely noticed or cared. We parted, shook hands, and I thanked him for breakfast.

XIX.   The INS

It was only a one mile or so walk over the Brooklyn Bridge to the Immigration and Naturalization office at 26 Federal Plaza. Perhaps the day wouldn't be a total waste. I decided to take decisive action! I would report the illegal alien in person. And so, I arrived at the Immigration and Naturalization Service. It is conveniently located in the lobby on the first floor. Unlike Landlord and Tenant Court, Immigration is a high priority item. I convinced the security guard that I really was a Federal employee and had a right to enter at the rear entrance, the employee entrance - it was closer. I showed him my DoD ID card. He scrutinized it, but he wasn't sure. He wanted to know what my business here was. I told him that I had to report an illegal alien. He looked at the card, then looked at me, and then reluctantly decided to let me in.

But now once in, where do I go? There was no one to talk to, only a long winding line of immigrants and a few security guards. One of them told me to get on the long winding line of immigrants. I walked over to the exit door and asked another guard where one would go to report an illegal alien, and again, I was told to get on the immigration line. I couldn't believe it! I was completely outraged! What a country this is! You go there to report an illegal alien, and they tell you to wait on line with the immigrants. So what was one supposed to do? Wait on line with the immigrants? I decided to make a bit of a scene. What could they do? They couldn't deport me, right?

"I AM AN AMERICAN CITIZEN!   I AM A

TAXPAYER! I AM NOT GETTING ON A LINE OF IMMIGRANTS!!!"

I got a lot of stares from the embarrassed INS employees, but the immigrants didn't know what I was saying. I was approached by a security guard. Would he escort me out of the building, or worse? He bent down over my shoulder, and then in a low, but audible voice said,

"7th, 8th, and 10th floors."

But the 7th, 8th, and 10th floors only offered more of the same - large auditoriums filled with immigrants completing their journey to citizenship. The investigations office was locked. There was no receptionist, information window, visitors' area, or anybody at all to talk to. I invited myself into an office at random and spoke to a clerk seated at the front desk. He gave me an investigations telephone number and a fax number, and told me to call the phone number from inside the building. I was told to use a pay phone located in the hallway! Why couldn't I just call from his office? It didn't pay to argue. I went to the pay phone, dialed the number, and got no answer. After trying several times, I had to give up. Midnite, the alien spirit wins again! A bit of Black-Magic from Trinidad. How could my Chanukah menorah compete with this? It seemed that this fifth candle, Judge Clancy's "candle of mercy," was burning brighter all the time.

I found myself back at work in the office. I wasn't doing much work anymore. I was too involved with my legal efforts. One does what one must. I faxed my letter to the INS after finally managing to talk to an Immigration Officer over the phone. Perhaps the wheels of justice were beginning to turn. Midnite would soon be out of the country, Kravitz would have his apartment back, I wouldn't have to pay him anymore rent, and I would get on with my life. But only if it would happen, only if it could be so...

XX. Kravitz vs. Cohen

The new court date was coming up fast. Kravitz called me in the office to remind me, and to make sure I would be there. It would mean another day off from work, another long trip into Brooklyn in rush hour traffic, and of course, all the stress involved with yet another court appearance. This time it would be for real, no more adjournments ... or maybe not. I thought it over, and came to the conclusion that I really had nothing to gain. I wasn't interested in continuing my tenancy or maintaining possession. Indeed, my purpose was to get rid of the thing. I decided that Kravitz and his lawyers would have to face Midnite alone, or Midnite and his lawyer, or whoever else found special delight in going to court again with or without their lawyers. And so, I simply ignored it all in blissful ignorance.

Also, as it happened, and almost by divine providence, the job called for me to be away for a week on TDY (temporary duty travel) in Hartford, Connecticut for training in Navy Nuclear contracts. I would be far away from the scene of all the action, and the other two litigants would have to do battle between themselves. The week went quickly. When I got back, the first thing I did was call Midnite, and to my delight, I heard the following message:

"The number you have reached ... 643-0875 in area 718 is no longer in service. There is no further information on 643-0875."

Yes! Midnite was gone! The trial actually did take place

this time. Kravitz was of course awarded Judgment of Possession. Kravitz, Sr. and his lawyers had somehow gotten Midnite to sign a Stipulation of Settlement to leave on January 20th. Since I had been paying my rent, there was no money judgment awarded. Nevertheless, my newly found "friendship" with my landlord had ended. Our non-aggression pact was terminated. The war was on. Kravitz was demanding payment of several thousands of dollars, plus court costs, interest, lawyer fees, and various other expenses. He started calling me even at home, and several times in the office. Even though these expenses weren't awarded at the trial, it looked like he was getting ready to sue. If he sued, it would be on eastern Long Island, my district, and about a seventy mile drive from Brooklyn. I'd get an adjournment, just like Midnite, and then we would do it again. But why let it get to that? It was time to take defensive action, just in case.

In order to evade the process servers, I would change the number on the house, "borrowing" someone else's number, and using it as my own. Actually, it was a simple thing to do because the numbers were screwed into the posts with only two screws. Who's to know? And I changed the name on the door using *"Earnshaw,"* a name that I just happened to remember from college English in <u>Wuthering</u> <u>Heights</u>. The name didn't even sound Jewish. They'd never find me! Nobody was ever able to find their way around this condo anyway, even with the right numbers! Next, I would change my phone number, or better yet, disconnect it, and then, request another duty station on the job.

I was right. Kravitz's certified letter demanding payment came shortly afterward. That same sickening, nauseating feeling returned. Oh! How stupid of me to have had breakfast with him! Let's see. What did I tell him? I think I told him that my job was subject to five year rotations. He misconstrued it to mean five years of subletting and that also was in his letter with the cute phrase, "as you advised," and therefore he padded the bill with extra charges for that too! And the ride that he asked me for from the court to his apartment building - Oh! Stupid me! He didn't need a ride. It was a short walk. He wanted to get the plate number of my car. It was an asset to be seized to satisfy an expected judgment! (That was assuming of course that Old Faithful was an asset worthy of being seized.) No, it wasn't over yet and things weren't looking good. Kravitz's letter needed a firm, honest, and well thought out response. It would be my swan song. It would be my farewell. What would happen, would happen, as Kravitz had so eloquently put it at the court. I wrote my letter.

Dear Mike,

This is in response to your letter of January 14th with reference to Apt 1C at 63 Clark Street.

The trial which took place on December 23rd did not require me to pay additional rent, use and occupancy costs, legal fees, or additional charges for alleged five years of subletting. Indeed, it is inconceivable how you or your agent would not have known of such alleged subletting. But this only serves to demonstrate the serious lack of supervision, security, and care which this building received during the thirteen years of my tenancy.

At the court session which took place on December 5th,

Judge George M. Clancy stated unequivocally that the landlord should pay his own legal costs.

I have cooperated with you fully in every possible way to achieve the removal of Mr. Neville Michaels, the squatter, and have incurred my own costs, court fees, etc., although without the benefit of a lawyer. I have provided you with copies of my correspondence with Mr. Michaels and the petition and notice served on him in an effort to hasten his removal. If a landlord chooses to hire a lawyer for his own convenience, it is the responsibility of that landlord to pay for his own lawyer.

I have complied to the best of my ability with your request for me to vacate no later than October 14th, as indicated on my letter of September 12th. Such vacating has been acknowledged by you in the Petition. Mr. Michaels was an unfortunate occurrence and his origins still remain something of a mystery.

I deny that any landlord-tenant relationship ever existed between us as may be evidenced by his inability to produce a lease or proof of rent paid at the trial. An order to vacate by a landlord, and compliance with that order by a tenant, terminates a lease and relieves a tenant of his obligation to pay additional rent. Nevertheless, I continued to pay my rent. I am now requesting that two month's rent be returned to me, together with my security deposit plus interest in the amount of $581.64 for a total amount of

$1,556.94.

During the thirteen years that I was your tenant, I had paid my rent every month, faithfully, and on time. Also, , I had suffered through severe roach infestation, mice, sewer leaks from an upstairs apartment, gas leaks, inadequate heat, lack of security, assorted and unauthorized persons roaming the building, various plumbing problems, general building neglect (as you advised), and strange, unpleasant odors emanating from a basement filled with garbage, dog feces, and dead animal carcasses.

My employment requires me to be in a travel status for varying and unspecified periods of time. Having a friend stay at my apartment for these short periods does not constitute a substantial violation of the lease or the rent stabilization laws. At our conversation over breakfast (which I found to be quite pleasant), I had indicated to you that I was subject to five year rotations. This did not mean five years of subletting. The fact is, I wore out my Honda commuting from Brooklyn to Long Island all these years.

It was through our mutual cooperation and interests that the squatter has been removed and the apartment returned to you in good order. I am now returning one set of keys and hope that we may part friends. I wish you success in your real estate career, and a good life.

Sincerely,
Jonah Cohen

Kravitz called me again after receiving my farewell letter. He didn't like it. His tone was unfriendly. There were more threats of litigation, demands for additional rent charges, and then he summed it all up.

"You know, that letter ... that letter! ... You'll be hearing from us, Mr. Cohen. You'll definitely be hearing from us. It's gonna cost! It's gonna cost!"

He hung up the phone in defeated frustration, and stuck with his own lawyer fees. He was right - It was "gonna cost," but now it was between Midnite and me. It was now Cohen vs. Michaels.

XXI. Skip Tracing

Kravitz was out of my life. I never heard from him or his lawyers again. It had been seven or eight weeks since I had last spoken with him and I had received nothing from him - no case. But Midnite out of my life? Never! Just because the United States Postal Service didn't know where he was, or the NYS Department of Motor Vehicles, or the Consulate General of Trinidad and Tobago, or even the U.S. Immigration and Naturalization Service, that didn't mean that he was unfindable, and that certainly didn't mean that I wouldn't find him. Justice would prevail! The rent would be paid!

My own case against Midnite had resulted in a Default Judgment from the Landlord & Tenant Court, since he did not bother to show up. Unfortunately for the claimant, the judgment was an award of possession only. There was no Money Judgment. In order to be awarded a Money Judgment, service would have had to be made by personal service - papers handed to him personally. Service here was made by conspicuous service - papers slipped under the door. So in effect, I was awarded nothing. The apartment was happily handed back to the landlord, and the case ended. In order to get a Money Judgment, I would have to sue in Small Claims Court.

Small Claims Court is nice. It's fast, cheap, and best of all, no lawyers. At the time, it was only $5.58. And since I didn't know where Midnite was, I had to use his last known address - Clark Street. It could work. The Court sends out two summonses. One by first class mail and the other by certified mail, return-receipt-requested. Since it is well known that deadbeats never answer certified mail, making the usually correct assumption that nothing good ever comes by certified mail, the Court relies on the regular first class mail. If the summons sent by first class mail does not come back to the Court marked "undeliverable" within three weeks, then service is assumed. It was worth a shot.

But of course, nothing in this world is easy - it came back to the Court. Personal service was needed and Midnite would have to be found. The search was on. I started with his old address, the one printed on his checks. It was 977 South 9th Street. There was at least a reasonable chance that he returned to the place from where he came. It was a terrible neighborhood, bearing more resemblance to burned out, bombed out Beirut than a major city in the U.S. It was awful - rubble and debris everywhere, abandoned buildings in serious need of repair and almost ready to collapse, and a few scrawny stray dogs - I guessed that he actually did live there once. It fit his lifestyle. I looked for the motorcycle, but of course it wasn't there - only a few abandoned cars on broken pavement. Nevertheless, 977 South 9th Street was a fairly well kept brownstone. On one side it adjoined an empty lot filled with garbage. On the other side, the building propped up an old run-down church - the Church of Light, or something like that. It blended in well with the rest of the neighborhood. It was so sad, it was almost funny. Thus was Midnite's old neighborhood.

I planned my investigative work to coincide with my dental visits so that the trips would not be a total waste. I visited the apartment building, the scene of the "crime," and searched for any clue, or anything at all that might lead to his whereabouts, but nothing. Kravitz had fixed up the apartment with new windows, new painting, etc., but he hadn't yet rented it out. I tried calling the references that Midnite had originally given me, but without any success. Either there would be a telephone answering machine, a disconnected phone with no forwarding number, or a useless response like, "Yes, he lived here, but I don't know where he is now."

I needed a good address to get him served. Midnite's social and business life (assuming there was any business at all) revolved around the telephone. It was a good bet that he would have a telephone in his own name, but if so, then how would I get the number ... or better yet the address? Now, it wasn't my style. I had never done anything like that before. I wasn't even sure if it was legal, but I had to try it. It just might work. I called the telephone company.

"Good morning. How may we help you?"

"Good morning. This is Neville Michaels."

"Telephone number, please."

I, of course, didn't have his telephone number. I had to give them the old number and hope it would work. The young lady at the phone company was very patient and especially friendly and helpful.

"Well, the number is (718) 643-0875 ... you see ... I just moved, and I haven't received my telephone bill."

"Let me look it up, just a minute ... Here it is. We sent it out four weeks ago."

"That's strange. I think I should have gotten it by now. Did you send it to the old address, to 63 Clark Street? It should have been sent to the new address. Could you tell me where you sent it?"

"Yes, we sent it to 21 Phlox Place in Flushing."

SUCCESS!!!!!!!!!!!!!!!!!!!!!!!!!!!!!!!!! It worked! But I wasn't sure if I heard it right. What was a phlox anyway? I needed to verify it, but already she was on to me, an exposed imposter. I groped my way through it and tried again.

"Did ... did you say phlox? How do you spell that?"

Her tone changed. I was the enemy. I was the bad guy, the spy caught red-handed, but she had already completely fallen into my trap.

"Why don't you give me the information ... SIR?"

"Uh ... Well ... Thanks for your help. Thanks a lot."

The crucial piece of personal information had been carelessly leaked out. Phlox is a flower, and Phlox Place was really on the map. That same afternoon, I went into Queens to check it out. It was a six story apartment building opposite a park. I didn't have the apartment number, and the name wasn't on the lobby directory. Getting into these buildings is amazingly simple. One method that usually works is to just ring all the buzzers. Somebody is bound to buzz you in. The other method is to just follow someone else into the building. People are usually very helpful. Also, it helps to have a key, any key in you hand. It makes you look like you belong. And so, I made my way into the building, but again, the name was not on the mailboxes, or it might have been someone else's name. Investigative work is not easy. I needed to know the apartment number to get him served. The only way was to start on the first floor and to work my way up, hoping that I would see his name on the door. Luck was with me. On the fifth floor, on the door of apartment 5G, appearing under the peephole, handwritten in light blue ink were the names of the two occupants, *Marciano & Michaels.*

SUCCESS!!!!!! Midnite had been found! He could now

be served. Just to make sure, I tried looking up Marciano in the telephone directory. Again, SUCCESS! I went to the Queens County Small Claims Court, waited on line, filled out the papers, and paid the fee for a new claim. My case was now in progress - Cohen vs. Michaels a/k/a Midnite. The court clerk looked at the papers and then looked up at me in disbelief.

"Is that the name of your adversary? Midnite?"

"Yup, that's his name. That's what they call him."

Service of process was done by the court by first class mail and certified mail. Since the papers did not come back to the court, service was assumed. The case was put on the calendar and set for trial. Court date: March 26th.

XXII. Small Claims

It had to be some black magic from Trinidad and Tobago. The forces of nature were against me. Nothing was going right. The day before the trial Old Faithful had sprung a leak in her right front brake caliper and I broke an irreplaceable bolt while trying to get it out. With nighttime approaching, it was looking frighteningly hopeless. Visions of taking the moped into Queens, or perhaps worse yet, the Long Island Railroad, danced through my head. The spirit of Captain Midnite was upon me! Fortunately, and at the last minute, my friend John came through, and the two of us managed to get the old car back on the road.

I got to the court two hours early, which gave me plenty of time to familiarize myself with my surroundings and also to do some last minute preparation on the case. The bulletin board had the cases for the night session posted. We were on the calendar. There it was: "Claimant: Jonah Cohen Defendant: Neville Michaels a/k/a Midnite." I found a comfortable spot on a window ledge about a half flight up the stairs where I was able to get a panoramic view of all the people - lawyer, litigant, or anybody else - entering or leaving the building at the main entrance. I scanned every head coming or going - there was no Midnite. Surely he wouldn't show. I would without a doubt get an easy default judgment. Morty, a friend from the office, said that he would meet me at the court at 6:30 P.M., just to provide some encouragement, or to help in any way that he could, or maybe it was just for his own personal entertainment. Anyway, as 6:30 P.M. approached, there was still no sign of

Midnite. It looked good. Morty, true to his word, showed up at exactly 6:30 P.M. The calendar call took place in room 138. As I sat with Morty at the rear of the room, still scanning heads, there was still no sign of the alien from Trinidad. Yes, I would have an easy default judgment and it would soon be over.

The calendar call began and progressed. I was so nervous that I thought I might go into fibrillation. Finally, we came to the case and I heard my name.

"Jonah Cohen."

I paused, just to make sure that I heard my name correctly, and then, after a slight nudge from Morty, and in a voice so powerful, determined, and tinged with revenge, I'm sure,

"READY."

The court officer then announced the respondent's name.

"Neville Michaels."

A response came from behind. It came from somewhere in the vastness and emptiness of outer space. It was faint, but audible, and very real.

"Application."

He was there! To my absolute shock, horror, and amazement, he came. Yes, there he was, the spirit of Captain Midnite incarnate. The impossible, the unthinkable had happened.

Midnite had been there all the time spying on my conversation with Morty. What did I say? What was revealed? And why was he there? Did he actually have assets to protect? Sometime later, as the courtroom emptied, the request for adjournments came up. We changed seats, but again, Midnite was right behind, still spying on our conversation. I raised my voice slightly so that he would have no trouble hearing while I continued speaking with Morty.

"Oh, I called the INS and spoke to the Immigration Officer. They've already completed the papers and started the deportation process. We should be getting a court date for the hearing in a couple of days ..."

He probably thought that Morty was my lawyer. It looked great! It must have scared the crap out of him, but now it was time to approach the judge. Morty did give me some encouragement and good advice.

"Don't let him have the adjournment. Say you can't make it. Say you'll be out of town on Government business. Say anything. Just get the trial going."

Midnite waved the summons in front of him, said that he just got it, that he was not living at that address anymore, and that he needed to get a lawyer. The argument was weak. If he showed up for the hearing, of course he was served. It was the same song and dance that he pulled in Landlord-Tenant Court. And then he had the *chutzpah* to request a court appointed lawyer at taxpayer's expense - my tax money paying for my opponent's legal expense! And finally, he asked for an adjournment until December ... or January ... or possibly later. He said that his band would be on tour in October and November. Band? On tour? Midnite was actually making some money? There was hope.

Next, the judge turned to me.

"Your Honor, the events in this case are now over a year old. I see no reason for further delay and I'm ready right now. Also, I'll be away on Government business in December and January."

The trial was rescheduled for the following Tuesday, October 27th. The judge was visibly annoyed with Midnite, and gave him only a week. Nevertheless, he got his adjournment. The court encourages litigants to settle a case between themselves before it goes to trial. It's probably a good policy to follow because it eliminates the stress, expense, and uncertainty of outcome. I followed Midnite out of the courtroom, and out of the building. Morty came with me for protection. I shouted out to my adversary,

"Hey, Midnite!"

The tall, nearly invisible black figure slowly emerged from out of the darkness. We approached each other.

"Wanna settle?"

"Settle what?"

"You owe me some money. Make me an offer."

"You're a dead man."

At that, Morty, my friend and protector, took off in a rush with parting words of farewell.

"See ya."

I guess Morty had had enough entertainment. You can always count on friends when you need them most. I was there alone in the dark with Midnite. What did he mean by I was a "dead man?" A settlement was not to be had. Was the threat to be taken literally? Was I in any danger? Never show your enemies fear. There was nothing further to be said. I pointed my index finger at him.

"See you next week! Be there!"

We parted, the spirit of Captain Midnite disappearing into the darkness once again, but the phantom's image reappeared as he crossed Queens Boulevard. He started up the motorcycle with a tremendous roar that reverberated against the apartment buildings and grew to a deafening crescendo. It was the same old, beat up BMW. I watched as he sped up and disappeared into the traffic. I too crossed

Queens Boulevard, now with Midnite's last words still ringing in my head, *"You're a dead man."* I headed into a dark, desolate street, and realized the folly of this. A native New Yorker should know better. I turned around, looked behind me, walked quickly to the Dodge, and started her up. Old Faithful proved to be more reliable than Morty. I began the long drive back to Long Island, meditating on the events of the day. Trial date: October 27, 1992 - 6:30 P.M. Would the Phantom of Captain Midnite show?

XXIII. The Trial

The trial date was October 27th. I got to the court about an hour early, found my usual spot on the gray marble window ledge, about a half flight up the stairs, and sat, watched, and waited. Then, at 6:20 P.M., the Black Phantom, silhouetted against the dimly lit pavement, passed into my line of sight. He made his way up the steps and approached the main entrance. It was him. Damn it! He came! But I expected him to come, even if it was just to deny me an easy default judgment. My eyes followed him through the doors of the court building. I studied him as he slipped through the lobby and walked down the hall. Yes. Midnite had come! There he was! His long straight black hair was cropped closely to the sides of his skull and tied into a pony tail, and tied to the pony tail was a black and white silk scarf nearly reaching to the floor. There was a gold earring, now one in each ear. Midnite had prospered over the past year. He doubled his assets! He wore faded blue jeans, ripped in the back exposing bare black flesh, and he wore black leather boots with bells. Here was my opponent - the Phantom incarnate!

I remained at my window ledge a few more minutes, watching the rats scurrying back and forth on the outside court steps. They seemed to ignore the occasional lawyer or litigant who happened to be walking up or down. Brazen little bastards! I would have stayed there and watched, but it was now time to get on with the trial.

Calendar call took place at 6:30 P.M. I sat far back this time and watched as Midnite seated himself up ahead. The

Phantom's head turned and he recognized me instantly. Did he think that I wouldn't show? My eyes darted to the front staring blankly, refusing to meet his. The calendar call progressed, and then,

"Jonah Cohen."

"Cohen, READY."

"Neville Michaels."

"Michaels, ready."

"Room 119."

We were on. I found myself following the Phantom who was hunting aimlessly for room 119. But why was I following him? I turned, walked the other way, and now he followed me. But I was lost too. Eventually we parted company. (He found room 119 first.) I decided that I liked room 119. It was a cozy little court room with not too many people. I envisioned myself going through my Perry Mason courtroom theatrics, somewhat confident, and almost looking forward to this. I stared at my opponent across the aisle. Was he human? Did he get nervous? Why was he here? He had no defense, and of course, no lawyer. His legs were crossed and he was tapping the fingers of his left hand on his knee. Yes! He did get nervous. He was somewhat human - not completely spirit. Then, our names were called and we moved to a smaller room at the front. We had to sign a waiver of appeal and agree to have the case heard by an arbitrator, not a judge. We also filled out an envelope with our address where the decision would be mailed. I peeked over at Midnite in a futile attempt to see the address. He covered it up quickly with his large hand, as if we were in school and I was trying to cheat on a test. The address would remain a secret. Anyway, he could have had it sent anywhere, or nowhere. And then,

"Room 137."

Room 137 was not a court room. I was disappointed, but also somewhat relieved. I probably would not have been very good at Perry Mason theatrics. Room 137 was just a small conference room with a desk where the arbitrator sat. There were three chairs in front of the desk. The room was occupied, so we had to wait a short while, until our names were called out by the court officer.

"Niggle Michaels."

"Neville," he corrected.

The unintended racial slur passed without incident and we moved on. We were both led into the humble little room for the trial. So this was it? Well, what did one really expect for $5.58?

We entered room 137. Midnite planted his motorcycle helmet on the center seat with an audible thud, and took the seat on the right. I took the seat on the left. We were sworn in. The arbitrator introduced himself, made some introductory remarks, and gave instructions as to how the case would proceed. There would be no appeals except in the case of a bribe. The arbitrator continued, stopped, and then looked up at me. I was fumbling with my briefcase, a folder with papers, and a pen. It was a clumsy beginning.

"Yes, I understand."

There were some more remarks and instructions. The arbitrator completed his introductions. Does one address an arbitrator as "Your Honor?" Maybe not, but he does sit in the place of the judge and represents the court. It certainly wouldn't hurt.

"Mr. Cohen, you begin."

I began.

"Your Honor, this case involves the non-payment of

RENT on a studio apartment at 63 Clark Street, Brooklyn, New York, that I sublet to the respondent. The period that I am claiming is from September 15, 1991 through January 6, 1992 for the total sum of TWO THOUSAND DOLLARS."

The arbitrator asked if there was a lease.

"Yes."

I showed him the lease.

"It's a SIGNED, NOTARIZED LEASE. The RESPONDENT entered into this LEASE AGREEMENT in BAD FAITH. I have here two BAD CHECKS. The respondent has paid no money whatsoever on this lease."

The arbitrator showed the lease to Midnite.

"Is this your signature?"

Midnite took the lease, squinted, examined it, mumbled something about it being the lease that I took from him, and then confirmed that the signature was indeed his.

"Did you pay anything on this lease?"

"No."

More discussion took place. The arbitrator made some notes, wrote down numbers, and figured amounts. It looked very good. I was off to a great start, but then the next question was directed at me.

"Did you pay anything to the landlord?"

I was afraid of this, but prepared. I didn't want this case to degenerate into Kravitz vs. Cohen with his "illegal" subletting. I thought Kravitz vs. Cohen was another case. It was a good thing that Midnite had adjourned the case until October 27th - I didn't bring my cancelled checks to the previous hearing, but now I had them.

"Yes, here are the check receipts, and here are the statements showing the debits to my account."

135

The arbitrator then asked what I thought was a strange question.

"Why were you paying the landlord?"

I looked at him with a puzzled look and said,

"I had an obligation under my lease."

I didn't realize until afterward the effectiveness of this obvious and simple answer. Nor did I realize the point that the arbitrator was making. The lease was a contract. I honored my contract with the landlord; Midnite did not honor his contract with me, and after all, this case was all about honoring a lease agreement - a contract. Wasn't it? Also, I showed financial loss, and I was seeking restitution of money paid as damages. But then the bombshell that I had been waiting for hit.

"Did you have the landlord's permission?"

Oh, the dreaded question! How would I handle it under oath?

"The lease rider gives me the right to sublet," I responded. It did. More discussion took place, but there it was again.

"But did you get the landlord's permission?"

It was getting late. I hadn't had anything to eat all day, not even the cup of coffee that usually would get me through the day. My voice had now acquired a strange, raspy quality that seemed more alien to me than the alien adversary seated at my right. The stress was too much! My mind lost track. Everything seemed to go white, even Midnite, if that were possible. I was totally lost. I became silent, my mind traveling through space at the speed of light. Oh, the dreaded question! *"The landlord's permission!"* I thought about the silence. I thought about Midnite at my right. I thought about the arbitrator, and what the arbitrator was

136

thinking of me, and I thought about the whole subletting nightmare ... and then I thought about losing! Losing was an unacceptable outcome. I could not lose! I didn't know how long I was on my space trip, with Captain Midnite co-piloting at my right. It might have been seconds, or even minutes. But Einstein says that at the speed of light, time stands still ... but for me, not them! But then, just when everything seemed lost, Section 226b of the Rent Stabilization Act began to crystallize in my mind as it was burned into my brain for over a year now. I began to become aware of my surroundings. My space trip was over. I had touched down. I had recovered. I was back.

"There is a procedure that I should have followed, Section 226b of the Housing Law."

"The Real Property Law," the arbitrator corrected, and then nodded approval.

So he was familiar with it. Of course he was! I continued and began to enumerate the details of 226b.

"I'm supposed to notify the landlord by certified mail, send a copy of the lease to the landlord, ...but, I wasn't able to because, ... because, ... I didn't have a consummated, ... eh, a completed, ... an effective, ..." I began to stumble badly, but then I remembered my self-training and preparation. Don't get tied up in words. Be blunt. Say what you mean. And then,

"THERE WAS NO MONEY PAID ON THIS LEASE! I couldn't follow 226b because there was no money paid!!"

It was perfect. The arbitrator again nodded approval.

"Well, that about wraps it up."

But Midnite hadn't said much up until then, and he was moving in his heavy artillery.

"Can I say something?" he began.

"I have been harassed. I have had things stolen out of my apartment. He took my lease, and stole my passport, and my green card …" (I didn't have his stupid green card. I wished I did. I would have thrown it into a sewer.) Midnite continued. He wasn't finished.

"I filed a police report …"

I braced, didn't respond, faced the arbitrator, and remained absolutely expressionless, but it was the arbitrator who stopped Midnite.

"I don't mean to belittle what you are saying, but what I have in front of me is his claim against you. You have nothing against him. If you choose to do so, you may start an action, but this isn't the time or place …"

And so, Midnite's heavy artillery was shot down faster than Saddam Hussein's air force. But Midnite wasn't dead yet. With great bravado, he threw the settlement papers of Kravitz vs. Cohen & Michaels on the desk. The arbitrator picked it up and looked at it. Again I braced. He finished reading it and looked up at Midnite.

"What does this have to do with the case at hand?"

Nothing! The settlement showed that the rent was paid up, and that Midnite had agreed to surrender the premises. The arbitrator began to end the hearing. I then asked that the respondent be examined.

"What do you mean?" asked the arbitrator.

Midnite covered up the rip in his jeans with the settlement papers. He was getting nervous.

"That the respondent reveal his assets, should judgment be rendered."

It was what the Small Claims book said to do, but it isn't done in New York. That would come later in Supplemental Proceedings.

And so the case was presented. The Claimant rested. The Respondent rested. The papers were returned.

"Good night," said the arbitrator.

"Thank you. Good night."

I was thoroughly drained, and absolutely exhausted, but I followed Midnite out of the building. Again, the BMW motorcycle was parked across the street from the court building. I still didn't know where he lived. He started up the big bike with a tremendous roar. Would he go east or west? I found a dark area outside the courthouse, on the grass, and under a tree. He wouldn't see me there. I watched, but I perceived the whites of the Phantom's eyes staring straight at me like laser beams in the darkness, across all eight lanes of Queens Boulevard. A frightening chill went through my spine, and then I remembered the rats. It was time to get the hell out of there.

I found the Dodge. Old Faithful started up on the first try. The pendulum had swung. Fortuna's wheel had turned. Victory was in the wind, along with the sweet smell of a well deserved JUDGMENT.

Court Decision: Two weeks.

XXIV. The Second Trial

It didn't come as a surprise, but nevertheless, it was tremendously satisfying. Justice had been served. I won! But it wasn't enough. Because of the $2,000 Small Claims limit, I wasn't able to sue for the full amount of the rent due - there was another three weeks of rent owed to the now judgment creditor - but I was able to file another claim. So, that is what I did.

The second trial took place on December 1, 1992. I found myself standing in front of the Court Building at 6:25 P.M., my eyes darting wildly east to west, and then back east along Queens Boulevard for any sign of the motorcycle and Midnite. There was none. It looked good for a default judgment. I was approached by a stranger who needed directions.

"Which way is it to the Small Claims Court?"

"To file a claim, or are you here for a trial?"

"Trial."

"Through the doors and to your left."

I had become a pro at this. I gave one more quick glance at the Courthouse entrance, and then another up and down Queens Boulevard. There was no sign of him. It was very encouraging. Even the rats were gone. I went inside for the calendar call.

"Cohen."

"Cohen, ready."

"Michaels ... Michaels?"

"Room 129."

Room 129 was a small courtroom. The arbitrator sat on a

judge's bench. I sat and waited in the jury box along with all the other landlords and litigants. Room 129 was used for inquests - a one-sided trial with no opposition. It was here that the Default Judgments would be awarded. I listened to the other cases, mostly motor vehicle accidents, fender benders. The Haitian woman sitting next to me didn't know how to address the envelope that we were each given for notification of the court's decision. (I was the exception - they ran out of envelopes.) She asked me for help. Would I help her? Another of Midnite's color, kindred, and appearance? Of course! She was a landlord and about to become a Judgment Creditor, just like me, and all Judgment Creditors must stick together! But it was almost hopeless. I couldn't understand her, and she was almost completely illiterate. I took her envelope and addressed it as best I could hoping that the notification of the court's decision would somehow reach her.

Finally, I heard my name, grabbed my briefcase, and took my place at the table facing the bench. The claim was made for the full $2,000 Small Claims limit, but Midnite really owed me only another three weeks of rent, the amount Kravitz confiscated out of my security. But my lease with Midnite was to run about another eight months. There was doubt. I went for the full $2,000.

It was getting late and there were only a few more cases to be heard. The usual courtroom decorum was slackened a bit. The arbitrator loosened his tie, and took a long sip of Coke through a straw from the can on the bench.

"Mr. Cohen, begin."

"I'm claiming rent for the period from January 6th on."

I showed the arbitrator the lease, and the bad checks, but then I was asked a very embarrassing question. I didn't even attempt to answer it. No, I wasn't on a space trip like the other time. I was in complete control. I just felt a little frustrated and stupid. The question was,

"How could anyone rent their apartment to someone named 'Midnite'?"

But what was done, was done, and now I would soon have another judgment. I got an envelope for the court's decision, sat down on a bench outside in the hall, and addressed it. The Haitian woman passed by and thanked me. I wished her good luck.

XXV. Chasing Midnite

As expected, the Default Judgment came in the mail, and it was signed by the arbitrator. Total judgments with interest and expenses now totaled $4,495.14, but how was I supposed to collect? Midnite was gone - vanished into thin air - no trace. The alien spirit had exited the physical world again.

Midnite was no longer living at the Phlox Place apartment, but I really couldn't be sure even of that. He did have two or three other addresses in the last year or so. The registration and license records that I was able to obtain from the NYS DMV revealed some interesting information. The motorcycle insurance was cancelled for non-payment, and the motorcycle had been reported stolen. Midnite was even more loose and reckless than I suspected, having come to court on a motorcycle reported stolen, with expired registration, a suspended motorcycle license, and no insurance.

I had to start some place, and Marciano at the Phlox Place address was the most logical place to start. It might have been the logical place to start, but what was not logical was what brought these two together. What does a white Italian have in common with a black alien from Trinidad? Was it a landlord-tenant relationship? Was it a homosexual relationship? Midnite sticks it in and that's the rent? Or was it a business relationship? Maybe the band was for real and they would be making some real money for the judgment creditor! There was only one way to find out. I would have to talk to this Marciano. Certainly he had some information about Midnite. I called his number and he answered.

"Wouldn't you know it? As soon as I turn off the machine, the phone rings. Hello?"

The voice seemed friendly enough, and I too, in as friendly a manner as I could feign,

"Hi, is Midnite there?"

"No. Midnite moved. Who is this?"

"Where'd he move to?"

"Well, if you let me have your name and number, I'll have him call you."

"Uh … well, I'm a friend of his, and I'm calling from a pay phone."

"Who is this?"

"I'm just a friend …"

"Well, like I said, I'll have him call you back."

It was useless. We weren't getting anywhere. Of course he had information. At least he revealed that he was able to get in touch with him. And then again, the voice asked,

"Who is this?" I decided that I would have to play it straight.

"This is Jonah Cohen, Midnite's former landlord."

Several long seconds of silence followed. I know my name must have sent shivers up his spine. He knew the name because his apartment is where all the subpoenas, certified letters, and judgments were mailed. Surprisingly, the voice is still very friendly, but now more wary. The response finally came.

"What can I do for you, Jonah?"

"Frank?"

"Yes."

"Francesco M. Marciano?"

"Yes."

It was progress. Up until now, I could only have guessed with whom I had been speaking, but it was Midnite's associate, whoever he was.

"I have a judgment on him - nonpayment of rent. Was he paying you?"

"I'm not at liberty to reveal that information."

"Can you tell me anything about him?"

"I'm sorry, no."

I was hoping that Midnite might have screwed him too, maybe literally, but now we were at the end of our conversation. There wouldn't be any information forthcoming with a simple telephone call. In hopeless desperation I had to say,

"You know, I can have you served with an Information Subpoena."

"I wish you would."

"Thanks for your help, Frank." (Thanks for nothing.)

"You're welcome."

So, the next step was another trip to the Small Claims Court. I purchased two Information Subpoenas, one for Marciano, and the other for Midnite, and had them served by certified mail return-receipt-requested. Marciano, after receiving and signing for the subpoena, foolishly chose to ignore it. Midnite's came back undelivered. His would have to be served personally. After that, I obtained an Order to Show Cause for Contempt against Marciano. Unfortunately, most people do not take the Small Claims Court seriously, but should. It can be just as effective as any other court. The problem here was getting the Order served on Marciano by personal service, and the Information Subpoena served on Midnite. The service is the first and weakest link in the litigation process.

I thought of my friend John on eastern Long Island. But John is loose, on the edge, always, and in a very strange way, a mirror image of Midnite. But he is a friend and he would do the service for me. Through a variety of events, I guess you could say he had become a close friend. He helped me with my car when it broke down, we went fishing a few times, we had our Volkswagen restoration project, etc. Yes, John agreed to do the service. No problem. He would do it the following Monday. I called him the next morning to see how it went.

"Jon, I'm sorry. I couldn't do it. I had to work late yesterday. I'll do it tomorrow for sure."

I called John again on Wednesday morning for an update.

"Jon, I had some trouble with the car, but don't worry. I'll take care of it on Friday."

"You know, Friday is the last day. It has to be done by Friday.

"Jon, I'll take care of it. It'll be done. Trust me."

Friday was a bitter cold day, awful. It was the coldest day of the year with wind gusts of up to 30 MPH, but it was also a day when most people were likely to stay home at night, and therefore, a good day to serve. I could only hope that John had come through for me. When I called his house over the weekend, the news wasn't good. I was told that he was in the hospital, with severe stomach pains.

"But … what about the service? Was the service accomplished? What about the service …?"

No, the service wasn't done. I spent that night within the confines of my condominium raving like a lunatic, with only my goldfish, Moby Dick to hear.

"The IDIOT!!! That #@!%#! That SUPREME SCREW-

UP! That USELESS FOOL! THAT STUPID USELESS IDIOT!!! ..."

John called me from his hospital bed to apologize. I was furious! He said he tried, that he went there, that he couldn't get into the building, that he rang for the super, but the super wouldn't let him in, and then ...

"Are we still friends?"

I paused and thought for a moment. What did that say about me? A friend, the only friend who was willing to do this service for me, gets sick, maybe a heart attack for all I knew, and all I was able to think of was the service. John has more problems than anyone I know - money problems, job problems, mortgage problems ... and now medical problems. I shouldn't have given him this job. He didn't want to do it, but like a good soldier, he went into battle on the front lines. And so, like the proverbial straw that broke the camel's back, so it was the process service on Marciano that ruptured John's ulcer.

And again,

"Are we still friends?"

"Of course we're still friends!"

"What do you want me to do with the court papers?"

"Well, you should remove them very carefully from the envelope. Then fold them very neatly in half, then quarters, and then eighths ... and when you're done folding, take them and shove it up ..."

John laughed, recovered, and we remained friends.

Nevertheless, the two services had to be accomplished, or my case would have ended right there. John said that he would do the service on Midnite. Like I said, I shouldn't have asked him in the first place, but he said he wanted to do it, ulcer and all, to make up for the other time. I told him that he could to it anytime that he wanted, any place, and however he wanted to do it, and in the least stressful way possible. All I needed was a signed, notarized affidavit. The rest was up to him. John sent me the affidavit of service.

Now, what about the service on Marciano? It still had to be done. I took the next day off from work and drove Old Faithful into Queens to the Small Claims Court. I was able to request and to receive an extension for service of the Order to Show Cause. My excuse: My process server was in the hospital. (Process serving is a rough business.)

I found a professional process server, Apple Process Servers, in the Yellow Pages. At $42.50, it was the best price around, and next day service was guaranteed. True to his word, and with remarkable efficiency, Frank Marciano was served at 6:04 A.M. and within 24 hours. (They are good at what they do.)

That same night, there were three messages left on my telephone answering machine, all from Marciano. He sounded very upset, nervous, and concerned - he was calling about the subpoena.

"I received a copy? ... of some court papers? ... I don't know what you guys are trying to pull ... It says I have to come to court? ... I'll definitely show this to my lawyer. I will protect myself ... and he's a good lawyer! We never lose! Please call me at (212) ... *click*"

And at that, the damned answering machine cut him off, so that I never did get his new number, but the next and last message was,

"On second thought, I'll call you ..."

Marciano overreacted. He wasn't being sued. He was only being called as a witness. All he had to do was answer the questions. Marciano did call back, and we had a long, sometimes heated, sometimes amiable conversation. He threatened me with a lawsuit for harassment if I pursued the Contempt of Court action. I explained that Neville Michaels was my tenant and owed me unpaid rent.

"Perhaps there was some impropriety on your part."

So they were friends, of course. Midnite must have told him the whole ugly story. He knew everything. But now I was a Judgment Creditor, not just an illegal sub-landlord, or whatever you want to call it. I had the ruling of the court behind me, and that made me right.

"This was tried before an arbitrator in Small Claims Court. The court ruled in my favor."

Marciano it seemed was different than Midnite. He was a more legitimate type person. He showed some concern. In fact, he was scared out of his mind and volunteered some information. It turned out that he did meet Midnite in a band, that they played together for a while, that he did him a favor by letting him live with him for what he said was about two months. He then said something that sounded funny, but was painfully true.

"We're both guilty of the same 'crime.' We both gave Midnite a place to live."

He said he now had nothing that belonged to Neville Michaels, didn't know where he was, and didn't have any phone numbers.

"Then how did the court papers get to him?"

"I bet he didn't even show up."

"He did … with the Notice of Claim and Summons to appear! You must have given it to him."

"I … eh … I … eh, met him on the street."

Some people just don't lie well, but knowing Midnite, maybe it was on the street, or in the gutter in a cardboard box.

"Look, Frank, I'll tell you what. You give me some good information, reimburse me for my expenses, and I'll drop the Contempt of Court action."

The conversation rambled on. He said that he owned a business, that he worked hard at it everyday, and that he *schleps* to work everyday. I'm amused at how these Yiddish words have crept into the New York vernacular. I continued.

"Can you get me some information?"

"So you want me to do your investigation?"

"I want you to answer the questions with the subpoena. Either that, or come to court!"

"What's in it for me?"

"I'll drop the Contempt of Court action and we'll negotiate my expenses."

"How much time do you have?"

"I'll be here for a while."

"I'll call you back in a few minutes. I'll make some calls."

And in a few minutes, the phone did ring. It was Marciano with some info.

"Boy! What I had to go through to get this! Midnite is living with a woman in Manhattan. The number is (212) ... Hey, what's in this for me?"

"Like I said, I'll drop the Contempt action. Give me fifty bucks and a number ... or just give me a number ... just his number, and you're off the hook."

Well, I never did get the number, but shortly after that, I did receive a certified letter in the mail with the answers to the subpoena - and except for the name, all the answers to the questions were filled in "N/A" or "not known."

And following the answers, came a call from Marciano's

lawyer friend at Rosenthal & Myers. I know from experience that one should not talk to lawyers, and here there was nothing to gain. He wanted to know if I received the answers to the subpoena by certified mail.

"What answers? You call those answers?"

"The answers to the subpoena, did you receive it?"

"Yes."

"So, why are you starting a contempt action? Why don't you have the debtor examined?"

"LOOK, YOUR CLIENT ANSWERED THE SUBPOENA TWO MONTHS LATE, HE WASN'T TRUTHFUL, AND I DON'T HAVE TIME TO EXPLAIN THE LAW TO A LAWYER!"

"What are you shouting about?"

"I have a meeting I have to get to, ok? Have your client come to court. Gotta go."

He hung up first. And so, Rosenthal & Myers was put in their place.

The shouting is a defensive tactic I use to compensate for a generally mild manner, some shyness in spite of all the courtroom victories, and small build. Over the phone, you could be anybody. Perhaps my method for dealing with lawyers was learned during my conversations with Kravitz, my landlord. He used to shout at me and I was scared out of my wits! I guess in a very perverse way, I did admire Kravitz. (*And he loved Big Brother?*)

I happened to be in Brooklyn again for my annual dental visit, and while in Brooklyn, I checked out some more of Midnite's old addresses. 315 Berry Street didn't exist. It was supposed to be between 290 and 318, or something, but no 315. They might have torn down the building. People there use only first names, usually not even their real names.

Some of the mail boxes are just holes in the wall, literally. And there was a Sears (not Roebuck) scribbled on the directory of 73 5th Avenue, but I couldn't find a telephone listing. It was a mild day, so a walked over the Brooklyn Bridge on to Washington Square Park near NYU in Greenwich Village in the faint hope that I might spot him, but there, everybody is a freak! There must have been almost a hundred that looked exactly like him. I walked up to 17th Street and checked out a certain Christine Kingston at 23 West 17th Street who sold him the BMW motorcycle, but she wasn't there anymore. It was now getting time for my dental appointment, so I hurried back into Brooklyn and passed by the old building that I used to call home. The old apartment was now fixed up with new windows, new paint, and a clean appearance. I happened to see Mrs. O'Malley, the nice old lady that lived across the hall from me. Should I have said hello? Was I still that nice young man who lived there as her neighbor all these years. Or was I the one who let that dope peddling deadbeat into the building, thereby endangering the lives of all within? I walked past the building, eyes straight ahead, as if 63 Clark Street and I had never intersected in the journey through time, space, and the L&T Part of Brooklyn Civil Court.

XXVI. In Contempt

The contempt hearing took place as scheduled, on April 9th at 11:00 A.M. While waiting outside the courtroom, fragments of the conversation that I had had with Marciano ran through my mind.

"I'll come to court in a suit, and I'll look the judge in the face with my big brown eyes ..."

"Your opposition has arrived and is waiting outside."

The court clerk announced his arrival. Marciano entered, we eyed each other for the first time, and neither of us spoke. He showed the clerk the certified mail return receipt for the answers to the Information Subpoena. The signature on it was my own. I did sign for it. He also showed the clerk a Christmas card, but I never knew from whom it was or what it was supposed to prove.

The clerk examined the two items, and looked up at me.

"So what's the problem? You have the answers."

I responded using the Kravitz method.

"The SUBPOENA was answered TWO MONTHS LATE, the answers are UNTRUTHFUL, were answered only in response to the ORDER TO SHOW CAUSE, and I have incurred EXPENSES, which need to be reimbursed." The clerk, in his bored, detached, and indifferent manner responded,

"I guess you're gonna have to see the judge."

As we entered the hearing room, Judge Lastrada introduced himself. We shook hands with him, and we were seated. I thought that was odd - a judge doesn't normally shake hands with the litigants. Furthermore, I noticed that he wasn't wearing a black robe. Don't they wear black robes anymore? And then I noticed that neither of us, especially the witness, was sworn in. I didn't say anything because I thought it would be impolite and improper to question procedure. I handed the judge the papers and began my speech.

"Your Honor, the subpoena was answered two months late, the information is useless and untruthful, and in fact the witness knows ..."

"STOP! STOP THIS IMMEDIATELY. I'M CONDUCTING THIS HEARING, NOT YOU!"

I was cut off at the beginning of my opening speech. I had incurred the wrath of "His Honor." I was dazed. I'm not sure what happened after that, but the hearing went extremely poorly. I think Marciano said something and I answered with,

"You have to know where he is because you've been forwarding his mail and his phone calls."

At this, the judge's wrath only continued to flare and things got worse. It was a total fiasco. It seems that I was out of order. I wasn't supposed to say anything to the witness. I thought I was doing quite well, but the judge thought otherwise.

"DON'T YOU THINK I'M MORE QUALIFIED THAN YOU ARE TO QUESTION THE WITNESS?!"

The words of reproach were directed straight at me. I had to endure what seemed to be a good five minute lecture about how and who is to question a witness, when to speak and when not to, and to have respect for "His Honor." Well, Marciano comes to court to show cause as to why he should not be punished, and it turns out that I'm the one who's being punished. I stared the judge down, stone faced, and pretended to listen. It reminded me of the time when I served on a jury in Brooklyn on a medical malpractice case. I thought of Mr. Schmeizer, attorney for the claimant, and all the screaming, lecturing, and verbal abuse that he had to endure at the mouth of the judge, but then came springing back as obnoxious and determined as ever ...

"Your Honor, I have here documented proof, medical books and journals ..."

Mr. Schmeizer walked over to the table upon which was a briefcase stuffed with books and journals, all carefully bookmarked, and was about to pull them out for presentation.

"Counselor, stop. Stop now!"

"But Your Honor ..."

"Counselor, I said STOP!"

"But ... but Judge ..."

"NO! Put it away NOW! I said NOW!"

"But Judge, this will reveal the most important ..."

"Did you hear me, Counselor? I SAID PUT IT AWAY! Put it away now, or I'll put you in contempt of court!"

"But ... but Judge ... please let me ..."

In the end, the jury split the claim down the middle, so Schmeizer actually won $750,000 for the plaintiff. Yes, perhaps I would yet spring back like Mr. Schmeizer, and win.

Judge Lastrada continued on with his lecture, and things continued to get even worse. It was like one of those college courses you'd drop in the first day or two because you knew it was hopeless. Finally, the judge concluded his tirade of discipline and it was time to continue on with the hearing. The judge stood up, held the paper with the questions attached to the subpoena, and read each verbatim to the witness.

"Question 1 - Please provide the debtor's full name as indicated on his application." Marciano dutifully provided the answer.

"Neville Michaels."

The name was incomplete. There was a middle name and an A/K/A. The full name as required by Question 1 was not given. I had to interrupt.

"Excuse me, Your Honor. May I say something?"

"No!"

I guess I was out of order again. The judge continued with the next question.

"Question 2 - Please set forth the last known home address and telephone number for the debtor's residence, if different from the address shown above."

The address and telephone number were the same as his. The remaining questions were read in the same manner, to which all the answers were "no" or "I don't know." At the conclusion of the reading of the questions, I was given a chance to say something. I again asked about the name, the middle name and the A/K/A. The answer given was,

"I don't know."

I moved on to Question 2.

"Question 2 - On March 26th, I had a telephone conversation with the witness and the witness indicated to me that if I would drop the Contempt of Court action, he would give me the judgment debtor's phone number, that he knew where he was, and that he was now living with a woman in Manhattan."

The judge directed his question to Marciano.

"Do you have such a number?"

"No, Your Honor."

Of course he had the number! If only I could have just

gotten it out of him. I continued on.

"In a telephone conversation on or about January 12, 1993, the witness said he would have the judgment debtor call me back."

And again,

"Do you have such a number for the debtor?"

"No, Your Honor."

"Do you recall such a conversation ever taking place?"

"Vaguely."

And then I tried to show that the Small Claims Summons for Midnite somehow found its way to Midnite, because he showed up in court with the summons. Someone would have had to have given it to him. It could only have been Marciano, but His Honor was no longer interested, was very bored, and deigned to end it all.

"Any more questions?"

"I am requesting reimbursement of expenses, and that a fine for contempt be imposed as the law requires."

> *"A pound of that same merchant's flesh is thine; The court awards it and the law doth give it ... And you must cut this flesh from off his breast; The law allows it and the court awards it ... Take then thy bond, take thou thy pound of flesh ..."*

(Merchant of Venice, Act IV, Sc. I - Wm. Shakespeare)

"DENIED!"

I believe that I might have blushed a bit at that, and after holding up so well. It was all over, and absolutely nothing gained. Zero-zilch - nothing. Marciano got up to leave, and turned to Judge Lastrada.

"Happy Easter, Your Honor."

I just sat there dazed for a few moments, but then the judge turned to me as if I too were going to wish His Honor a "Happy Easter." *Go to Hell, Your Honor!* The words very nearly came out, but then it would have been I who would have been in contempt. And so, the money grubbing Jew left without his "pound of flesh."

The clerk saw me on the way out, and asked how I made out.

"I got nothing. Absolutely nothing."

He told me that judges don't like to put anybody in contempt, especially witnesses. He also mentioned that he had seen me around the court a lot. I told him about Brooklyn Landlord & Tenant Court, and Queens County Small Claims Court. I began to take my frustrations out on the clerk, realized what I was doing, and apologized. But he wasn't angry, and sympathized with me. That's just the way things are in this farce of a legal system. The words were unspoken, but understood. I thanked him for his assistance.

"You're quite welcome."

XXVII. The Lost Alien

The contempt hearing with the witness, Marciano, was pointless and useless. One should never use the friend of a defendant as a witness. I did hear from Marciano again in the form of a certified letter. It was a bill for his expenses for coming to court, together with a demand letter for payment and a threatened lawsuit. I read over the itemized expenses with some amusement:

Cab Fare to and from the court *$29.46*
Tip *5.00*
Breakfast *9.29*
Tip *2.00*
Lunch *18.87*
Tip *4.00*
Postage and Miscellaneous Expenses *15.00*
Time off from work, lost wages *300.00*
Total $383.62

Needless to say, I wasn't required to pay any of it, and none of it was ever paid. I never heard from him again. Marciano was, however, my best hope for finding the elusive alien. I decided to make another visit to the apartment building on Phlox Place. I didn't know what I was looking for, any clue, anything at all that might be useful. I got there in the afternoon and parked opposite the apartment building. There was no sign of the BMW motorcycle. The apartment was on the fifth floor, in the front part of the building. It was a corner apartment. The windows were open with curtains blowing in the breeze. Residents were entering and exiting the building. I could have asked any one of them if they knew Midnite, but I thought that would have been useless, and would have sounded silly. I waited until dark. Perhaps I would be able to see who was actually in the apartment, but as darkness fell upon Phlox Place, the apartment too remained dark.

April turned into August, and August into January, and there was no sign of Midnite. The winter of '94 was the worst winter in two decades turning eastern Long Island into a frozen, frigid wasteland. I curse January! Old Faithful was again up on jack stands, the result of a failed rear axle bearing. Now stuck in six inches of ice, the residue of the terrible ice storms and sub-zero degree weather that took place, she wouldn't be going anywhere for a while. And like Old Faithful on ice, so was my collection action against Midnite - frozen solid and going nowhere.

There was no clue, no lead - nothing. The elusive alien could have been anywhere, anywhere at all. He could have been anywhere in the country, or maybe even out of the country. Maybe he went back home, wherever that might be. Maybe he escaped this terrible cold and went someplace where it's warm. Perhaps he went back to Trinidad and Tobago ... palm trees, blue lagoons, sunshine ... Trinidad ... Trinidad ... Trinidad ...

I find myself on a street in Trinidad. It is at night. The air is warm and heavy, typical of the tropics, but quite pleasant. The gentle breeze rustles the palm branches. There is a full moon over Trinidad casting its silvery light over the palm trees and over the waters. I hear music in the distance. The sound is faint, but the music is that heard in the West

161

Indies. It seems to be a strange blend of rock, reggae, and afro, played on steel drums and electric guitar, with some brass. The street is dark, as it is in the shadow of the moonlight. I can hardly see. I find myself walking toward the music, and as I walk, it appears to get louder. This is not my kind of music, but I am mysteriously drawn towards it. I pick up my pace and follow it to its source. I arrive at a basement club off the main street. I walk down the stairs and enter. The music is now loud, intensely loud, and it is coming from a stage at the rear. I seem to be unaware and unconcerned that I am the only Caucasian there as I continue to concentrate only on the music, and still mysteriously drawn to its source. The club is dark, except for the stage and the musicians. The air is so thick that it is almost unbreathable, made all the more so by the thick tobacco and marijuana smoke. And the room is crowded, oh, so crowded. People are packed together tightly, sweaty flesh against flesh. I can hardly breath, and I can't see except for the light on the musicians. Why don't I leave? What am I doing here in this land of aliens? Ah! But here in Trinidad, who is the alien? Nevertheless, I am still hopelessly drawn to the music, and in particular, to the percussionist. I push and slide past sweaty black flesh toward the stage, toward the drummer, toward the silhouetted image, the source of the mysterious alien music. I fight my way closer and closer, while the music kept getting louder and louder. I am now experiencing fear, a growing intense fear. For some bizarre and inexplicable reason, the entire episode began to remind me of the revelation on Mount Sinai, where there was thundering and lightning amid the deafening sounds of the Shofar or trumpets, and a thick, dense cloud over the mountain. The people stood back and were afraid. I think: "Man! This is not the revelation on Mount Sinai, and the dark alien up there isn't Moses!" And so, I push on, past the forbidden boundary line at the foot of the mountain, or the foot of the stage, so that the light is also on me. Our eyes meet! The mutual recognition is unmistakable. It's him! It's Midnite! I want to call out to him, but I can't. The words don't come out, as if my vocal cords had been severed. I try again in vain, "M ..., M ..., Mm..." The music stops. The musician rises from the steel drums and the strange assortment of other percussion instruments. He is dressed all in black, his boots are black, and the bandanna is black. The dark, slender image walks toward me, and the growing fear within me is awesome. I am sweating wildly, and it is so hot, oh so damned hot! The alien figure continues to come toward me until I can almost touch it. It extends its right arm toward me, the index finger pointing straight at me. It is like the finger of G-d in Michelangelo's painting on the ceiling of the Sistine Chapel. Again I think: "Man! This is not G-d, this is my tenant!" I reach out to touch the finger, but instantly upon contact, the image vanishes. All that remains is a miniature, lifeless rag doll in the image of Midnite. With an unknown, supernatural, invisible force, it is picked up and thrown unceremoniously against a red brick wall. But at this, the words finally do come out, and come out they do with tremendous power ...

"MIDNITE, YOU OWE ME RENT!!!!!!!!!!!!!!!!!!!!!!"

The room is now dark, cold, and silent. The sweat is my own. And now the Spirit of Captain Midnite had not only vanished in the dream, but the dream had disappeared into the world of dreams.

163

XXVIII. The Marshall Islands

If nothing else, my real estate misadventures were always a good topic of conversation with my friends at work. I happened to be discussing my disaster with one certain individual who worked part time for an insurance company and happened to have access to the company's data bases. Well, we weren't sure what we could do with this, and it was a long shot, but my friend offered to run a check. I had Midnite's DMV report showing Progressive Insurance as his insurance company. The policy was cancelled for non-payment. We ran the check with my friend's insurance company, State Farm, not knowing what it would reveal if anything, but as it turned out, my judgment debtor had been involved in a serious motorcycle accident. This was tremendous news! Motorcycle accidents could mean big bucks!

I was able to obtain a copy of the police report of the accident from the NYPD. The report revealed that Midnite had rear-ended another vehicle on the Brooklyn-Queens Expressway. The BMW and Midnite went down and he had suffered injuries to the right arm and shoulder. I wasted no time in calling State Farm Legal Department to try to get more information on the accident. As expected, they would not discuss the accident, nor give out any additional information concerning the accident, but the State Farm attorney did say something interesting.

"Why don't you ask his lawyer?"

His lawyer? Midnite had a lawyer? It's amazing! All deadbeats always have money for lawyers. I asked the question.

"Who's his lawyer?"

"Rosenthal and Meyers, ok?"

"Sure. Thanks."

Of course! It was so simple. Rosenthal and Meyers was Marciano's lawyer, and now he was also Midnite's lawyer. I called Rosenthal and Meyers. I knew that they weren't able to give out any information, but now I was able to get the name of an individual upon whom to serve an Information Subpoena, Frances Suarez, a legal secretary.

At my first opportunity, I went back to the Small Claims Court, purchased an Information Subpoena for $2.00, and had it served by certified mail on Rosenthal and Meyers. Banks and law firms are super in their compliance with Information Subpoenas - friends are not. The subpoena with the questions came back to me within the required seven day period. Midnite had a job! And an address! The answers to the Information Subpoena revealed that the elusive alien was now living on the West Side at 501 West 46th Street and worked at the Hudson Grill at a job they called "security." Midnite was a bouncer. Ironically, the Hudson Grill was right across the street from the DoD DCASR-NY headquarters on Hudson Street. Midnite wasn't in Trinidad. He was right here in New York, practically right under my nose!

And so it was that Rosenthal and Meyers, Midnite's own lawyers, threw him to the wolves. Never trust your lawyer! I obtained two more Information Subpoenas, one to be served on the employer, and the other to be served on my judgment debtor at his new address. Things were starting to happen. I got an Income Execution and a City Marshal.

The office of City Marshal is an unusual one. They are

not employed by the City, or anyone else for that matter. They are private entrepreneurs, independent contractors who work for themselves, taking a cut of anything they collect. The collection process had begun.

A long and tiring day had come to an end. I had a late supper, a bottle of beer, and stretched out on my favorite chair to watch Nightline with Ted Koppel. It was an interesting show. It was about the inhabitants of the Marshall Islands and the health hazards that those unfortunate people suffered due to the nuclear bomb testing that took place after World War II during the Cold War. The resulting high levels of radiation had caused high cancer rates and birth defects among the population. I heard Koppel ask his guest,

"Don't you think that the people of the Marshall Islands should be compensated? ... Should they be compensated?"

"Well, one should consider several important facts concerning this. Compensation would be required and appropriate if ..."

The guest continued on in a lengthy, but somewhat ambivalent discussion. Koppel wanted an answer.

"Well, should they be compensated? Should the people of the Marshall Islands be compensated? ... Marshall Islands ... compensation ... marshal ... compensation ... marshal ... marshal ..."

I'm in a strange apartment and alone, but not alone. There is a presence in the room, an unseen presence, and the low hum of voices in the background. I can't see it, hear it, or smell it, but I know it's there. I am not alone! I begin to concentrate on the room, on the gentle hum of voices, and on the unseen presence. Suddenly, it appears in full view from behind the couch. It's the alien!! But he has a silly grin on his face. Why is he smiling? And just then, my Marshal appears in full uniform with shiny silver badges. My Marshal is just outside the window and he has pointed at the alien a huge rifle with a five foot barrel. I think, "Ah! Justice will be served!" But why is the alien smiling? Victory is mine! Why is the alien still smiling? My Marshal cocks the hammer of the rifle. "Oh, no! There are no assets." He takes careful aim. "Oh, no! Oh, no! No! THERE'S NO WAY TO COLLECT A JUDGMENT FROM A CORPSE! NO! NO! NOOOOOOOOOOOOOOO!"

"And this is Ted Koppel in Washington. Good night."

XXIX. Hudson Grill

The Hudson Grill is a nice, clean place. It looked to be completely legitimate. It appeared to be fairly new and well kept. It had a dining area, a bar, a lounge, and a couple of pool tables. Midnite never had it so good. He would never leave it, even if they did garnish ten percent of his wages.

The Information Subpoena sent by certified mail to the Hudson Grill was ignored. The next step would be a contempt action, but contempt actions are best to be avoided, if possible. I tried sending the subpoena again, and this time it was returned, the questions being answered with "unknown," blanks, or "no." It had to be followed up with a phone call. A young woman with a friendly voice answered.

"Hudson Grill."

"I'd like to speak to someone in charge of personnel. I'm calling for a reference on an employee."

I was switched, presumably to someone who was supposed to be in charge of personnel.

"Hello?"

"Yeah, I'm calling for a reference on Neville Michaels? Does he work there?"

"Nobody here by that name."

"Well, he uses the name 'Midnite.'"

"Oh, why didn't you say so? Sure, he works here."

"He wants to rent an apartment from me. Can he afford $500 per month in rent?"

"Oh, sure."

"And he works there now?"

"Yeah."

"For how long?"

"Oh, a year and a half, on and off."

"Ok, thank you."

And with that, before the electrons had finished flowing through the telephone lines, I called my Marshal, and the Marshal served them with an Income Execution for the wage garnishment. Unfortunately, days and weeks passed, and nothing was collected. Collecting on any judgment is not an easy business. I had to follow up again with another phone call to the Hudson Grill.

"Hudson Grill, Cheryl speaking."

"Hi, is Midnite there?"

"Who is this?"

"This is Frank. I'm a friend. We used to play together in the band."

"Midnite doesn't work here anymore."

"Oh? When did he leave?"

"A couple of weeks ago, but if you want to leave a message or something for him, I can give it to him, or you may catch him here sometime in the evenings."

"When is a good time to come?"

"Try Friday or Saturday nights."

So, after the garnishment was served, it appeared that he didn't work there anymore, and yet he still seemed to hang around there. Strange! I had to call the Hudson Grill again. This time I played it straight. There was nothing to lose.

"Hudson Grill."

It was Cheryl's friendly voice, but I had to make sure.

"Cheryl?"

"Yes?"

"My name is Jonah Cohen. We spoke yesterday about Midnite? I have a judgment against him from the Small

Claims Court."

Well, at this, Cheryl's friendly manner turned colder than Long Island's January ice. People don't like to hear about courts and judgments. Maybe it was clumsy, but I already established that he worked or had worked there, and now we had to move on. And I really couldn't be sure whether or not the Hudson Grill would comply with the Marshal's execution as any truly legitimate business would, or if they would protect him, or if even Cheryl would protect him. I fired away with my questions.

"Do you have an address for him?"

"No."

"Well, you employed him. Where does he live?"

Cheryl became very nervous, and she wasn't able to lie very well, but now I was no longer a "friend," I was the enemy, and I betrayed her trust. And again,

"Where does he live?"

My questions seemed to flow with rhythm. Maybe I would have made a great prosecuting attorney after all.

"He moves around a lot, lives with different girlfriends."

Different girlfriends? How many? There had to be something magical about my alien from Trinidad. I didn't even try to understand it. Apparently, I wasn't the only one who got screwed. I continued to badger Cheryl. That's what lawyers do, isn't it? They badger the witness.

"Was he on the books?"

"Yeah … with us he was…"

On the books? Oh sure! I'll bet! She was still not sure of how, or whether to answer the questions. I finally got her to hang up on me.

"For how long?"

"Click."

I waited another week or two before calling back. This time I got to talk to Ritchie. Ritchie was either the owner, or the manager of the place. He was friendly - at least on the surface - a smooth talker, and lied very well, but lied nevertheless.

"Midnite left summer of '93, worked here only 4 or 5 weeks ... and only one day a week ..."

And as he continued, the memory of Captain Midnite faded further and further into obscurity.

"Do you have an address or a phone number for him?"

"No address. He was a freelancer."

"Freelancer?"

"Yeah. That's what he told me. He had his own business ... I called him when I needed him ... I have to go back to the '93 files. I'll get it for you ... I'll get back to you on this."

Oh sure you'll get back to me. Ha! I made one more call to the Hudson Grill, the last. It sounded like Cheryl again. We went through the same routine, but there was no progress. Everybody is on a first name basis these days. It's not just to be friendly; they're all afraid of lawsuits.

"What's your last name, Cheryl?"

"Cheryl?? This is Suzy at the bar!!"

When you blunder, just keep going.

"Does Midnite work there?"

"Midnite left ages ago."

And so, from he works here now, to he left a couple of weeks ago, to about a year ago, to ages ago, the memory of the dark alien continued to fade into the dark, distant past.

I couldn't be sure if he was really there or not, or maybe occasionally there. But I had his address, the one on 46th Street. I sent my former tenant a letter, demanding payment.

Now, of course I knew that this wasn't going to result in immediate payment. The purpose was to see what would happen to the letter. I did expect it to just get lost, not forwarded, or returned. (Deadbeats do not file forwarding addresses with the Post Office.) But that's not what happened. The letter was returned, and written on the envelope, in his OWN HANDWRITING:

"RETURN TO SENDER - NOT AT THIS ADDRESS"

I had found Midnite!

It was Passover, and I had taken some time off from the job. I hadn't been in the City for nearly two years. It would be a good time to do some investigative work. The Hudson Grill was still there, but there was no sign of Midnite or the motorcycle. I took the subway up to his new address on 46th Street, the address given to me by his lawyer. The old trains of pre-World War II vintage were now gone, replaced with new, stainless steel clad, graffiti-proof trains with LCD displays. But I missed the old trains, with their incandescent lighting, ceiling fans, cane seats, and porcelain hand rails - all miraculously held together with rust and dirt. 501 West 46th Street really did exist. It looked like a well maintained building, but within its confines, the alien was kept well hidden, protected by a wrought iron fence with a locked gate and an intercom system. There was no access, and again, no sign of the motorcycle.

I walked back downtown, through the Chelsea district, and found myself singing Joni Mitchell's Chelsea Morning, then on through the Village, through Washington Square Park, and then back to the Hudson Grill. There was no sign of the elusive alien. I called the Marshal and discussed with him my findings. He suggested that I meet him there at the Hudson Grill, and so, I agreed to meet the Marshal there between 9:30 P.M. and 10:00 P.M. on the next Saturday night. A more dedicated, enthusiastic, and gung-ho Marshal could anyone find anywhere?

"If he's there, we'll levy the execution on them!"

It was after the two Seder nights. I especially remembered the part of the Seder where we stood up to welcome Elijah the Prophet into our houses, and we chanted,

> *"Pour out thy wrath upon the nations that know Thee not,*
> *And upon the kingdoms who do not call upon Thy name.*
> *For they have devoured Jacob, and laid waste his habitation.*
> *Pour out Thine indignation upon them, and let the fierceness of Thine anger overtake them.*
> *Thou wilt pursue them in anger and destroy them from under the heavens of the Lord."*

> *(Psalm 79:6, Psalm 69:24, Lamentations 3:66)*

Sh-fawch chamaticha el ha-goyim - Yes! Pour out Thy wrath upon these alien nations!

Midnite should not have fooled with this child of Zion!

XXX. Mr. Bazzel

The raid on the Hudson Grill was a bust. I was there at
9:00 P.M. and waited until 11:00 P.M. Midnite didn't show
up. My Marshal didn't show up. I was the only one who
came to the party. I called the Marshal to see what went
wrong.

"Please forgive me. I forgot all about it."

*"Israel trusts in the Lord, He is their help and their
shield ... All men are deceitful."*

(Psalms 115:9 & 116:11)

Shortly after this, I received a letter from the Marshal.
They were going to close the case.   Any additional
information that I would have to send to them regarding
collection actions would cost me in additional fees. I had it
out with Charlotte at the Marshal's office. There would be
no more additional fees, but the case was closed, at least for
the time being.

I had to give up on getting anything from the Hudson
Grill. The next step was to get the Order to Show Cause for
Contempt served on Midnite. Now, all I had was the letter
that I sent to Midnite at the 46th Street address that was
returned with his own hand writing, and the Information
Subpoena from his lawyer showing his address. At any rate,
it was the last known address, and I had to move the case on.
I called National Process Servers.

"Well, I do have proof that he's living there now, at

Apartment #5. I haven't seen or spoken with him, but I'm pretty sure he's there."

I gave the process service company all the information that I had. Personal service was desirable, but the so called "nail and mail," or substitute service would be satisfactory. I also had a special request. It was included in the fee.

"Please have the process server look around for a black BMW motorcycle. It may be in the basement, in the courtyard, or even in the hall or lobby."

They agreed. I waited anxiously for the results, which came about a week later. Midnite, if he was really there at all, could not be served by personal service, and there was no sign of the motorcycle anywhere, but on the third attempt, the process server found a neighbor who lived in the building, a certain John Garcia, who took the papers for him and confirmed that Midnite did actually live there. It had to be good enough. I was able to go back to the Small Claims Court, return the Affidavit of Service with the other court papers, and our contempt hearing was set for two weeks later.

My opposition did not show up for the hearing. This was both good and bad. Good because I was able to submit a Fining Order for $200.00 and put Midnite in contempt of court. Bad because I might not have ever found him again and only find myself with worthless and uncollectable judgments, and an unpaid fine.

And so, with Midnite now in contempt, the answers to the Information Subpoena ignored, the failure to appear for the hearing, and the fine unpaid, the final step was to have him arrested. Yes! I could have Midnite arrested! The thought came to me of an earlier time when it was Midnite who thought that he could have me arrested. The tables had turned, but before I could have him arrested, a judge would have to sign a warrant, and then I would have to know, really know for sure, where and when he could be arrested. I needed confirmation of the 46th Street address. Certainly the owner of the building, or the property manager, would know who was living in the building. But did Kravitz know who was living in his building?

I prepared the arrest warrant and submitted it for the judge's signature, but of course, it was rejected. The right words and format weren't there. It had to be done again, but this time with their wording even though the English and sentence structure didn't completely make sense. Professor Dunno would have graded it with one of his inexhaustible D minuses, but that's what they wanted, and that's what worked. The second time around it was signed. The warrant itself was indeed a genuine work of art. It read as follows:

-----------------------------------*x*

Jonah Cohen, Plaintiff

                              WARRANT OF COMMITMENT
vs.   **SCQ NO. 9999/92**

Neville Michaels a/k/a Midnite,
                 Defendant
-----------------------------------*x*

 Plaintiff having applied for an order committing the defendant Neville Michaels for failure to comply with the prior order of this court.

 Now, upon reading and filing the order of Judge Hon. Benton T. Greenberg dated 7/29/94, the affidavit of Mary

Ambrosia sworn to 9/29/94 showing due service of the annexed order upon the defendant, and the affidavit of Jonah Cohen dated 10/17/94, and upon all the proceedings herein, it appears to the satisfaction of the Court that the defendant has failed to comply with the aforementioned order. It is on motion of Jonah Cohen, plaintiff,

__ADJUDGED__, that the conduct of the defendant was willful and was such as to defeat, impair, impede and prejudice the rights of the plaintiff, and it is further,

__ADJUDGED__, that the defendant, Neville Michaels, has failed to purge himself of the contempt by payment of the fine imposed by or otherwise comply with the order of the Court dated 9/29/94 and it is further,

__ADJUDGED__, that the defendant Neville Michaels remains guilty of contempt, and it is further,

__ORDERED__, that the Sheriff of any County wherein the defendant may be found, be and he is hereby directed upon payment of the statutory fee in such cases provided, to bring him before the Court or a Judge thereof, to be committed or for such other disposition as the Court in its discretion shall direct.

ENTER

Judge Benton T. Greenberg, JCC

The building manager was easy enough to find. They

were listed in the telephone directory as "401 West 46th Street Properties." I called the number and got the name of the manager, Ms. Maria Sanchez. I decided that it was time to come up front and out of the cold. I wrote a letter to Ms. Sanchez and explained in my letter all about the judgments, that I was Mr. Michaels' landlord (and we landlords have to stick together, right?), that he was in contempt of court, that he was an alien and might be dangerous and a threat to the other tenants in the building, … and that he was now living in apartment No. 5! The letter read:

Dear Ms. Sanchez:

This matter concerns a certain resident at a building owned or managed by you, probably without your knowledge or permission.

This person is Neville Michaels a/k/a Midnite and he is currently residing at 501 West 46th Street, Apt. No. 5, New York, NY 10036

I am Mr. Michaels' former landlord. Mr. Michaels occupied my apartment for several months as a squatter until he was finally evicted in Landlord and Tenant Court. I sued Mr. Michaels in Small

Claims Court, and received the attached judgment which he refuses to satisfy. Mr. Michaels is presently in contempt of court and a warrant has been issued for his arrest. Mr. Michaels, an alien from Trinidad and Tobago, is possibly dangerous, and the tenants in your building might be at some risk.

I have contacted the Sheriff's Office concerning his arrest, but we may need your cooperation in gaining access to the apartment at a time that he is likely to be home. Also, it would be extremely helpful if you would provide me with the telephone number at apartment No. 5, as well as the name of the legal tenant. This information can be subpoenaed, but it would be to our mutual benefit if I have your full cooperation.

The foregoing is true and accurate. I hope I have not caused you any alarm concerning this matter, but perhaps we can work together toward its speedy *resolution. I will call you shortly.*

Thank you for your cooperation in this important matter.

Sincerely,

Jonah Cohen

Of course, there was no response to the letter. I had to follow it up with a phone call. I didn't know what to expect, but there was nothing to lose.

"Ms. Sanchez? This is Jonah Cohen. Did you get my letter?"

It turned out that Sanchez was cooperative. She didn't know anyone named Michaels, or Midnite. The tenant who was living in apartment No. 5 was a Susan Samuels, but the apartment was now being renovated and Samuels had moved out at the end of August. A certain Bertram Bazzel had taken over the lease and filled out a rental application. He was living there now with a Linda Bennington. I told Ms. Sanchez that I had proof that Neville Michaels is or was living there until very recently. I told her of the lawyer's answers to the Information Subpoena giving the 46th Street address, the returned letters with Midnite's handwriting, and the neighbor who confirmed Midnite's address with my process server.

It was all too much for her. She was confused. She didn't know who this Neville Michaels was, but she thought that it might be this Mr. Bazzel. She said she would call me back after discussing the matter with the owner of the building. I asked her if Mr. John Garcia, the neighbor who accepted the Order to Show Cause from the process server to give to Midnite, was a tenant in the building.

"There is no such person in this building, but I'll surely get back to you."

"Thank you Ms. Sanchez. You've been very helpful."

Well, a week went by, and of course, once again, Ms. Sanchez didn't call back, but I did. Communication had been cut off! There would be no more information forthcoming. And again, I had become the enemy. All that she would tell me was,

"Talk to my lawyer."

Talk to my lawyer? Oh, these damned lawyers! So, now here I was with a whole assortment of new names, an arrest warrant, and nothing useful. I thought Bazzel to be a very odd name. There were no "Bazzels" in the phone book at all. I thought about it, and I thought about it some more. I dreamed about it, and I tried to figure it all out. Who was this Bazzel? Was Sanchez right? I thought about it when I went to bed, and again when I woke up. I thought about it when I was stuck in traffic on the LIE, and when I had my first cup of coffee at my desk. Bazzel … Bazzel … who is this Bertram Bazzel …???

"YES!!! Of course! That alien deadbeat! It was just like him - his *modus operandi*. He slipped in under someone else's lease with an assumed name: Neville Michaels a/k/a Midnite a/k/a Bertram Bazzel. Trinidad was a British colony. If he had to pick an assumed name, why not British? Basil is a British name. Midnite is illiterate, so he must have misspelled it. That's why there are no Bazzels in the phone book. Bazzel exists only in Midnite's illiterate brain!

BERTRAM BAZZEL IS MIDNITE!

And yes, I will talk to Ms. Sanchez's lawyer.

XXXI.   A Talk with the Lawyer

I did call Ms. Sanchez's lawyer, the attorney representing the building owner at 501 West 46th Street. We had a long and interesting conversation. Harry Rosen was the talkative type, as are most lawyers, but Rosen was special. In a way that's good. You don't have to say a lot, just listen. He told me that Ms. Sanchez was not able to give me any information out of fear that she could be sued by the people on whom she would be giving the information. He said that it would be necessary to obtain an Information Subpoena from the court.

He went on to tell me a little about Ms. Sanchez, that she was basically a good building manager, but perhaps too lax with the tenants, not doing a proper investigation, and not really knowledgeable about who was in the apartments. He talked about the West Side, the "Hell's Kitchen" area, that people there don't usually sign leases, sometimes don't pay rent, and that they tend to move around often, sometimes right next door, or across the street. He related several specific stories, one about the FBI and the Cold War, and a ring of Russian spies. I would have liked to listen, but I was unable to focus on it and totally lost it. I had to move on with my own case.

"Mr. Rosen, I will be willing to get this Information Subpoena, but ..."

The lawyer hardly let me say anything and interrupted.

"I know, I know ... You have to go into the City, wait on line, waste time ..."

"Mr. Rosen, I will do this, but I don't want the subpoena

coming back to me with blanks and 'No … No … N/A … No.' If you could just tell me if this Bertram Bazzel is Neville Michaels, then I will get this subpoena."

I faxed him over the judgments and all the information I had, including Midnite's driving record from the DMV. Rosen agreed to get the lease application from Sanchez. I was now getting somewhere with him. It looked good. I called him back late that afternoon.

"Mr. Rosen, I don't expect you to give me his social security number, but if I give you Michaels' social security number, perhaps you could tell me if it matches the one on the application."

He agreed! Great! I fumbled ineptly through my papers. Where was the damned social security number?

"Well …?"

"Ok, ok … I'm looking through my papers here …"

I couldn't find it. It's always like that. When you need something, you can't find it. Panic was about to set in, but then came words of relief from the good lawyer.

"It's ok, take your time."

I tried it from memory, but it was wrong. But just then it turned up on the Wyman Associates application, a private investigator firm that I had considered hiring.

"I have it!"

"Go ahead."

"031-65-2792"

"No."

No? So, the social security number didn't match, but he might have used another one. By this time, it appeared that Rosen didn't care about subpoenas or about being sued. He began to read off the information on the application.

"Bertram Bazzel, age 27 at top of application."

"No. My guy is 32."

"Well, sometimes people lie about their age."

I couldn't believe it. Rosen was on my side, even to the point of hopelessness! He continued to read on.

"Laura Bender, female, age 26 is also on the lease."

The name didn't ring a bell. My brain quickly flashed back to the time that I was in the apartment at 63 Clark Street. What was the name on the love letter? Who left a message on the telephone answering machine? I drew a blank. Kathy or Sandy, maybe, but not Laura. I couldn't remember. But there was more coming!

"Employers: Spoon Bread, Inc., Restaurants Associates, Tiger Management Restaurants ..."

And still more!

"Phone numbers: a pager, (917) ..."

He willingly, even enthusiastically rattled them all off, but disappointment set in.

"Mr. Rosen, it's not him."

He went on, nevertheless.

"Salary: $28,000 ... $5,000 ... $3,000. Reason for moving: Lease expired."

Midnite didn't have a lease or a salary. The employers didn't match, the social didn't match, the age didn't match - nothing matched.

"Mr. Rosen, to tell you the truth, it's not him."

But he wouldn't give up.

"Oh, here's something you'd really be interested in. A bank account! With money in it! $1,800!"

Well, now I knew for sure that it wasn't him, but incredibly, Mr. Rosen went on!

"Chemical Bank, but I think they closed that branch ... try it ... 11 W. 57th Street."

I listened, and took it all down feverishly in the vain hope that I could use some of it, and I listened for as long as he would talk, and talk he did.

"I give you credit," he said.

I liked that. A lawyer gave me credit. And yes, I had certainly come a long way since disaster broke. It had now been over three years since Kravitz, Midnite, and I all made our appearance together in Landlord and Tenant Court in Brooklyn. I told Rosen about the arrest warrant that I had on him.

"You know, you have to be careful with that. People don't like being arrested."

I think that I might have said something like this was a special case. He told me that the Manhattan House of Detention was now closed and they put them in the Bronx House of Detention.

"For how long?" I inquired.

"Until they pay the fine."

I liked that too. It was like debtor's prison. He went on for a while until he had a visitor.

"Look, I have to go."

The call ended abruptly, and I was barely able to get in,

"Thanks for your help, Mr. Rosen."

I had sent a Freedom of Information request to the Post Office for a new address for Midnite and Sandy Samuels, the suspected girlfriend, but these people don't file change of address forms with the Post Office, and don't usually pick up their mail. And so, it appeared that I had lost Neville Michaels a/k/a Midnite, the elusive alien, for the third time. All avenues closed. All methods exhausted. Rosen gave me credit, but I had nothing to show for it. The embodiment of Neville Michaels had once again turned into the spirit of

Captain Midnite, now disintegrated into the endless infinities of the cosmos. All the effort, all the court appearances, all the services, letters, calls, and research had yielded nothing. All that remained were the worthless case files, the uncollected judgments, the unexecuted arrest warrant, and the still vivid memories of my failed real estate and legal pursuits.

XXXII. Dickens' Ghosts

Time marches on as they say. It was Christmas Eve and I had nothing better to do than review the case files (now nearly a foot high), and write letters. I wrote letters to the INS, my congressman, a collection agency, the Consulate of Trinidad and Tobago, and the City Marshal's office. I suppose it wasn't at all in keeping with the holiday spirit. I feared that perhaps I would be visited by one of Charles Dickens' ghosts. Like the ghost of the old Jacob Marley, I had forged the links of my chain one by one. But why identify with Jacob Marley? I prefer to think of myself as Judah Maccabee wreaking vengeance upon the Syrian Greeks! The hell with the chains! And so the story of eviction, pursuit, vengeance, and ultimate justice continues.

My congressman lost the election, and all the letters that I had written to him were wasted. I guess I had made Giuliani's mistake - I had backed the Democrat when I should have backed the Republican. My congressman, lame duck that he was, did however follow through and I received a letter from the Acting District Director of the INS regarding a deportation hearing for the elusive Mr. Michaels:

"The subject does have legal status in the U.S. Therefore, this matter does not fall under the jurisdiction of the INS."

The INS is just plain useless.

And my Marshal sent me another letter saying that they were going to close the case permanently as uncollectable. If I would be able to find any additional information, it would cost me additional fees for a new property execution.

And now, even though I had a Warrant of Arrest, signed by a judge, the Marshal's Office would not do an arrest. They said that they were not authorized, or not equipped to handle it. I spoke to an attorney at the NYC Sheriff's office concerning an arrest. I was amused with the response.

"The Marshal is either off-the-wall, they're lying, or they don't want to do it."

"Will the Sheriff make the arrest?"

Yes is the answer! They would make the arrest, provided I would send them $65.00 together with a certified copy of the arrest warrant. In addition, after their review, the warrant would have to meet the requirements of the judicial code. Meet the requirements of the judicial code? The judge signed it! Wasn't that good enough? An explanation was needed.

"But what I have here is an arrest warrant signed by a judge!"

"Don't you think judges ever make mistakes?"

Well, that wasn't really a problem. Sure, they would have to review it. And for a fee of $65.00, they would make the arrest. The problem here was that I didn't even know where Midnite lived. And if I did know where he lived, there was yet another problem. This is America. In America, if you don't want to be arrested, you simply don't answer the door when the Sheriff rings. That's it! They would make three attempts, and if he didn't answer, then he wouldn't get arrested, and Midnite never answers the door for anyone. And since City Marshals are private contractors, working for themselves for a profit, but licensed by the City, who in their right minds would arrest anybody for $65.00? Can you blame them?

Then there was Albert, the computer hack at Wyman

Associates, my private investigators. He was always friendly and easy to talk to. I used them on a contingency fee basis - no information - no fee. Unfortunately, Midnite had no credit report, no address, no job, no bank - nothing - absolutely nothing. Even the old beat up BMW motorcycle seemed to have vanished from the records. Too bad. I was really getting to like Albert.

And lastly, there was the collection agency that I tried using. The term collection agency is something of a misnomer because they didn't collect anything. They gave up - outsmarted by the elusive alien. I found them in the Yellow Pages. After exhausting all the other possibilities, I found someone who might actually take the case. Yes! Mr. Burns was interested, but only for one fleeting moment.

"Is it a business?"

"No. It's Small Claims against an individual. I have a judgment."

"What does he owe you?"

"Well, about $5,000 now, including interest and costs."

"What does he look like?"

"Eh ..."

"Well, is he black?"

"Yeah ... about six foot two, 180 pounds, long black hair cropped close to the sides ... gold earrings in each ear, wears a bandana ... boots and bells ... Mr. Burns? MR. BURNS ... PLEASE DON'T HANG UP!"

It was really quite funny, but he took it all down, pretending to be interested, or maybe he thought there was just a small chance.

"Where does he live?"

"Well, his last known address was 501 W. 46th Street ..."

"Oh, a Westie. I know the area very well. In fact, I have

a friend at the police precinct. I'll check to see if there's a criminal record."

Mr. Burns never called back, but I did. There was no criminal record. Midnite was clean - completely legit - just a supreme deadbeat. Mr. Burns said that he would have to get a lawyer, and an investigator, and that I would have to pay $200 up front, just to start, with no end. He advised me to give it up and take it off my taxes, but I already did and continued to do so. I thanked him for his efforts, but I didn't give up.

And so, with the elusive alien unfindable and perhaps nonexistent, and with all avenues, opportunities, and possibilities exhausted, I had to consider my case on temporary hold. But give up? Never! A judgment is good for twenty years, and the pursuit of justice would continue. A long, hard winter was ahead of us, and a new year approaching. Who knew what it would bring?

XXXIII. Dealing with the Telephone Company

Winter recess was over, and I was back at the job at the plant. Things were slow and production had not yet started up. It was the beginning of the month, and the beginning of the year. It gave me some time to get back to the case. And so, on one of those lazy, do-nothing afternoons, I decided to give it a shot. Why not? There was nothing to lose. I dialed directory assistance, 9-1-212-555-1212.

"Listing please?"

"Neville Michaels."

The recording followed.

"The number ... is non-published ... at the customer's request."

HALLALUYAH! NON-PUBLISHED!

January 15, 1994, 4:37 P.M. - A great day! Midnite had a telephone listing! And maybe he had a job and an apartment also. I was dealing with a real person again! The information would be made available when an Information Subpoena would be served upon the telephone company. And so, that is what happened. An Information Subpoena was served on NYNEX, the telephone company.

Of course, nothing is quite that simple. You have to experience the system to appreciate it. Nobody, not even the telephone company, when required to do so under a court ordered subpoena, likes to give out information on deadbeats. I wasn't exactly shocked when the answers to the subpoena came back stamped, "No Information." Of course they had information! They're the telephone company! Where are they sending the bills? Who does he call? They must have his credit report. Midnite had a credit report? NYNEX had some explaining to do. I had to call their Legal Department. I asked for the Subpoena Group.

"Mrs. Petersen speaking. How can I help you?"

"Mrs. Petersen, this is Jonah Cohen. I'm a judgment creditor from the Small Claims Court. I'm calling about the answers to an Information Subpoena that you completed?"

"What is the defendant's name, please?"

"Michaels, M - I - C - H - A - E - L - S, Neville M. Michaels."

"One moment, Sir ... Sir, we have no listing for a Neville M. Michaels at 501 West 46th Street."

"I know. He moved."

"Where?"

Where? They want to know where? They're supposed to tell me where.

"I don't know where. That's why I sent you the subpoena!"

"Well, unless you give us an address ..."

"Mrs. Petersen, YOU HAVE A COURT ORDERED SUBPOENA AND YOU ARE LEGALLY REQUIRED TO PROVIDE ME WITH THIS INFORMATION!"

"How do you know that he has a telephone?"

"Directory Assistance told me! It's unlisted. And you have to provide me with the information."

"One moment, sir."

Several minutes passed by. I struggled to contain my rage. Nobody likes the telephone company, but my case was special.

"Sir ...?"

"Yes?"

"We have a listing for a Neville Michaels."

AH! SUCCESS! Of course they have a listing!

"But the subpoena says Neville <u>M</u>. Michaels. We can't take the chance that it might be someone else."

Well, I crashed - right into a fit of frustration. Everybody protects Neville Michaels, but Mrs. Petersen was surprisingly patient. It gave me some time to think. Of course Neville Michaels and Neville M. Michaels are the same person. How many Neville Michaels' with unlisted telephone numbers could there be in Manhattan, who have also just moved, and with Small Claims judgments against them? I was reduced to begging.

"Mrs. Petersen, please don't make me go back to the court to get another subpoena in the name of Neville Michaels ... or maybe even have to sue him again!"

It was then that my eyes dropped down to the papers on my desk ... the defense contracts, reports, forms, Government work, my own legal work, all mixed up into one insane mess, and what came into my eyes was Midnite's social security number on my copy of the subpoena. And so, like Moses coming down from Mount Sinai with the tablets of the Ten Commandments, so was I, enlightened with Neville Michaels' social security number.

"If you had his social security number, could you then give me the information?"

"Yes. What is it?"

"It's on the subpoena."

I read it off to her and it was no more than twenty seconds of listening to clicking keys on the NYNEX computers when the subpoena clerk returned.

"Sir, we have it. We'll fax this information right over to you."

True to her word, and within minutes, the answers to the

Information Subpoena came cranking over on IMC's fax machine. So the Spirit of Captain Midnite was a very real person, with a telephone, with an address, and with a job. Perhaps, not surprisingly, he still worked at the Hudson Grill. The address given was 71 Varick Street, only a couple of blocks away. How convenient for him!

With my pulse racing wildly, I called Midnite's unlisted number. A voice, with a faint accent of the West Indies came through the lines. It was the reincarnated voice of the alien spirit.

"Hello?"

I did not answer. I just paused to make sure it was him, but then again,

"Hello? Who is it, mun?"

I didn't want to blow my cover. Besides, I was too nervous and excited to answer. I just hung up.

"Click."

It was him.

I did not sleep well that night. My brain was feeding on the events of the day. IMC, the company where I was stationed was closing. With nearly all of the equipment and office furniture moved out of the plant, and most of the employees laid off, things had slowed down to nothing. I think reality set in when I saw them rolling out the Coke machine past my office. I began reading a book on Western Civilization of all things, maybe catching up on some of my lost college reading. I read about the ancient Egyptians, and about their religions. I read about their great sun-god Re or Amon-Re. I read about the cult of Osiris, who was the god of the Nile, agriculture, and nature. He was murdered by his son Set who cut up his body in pieces. Isis, the wife and sister of Osiris miraculously put the pieces together and restored him to life. His other son Horace avenged his murder and killed Set.

I also read about the Greek gods, especially Zeus, and how he wreaked vengeance on his enemies, and executed justice by throwing thunderbolts of lightning. It was a rough night ... a very rough night ...

I find myself in a strange neighborhood. I seem to be walking aimlessly. In the distance there is some activity, a street fair, perhaps. I walk towards it, and I see a tent or a booth. There is a tall, black man there. He is dressed in very bright orange, yellow, and light green clothes and he is wearing a bright orange hat with a tassel, a fez, like the Turks wear. As I approach, he appears to be training dogs to do acrobatics for some circus act. As I continue to go forward, I recognize the black man in the brightly colored clothes. It is Midnite! And now he too, recognizes me! We walk slowly toward each other. Eventually, we are standing opposite each other. Midnite extends his hand in friendship. I too, meet his, not in friendship, but by some inexplicable force of nature, or by an automatic reaction based on instinct or experience. It was like kissing your aunt, or like the time I almost kissed my gay neighbor at the Brooklyn Heights apartment. He got hold of me as I was coming home from work on Christmas Eve and kissed me. I very nearly kissed him back before I caught myself, but here I was not so lucky. My hand met his! Yes, my cold, nervous hand was suddenly in the warm, friendly hand of the black man from Trinidad. I took Midnite's hand ... and suddenly, a bolt of lightning flashed! It was the great Greek god Zeus wreaking vengeance on the forbidden union. All at once it was a challenge of opposites: black vs. white, American vs. alien,

Jew vs. gentile, landlord vs. tenant, plaintiff vs. defendant, creditor vs. debtor, and matter vs. anti-matter - all of this, amidst the wrath and fury of the great Greek god Zeus! There was terrible thunder and lightning threatening to split the earth wide open, but it was too late. The mortal sin had been committed. I had taken the alien black man's hand, and amidst the raging fury of Zeus came Midnite's cool, calm, collected voice, "Und how are you, mun?" And with this, the great god threw down another lightning bolt, the most powerful yet, to undo it all, but I could not release my hand from the alien's grip. And then ... and then ... the penultimate lightning bolt to undo the unholy alliance hit with terrible, resounding, crashing thunder ...

"CRASH!"

It was about 2:20 A.M. My idiot upstairs neighbor had just come home from one of his wild, drunken episodes, dropping his shoes on the hard wood floor. My thoughts: I have to get out of this condo lest Zeus hits me with a piece of falling sheetrock one day.

XXXIV.   The Arrest

It had come down to this. It had to succeed. In order for an arrest to be successful, one had to know with absolute certainty the exact location of the defendant. Now this was going to be a civil arrest for failure to comply with the Information Subpoena, and failure to appear in court after service of the Order to Show Cause.   In order to assure success, I decided to personally check out the defendant's new address.

I visited the building at 71 Varick St., but I wasn't able to find the apartment, 1G. The ground floor apartments had sidewalk entrances, some with steel doors and steel bars. The apartment letters went from A to F, north to south along Varick. Apartment F was on the corner of Varick. After F, there was a huge, roll-down type garage door. And just after the garage door were two small wooden doors, painted gray. There were no windows above the gray colored doors. The doors were unmarked. Where was apartment G? I happened to ask a few people whom I saw coming out of the building, but nobody knew where apartment G was. Perhaps it was one of the unmarked doors, or perhaps G meant garage? Did Midnite live in the garage? Did I really expect Midnite to actually live in a real apartment? Did Midnite even live here?

There was a motorcycle parked in front of the building, chained to a no parking sign, and covered with canvas. I wasn't able to tell if it was Midnite's '74 BMW. Midnite's bike had a distinctive headlight with a yellowed, plastic lens with a button-like center. Its color was black. What was the plate number? Would I dare to pick up the canvas and look? Was it his? It was at nighttime. The motorcycle was parked exactly opposite the brightly lit and mirrored lobby. I might have been seen - an attempted act of vandalism or theft. Perhaps it would be Midnite who would arrest me instead! I looked this way and that, and then I picked up the canvas. No, it wasn't his. I couldn't do anything further. I had to go with what I had.

The next day I was back at the job at my office. I was in my last waning days at IMC Magnetics. The flatbed trucks were in the plant loading up the last pieces of machinery. My transfer to the main Government office building in Garden City was imminent. Yes, IMC was finished, and I was destined for Garden City. It had been a long time since I had worked in the main office building. The trauma of working with supervisors, section chiefs, branch chiefs, and assorted military types was overwhelming. And worst of all, all my legal work would come to a screeching halt! What would it be like? I wondered what it would all be like ...

I find myself in my new cubicle, amidst a mess of unsorted and confusing papers. I have no idea what I am doing. We don't have a paging system here, but the page comes through anyway, "Jonah Cohen, please report to the lobby." Nobody ever reports to the lobby - there is nobody there, no receptionist and no offices, but the page comes through again. I am compelled to obey the instructions of the page and make my way to the elevator and descend. As the door opens, I find myself in a strange lobby, a place I had never seen or been to before. It is illuminated with a deep blue, almost indigo light. There is nobody there and the silence is absolute. A *minute passes, and the front door of the building suddenly slides open. A dark, familiar figure appears. It is Midnite in chains! And immediately behind is the Sheriff, in blue and gray uniform. Although the chains are heavy, and being dragged along the concrete floor, they make no noise. There is no talking. The Sheriff finds the key on a huge key ring and unlocks the chains. Midnite reaches into his pockets, pulls out his wallet, slowly counts out $216.00, and hands it over to the Sheriff. It is all done with one unhesitating motion. It is truly all he has. The Sheriff hands the money over to me. It is all in small bills, and it is a huge wad. There is only about $4,784.00 to go, plus interest and fees. I sign the paper for partial satisfaction of the judgment and hand it to the Sheriff who hands it to Midnite. The transaction is completed. The Sheriff puts Midnite back in his chains. Midnite and the Sheriff depart. I return to work. It is all done under the cover of the protective indigo light.*

I awoke from my daydream and quickly got back to work, legal work. I called Rick Mosley, the attorney at the Sheriff's Office. Nothing happens unless you make it happen.

"Mr. Mosley? This is Jonah Cohen, Cohen vs. Michaels? We spoke a while back about an arrest?"

He seemed to remember vaguely. There aren't many people being arrested in Small Claims civil actions anymore, so they do tend to remember, but he needed some help.

"Refresh my memory."

"I faxed over an arrest warrant for your review. Did you get it?"

He did.

"This is an arrest warrant for failure to answer questions on an Information Subpoena. The subpoena was served and ignored, the Show Cause Order was served and ignored, and an arrest warrant was signed by a judge. I had a copy certified and I can send it to you."

"Was there a Fining Order?"

Fining Order? I had to think quickly. Yes, of course there was a Fining Order, but I hadn't mentioned it. Everything was covered and in order.

"Yes."

And then Mosley asked,

"Did you include these words on the warrant ...? What I am looking for is 'DEFEAT, IMPEDE, IMPAIR, and PREDJUDICE the rights of the judgment creditor.'"

"Yes, it's all there."

"Send me the certified copy, three additional copies, and $65.00 together with a cover letter."

"Ok, I'll do that. Thanks Mr. Mosley."

I called Mosley again a few days later to see how things were coming along. He was pretty sure that the warrant had already been given to a Deputy Sheriff. He gave me the number that I should call. Mosley was polite, mild mannered, and appeared to be somewhat interested in my particular case. I tried for some free lawyerly advice. The City Marshal wasn't able to collect from the Hudson Grill, Midnite's supposed employer, because he worked there "off the books." I asked Mosley if I would be able to hold the Hudson Grill responsible for the judgment.

"You would have to file a motion with the court. There is no Blumberg form. It's part of the CPLR 5231 statute."

Mosley wished me good luck. I liked that. Here was another lawyer who seemed to be personally interested in my cause. I seemed to have made many enemies in my role as judgment creditor, but I have friends among scoundrels, and Mosley wished me good luck!

I called the number at the Sheriff's Office that Mosley gave me, but the Sheriff's Office resembled a zoo more than an official government office. An Afro-American woman with a powerful voice and a heavy accent answered.

"Yo! Who deyah? … Hold on. Hold on."

I listened intently to the conversation in the background.

"You know why dey sent me ovah? Deese are de outstanding figures. Deyah ain't no mo', honey. If yo' want some mo' den yo have to go back to de court … All right, all right. We'll send somebody else ovah heya."

I tried to gain some insight as to how collections worked at the Sheriff's Office. There is no insight, only insanity. The woman from the Sheriff's Office came back on the phone.

"Call back in a month. We're backed up. Give us until about the third week in March. Can't find it in the computer - not in the computer yet."

I had been at this for nearly four years now. If someone tells you to call back in a month, you should call back in a few days, maybe sooner. I called the Sheriff's Office a few days later, and yes, it was in the computer. Case #734259 was assigned to Deputy Desoto. I liked Deputy Desoto. He spoke slowly and with determination in a low pitched monotone with a faint Hispanic accent. And that monotone ran chills up my spine. I was glad that Deputy Desoto wasn't arresting me! He sounded like he was about 250 pounds, 6 ft., 3 in., or so. With a Deputy like this, who needed a Sheriff? Deputy Desoto would do just fine. Desoto needed some information to aid in the arrest.

Midnite most likely lived at 71 Varick, but I really couldn't be sure even of that. I explained to Desoto the apartment configuration of the building, the unmarked doors on the sidewalk, and Midnite's strange and mysterious nocturnal schedule. I also had to tell him that I couldn't find apartment 1G, if it existed at all.

"But look for that BMW motorcycle. It could be in the garage. If it's there, he's there."

I suggested that perhaps the best time to make the arrest would be in front of the Hudson Grill, just before 5:00 P.M., when Midnite would be reporting for work. The answer was no. Deputy Desoto informed me that the courts close at 5:00 P.M. and that there would be no place to put him! America is a strange place, a very strange place, indeed. In a civil arrest, they can't break down doors, and an arrest has to be made in the morning, to allow time to get to the court before it closed. I tried to explain Midnite's vampire-like schedule, that Midnite slept all day and would only come alive at night, but Desoto assured me.

"Don't worry. If he's there, we'll get him."

The Deputy explained the procedure. An attempt would be made on the employer, and at his residence. If the arrest is made, I would have to be in court in order to present my case. Present my case, again? I thought I had already won! How many times would I have to present this stupid case? He was in contempt, and I would collect my money. That's the case!

Desoto said that he would call me if the arrest were made. I would have to be in court within one hour after the arrest.

"Can you be there?"

Be there?! If I were in a space ship orbiting the great galaxy Andromeda M31, I would find a way to be there! There was no question about it.

"Yes! Of course I'll be there."

It was March 8th at exactly 3:30 P.M. The call came from Deputy Desoto.

"Mr. Cohen, this is Deputy Desoto."

"Yes, Mr. Desoto, eh … I mean Deputy Desoto."

I was too nervous to think straight, and I wasn't yet used to addressing anyone with the title of "Deputy." I was just beginning to feel comfortable with "Your Honor." The slight error went unnoticed, but the Deputy called and I knew that it had to be something big, and here it was.

"Mr. Michaels has agreed to turn himself in to the Sheriff's Office at 253 Broadway, corner Warren Street, tomorrow at 8:30 A.M., Room 600.

Desoto would call me when and if this would happen. I was supposed to meet them at Queens County Civil Court. Well, it wasn't exactly what I had expected. I was hoping for some action, maybe a fight, or a shootout, but then the arrest could have failed altogether. And it wouldn't do any good to bring a corpse into court. Besides, I would be out the $65.00. March 9th - 9:00 A.M. The call was from Deputy Desoto.

"Mr. Michaels has turned himself in."

I had to question the Deputy to make sure that I heard it right. I couldn't believe it actually happened. The Spirit of Captain Midnite transformed into a humble mortal in the custody of a New York City Deputy Sheriff.

"The defendant is in your custody … NOW?"

And the answer to my question was,

"Yes."

Old Faithful, don't fail me now! PLEASE don't fail me now! I called my office immediately and got the secretary.

"Susan, put me down for five hours of annual leave ... got an emergency ..."

And without waiting for approval, it was Old Faithful and I barreling up the LIE on our way to the Queens County Civil Court. I recalled more of my conversation with Deputy Desoto.

"What do you look like?"

"I wear glasses, mustache, and a brown leather jacket."

And the Deputy responded,

"I wear a blue uniform."

I wondered if it was indigo.

I found myself in the lobby of the Queens County Courthouse that I had come to know so well, but there was no sign of the Deputy or Midnite. Where the hell were they? I waited a while, looked, and then took my usual position on the landing of the stairway to the second floor. There was a window there where one was able to look out into the courtyard, or down into the lobby, but there was no sign of either. I walked down the stairs and was suddenly approached from behind.

"Mr. Cohen?"

"Yes."

"Deputy Desoto."

Deputy Desoto, it turned out, was shorter than I was, maybe by two inches, and the uniform looked more gray than blue or indigo. The Sheriff's Office had sent a rookie! No matter. And with him, hands cuffed behind him, was the alien, the genie from Trinidad, reduced to the status of common prisoner. Midnite, all 6 ft., 2 in. of him towered above everyone. He was very nearly exactly as I saw him in this very same court building almost two and a half years ago. He wore the same gold earrings. His long straight black hair was cropped close to the sides. Torn blue jeans, bandana, and motorcycle boots with bells completed his courtroom attire. My description of him to the Sheriff's Office was perfect. The only additions were a New York Knicks cap and new wrap around designer sunglasses.

"Follow this way!"

The Deputy gave the order. Midnite held his head up expressionless, towering high above Deputy Desoto, myself, and everyone else. The bandana seemed to fly behind him as he was being escorted. It was a sight that caught the stares of the crowd. It curtailed their conversation, and stopped them in their steps. An arrest in a Civil Court is unusual. My own eyes transfixed on the cuffed hands, the whites of the palms turned outwards. There were rings on the middle fingers of both hands. I watched as the fingers of the large cuffed black hands moved. They curled up, stretched out, and relaxed. And then, the process was repeated. I watched the cuffed hands during the entire walk to the courtroom. I knew that whatever the outcome of the court would be, this had to be my ultimate and total victory. I had the alien in chains. This was my victory!

I was told to wait outside. I didn't know what was happening in the courtroom, what questions they might have asked him, or how they might prepare a prisoner for a hearing. I could only imagine. Perhaps they would attach electrodes from a lie detector to his genitals!

Yes! This was my victory! Even Kravitz would have been proud of me at this moment! Neville M. Michaels a/k/a Midnite had been apprehended, arrested, and chained.

Paying the price

Severe penalties used

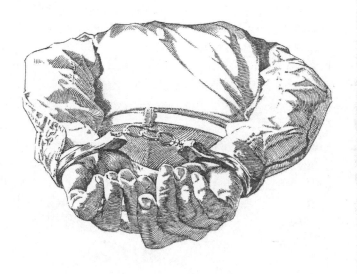

XXXV. Supplementary Proceedings

The hearing was about to begin. I was called into the courtroom by Deputy Desoto. The judge who would preside over the hearing was already seated on the bench. There were two court officers present, and standing handcuffed between them was Michaels, the defendant. He still had the Knicks cap on his head, and wore the designer sunglasses, earrings, and bandana. One of the court officers unlocked the handcuffs. Michaels rubbed each wrist with the other hand in an attempt to restore the circulation. He looked at me, and with this, I thought I caught a wry smile. He must have been handcuffed for hours, and was now probably in some pain. It made me glad. I saw the judge look Michaels up and down as if to say, *"Is this guy for real?"*

We were soon seated before the judge, who didn't really look like a judge. They don't wear black robes anymore, or at least, he wasn't wearing one. I had prepared a short speech and expected the hearing to begin with the judge saying,

"Plaintiff begin."

It didn't happen like that, and I didn't get to use my prepared speech. The judge instead began the hearing with some small talk with the defendant.

"Are you a Knicks fan?"

Michaels responded in a low tone, and with a shrug of the shoulders.

"Yeah."

"They lost badly in their last game. Did you see it?"

Michaels smiled slightly, and responded almost

inaudibly.

"No."

The judge looked him up and down once again. There was a long pause as the judge continued to study Michaels. At last, his silence was broken. The words were directed at Michaels.

"Just answer the questions. You'll be out of here in a few minutes."

Did I hear that correctly? Out of here in a few minutes?!! It must have taken almost two years to put this together, and this judge is ending it in a few minutes? Two years of skip tracing, phone calls, process services, court appearances ... and now, a few minutes? Well, this was supposed to be a hearing for contempt of court, to answer questions, to be examined, to pay fines, judgments, and maybe even go to jail. And now, here they are discussing the damned Knicks? Or did I misunderstand? Perhaps it was a hint to remove the stupid cap! But then it was the court officer who asked Michaels to remove the cap, and also the silly wrap-around sunglasses, which he did.

The judge then asked if there were any lawyers present. No, thank goodness, no lawyers. Did they expect me to pay a lawyer to take part in this ridiculous comedy act? The preliminaries being dispensed with, the contempt hearing began. Michaels was asked the questions on the Information Subpoena. The judge read them off one at a time in succession, and the defendant answered.

"Question 1 - Where do you live?"

"71 Varick Street, Apartment 1G, New York City."

"Question 2 - What is your Social Security Number?"

"279-26-5160."

"Question 3 - What is your date of birth?"

"12/08/62"

It was all going very fast. We were already a third of the way through the questions. I had a clipboard on my lap and a pen in my hand, but I wasn't taking down all this vital information. I must have been looking up, my eyes glazed over, apparently lost. The court officer noticed this and interrupted.

"Are you taking this down?"

I nodded to the court officer. He was only trying to be helpful, but I obviously already had all this information. I couldn't have had the defendant arrested if I did not. And then at this zoo of a hearing, the court officer realized as an afterthought, that nobody had been sworn in! But then, they all lie anyway. The defendant was quickly sworn in, and we were ready for the next question.

"Question 4 - Do you own or rent the place where you live?"

"I'm living with someone."

I dropped my pen. Here we go again. Another "illegal sublet?" A girlfriend, perhaps? Somebody from the band? The telephone was in his own name! We went on. It might have been that the judge thought that I wasn't paying attention. His Honor looked at me, and replied with a very loud and disgusted,

"OK?!!!"

I nodded. We continued.

"Question 5 - Are you a union member?"

"No."

I slouched down in my chair. It was all so useless. Midnite a union member? No, I didn't think so. My mind began to wander, and I even began to wonder why I ever did this. It was all a waste.

"Question 6 - Do you have any bank accounts?"

"No."

What a stupid question. Of course he had no bank accounts! And then we came to Question 7.

"Question 7 - Do you own an automobile?"

"No."

Ah hah! Now we were getting somewhere. This was the question that would make it all worthwhile. I knew that he still had the motorcycle. I was able to prove it with the DMV registration and title records. This was my question! But it was Midnite who continued, providing the needed clarification regarding his motor vehicle assets.

"... but I do own a motorcycle..."

The mystery of the motorcycle, its whereabouts, and its present condition would soon be unraveled, but hidden in the back pages of the New York Post at an earlier date ran the following article:

It was a cold, rainy night at 4:30 A.M. when a 32 year old black male, driving without a license or registration, lost control of his 1974 BMW motorcycle on the rain slicked Brooklyn-Queens Expressway and crashed into the rear of a 1993 Honda SUV. Brian Kelly, an NYPD police officer on the scene said that the cause of the accident was excessive speed. The driver of the Honda SUV was unhurt, but the motorcyclist suffered an injured right arm and was taken to Brookdale Hospital for treatment. It was not known if drugs or alcohol played a part in the accident. The extent of his injuries was unknown. The BMW motorcycle was picked up by a flatbed tow truck operated by City Boys Towing. Its whereabouts or condition could not be determined.

"...yes, I do own a motorcycle, but it's in pieces, and it needs an engine."

The alien smiled. It was a smug, confident smile. The hearing was nearly over, and now the most important question was being shot down. I didn't believe him. And the judge, now even more disgusted, directed his entire wrath toward me, and now with a voice even louder than before.

"OK?!!!!!!!!!!"

I responded,

"Where is the motorcycle?"

This was the only time throughout the hearing, or even the entire arrest process for that matter, that Midnite showed any stress or emotion whatsoever. The alien spirit from Trinidad and Tobago had cracked. The smile was gone. Serious concern set in. An asset that could be seized had been identified and soon located. The interchange was fast and the pace quickened.

"Why do you have to know this?"

"It's my right to know!"

And now Judge Greenstein looked at the alien.

"Answer the question!"

And after a short pause,

"It's in the basement at 71 Varick Street."

We went on to the employment question.

"I'm unemployed."

The judge turned toward me in his bored and disgusted way.

"OK?!!!"

I had two Information Subpoenas with the answers with me. One was from his lawyer in the motorcycle accident; the other was from NYNEX, the telephone company. The two sets of answers to the Information Subpoenas gave the

Hudson Grill as the employer. I didn't want Midnite to know where or how I was getting my information, so I didn't present the copies to the judge, but the employment question was important. It was time for the claimant to respond.

"Your Honor, I have two separate pieces of information that indicate that the defendant works at the Hudson Grill."

The judge turned toward the alien.

"Do you work at the Hudson Grill?"

Midnite squirmed in his seat, but responded in a manner that was sure to evoke the sympathy of a liberal New York judge on a poor oppressed black man. He played the part well.

"Well, I don't really *work* there. But I am there often … I hang out there. If they tell me to do something, then I'll go and do it. Maybe they'll give me a little something … you know … I'm just there, and I help out … but I don't really work there."

The speech was slow and drawn out. It was presented in acceptable English, but in the presence of the "rich" white man, and the liberal New York judge, in parts it sounded more like,

"If dey wan' me to do it, den I goes an' doose it."

Midnite didn't just have to act the part (which he did like a pro), the characters were cast and the scenery set. And now the claimant was even more disgusted than the judge. I knew that he worked there! I recalled some of my conversations with Richie, the owner of the Hudson Grill, and also with some of the other people who worked there.

"When does he start?"

"Five o'clock."

I thought of how I might present it, but saying I said this and he said that is not the kind of evidence that impresses judges. And now the judge actually growled at me with a loud and terrifying growl.

"OK?!!!!!!!!!!!!!!!!!!!"

The employment question was lost.

"Yes, Your Honor."

Next was the property question. Did the defendant own any real property? Ah … if it could only be, but perhaps it was! Images of rolling green hills, palm trees, and blue lagoons flipped through my mind. Perhaps it actually was …

And I saw before me endless acres of land in Trinidad, planted with groves of avocado and kiwi trees, lush and beautiful; ready for harvesting, sale and export. It would be a harvest worth hundreds of thousands of dollars. And there was Midnite, standing along side a new Moto Guzzi motorcycle - California Vintage - in front of a gleaming white mansion. He was dressed in a white suit like that of a plantation owner, the proud and prosperous owner of it all. He had to be worth millions.

"Do you own any real property?"

"No."

The images of palm trees, blue lagoons, and kiwis vanished. The avocados rotted away on the trees instantly.

We were up to the last two questions. Midnite was asked if he had any lawsuits pending. I knew from the DMV records that there was a motorcycle accident. If he were a claimant, I could have had a City Marshal levy on the award. His answer was short and simple.

"No."

But what about the accident? Surely there was litigation. It would have to be pursued at another time with another judge. And then finally,

"Are there any other assets?"

"No."

With the questions to the Information Subpoena completed, the judge asked me for the amounts of the judgments. I had an itemized list of expenses on my lap and read it all off.

"Your Honor, there are two judgments, $2,000 each ..."

"TWO JUDGMENTS?"

The surprised interjection came from Midnite. I guess he did care, a little. It was encouraging. I continued.

"Two judgments totaling $4,000.00, interest and expenses of $876.89, Marshal fees $50.00, Sheriff fees $65.00 for the arrest, plus various other costs and expenses, in addition to the Contempt of Court fine of $250.00."

The plaintiff's case was presented. It was now up to the judge to decide on the defendant's punishment and payment of the judgments and the fine. What followed seemed like long seconds of inactivity. And after carefully considering all the facts of the case at hand, and making a deliberate and well thought out unbiased decision, based on law and the rights of the judgment creditor, all in accordance with the Civil Practices Law and Procedure of the State of New York, the judge at last spoke.

"RELEASE THE DEFENDANT!"

I sat motionless in a state of shock. Empowered with the voodoo magic contained within his bandana, Midnite vanished faster than my images of palm trees and blue lagoons. It wasn't supposed to happen like that. I remembered my readings, where a judge could make a debtor turn his pockets inside out and confiscate all cash. Anything of value could be taken from him. I remembered that Midnite still had the gold earrings. I shouted out,

"I'LL TAKE THE JEWELERY! LET ME HAVE THE GOLD EARRINGS!

But the alien was gone, and Judge Greenstein wasn't about to do anything. I went up to the judge with the Fining Order, $250.00 plus $10.00 court costs. I read the Fining Order to the judge and surprisingly, he listened. Obviously, the response wasn't what I wanted or expected.

"He doesn't have any money. What do you want me to do?"

I was furious. But this is America! In America, nobody goes to jail, certainly not in Small Claims anyway. And if Midnite wasn't going to jail, then neither was I. In my rage, I spoke up to His Honor, or lack thereof.

"This is one farce of legal system you're running here!"

The judge was so shocked that all he was able to do was shrug, but the court officer heard it

"PLEASE LEAVE THE COURTROOM!"

And so, this is the end, the end of the subletting misadventure, the end of the trials, the end of the court appearances, the end of the process services, the end of the arrest, and finally with the arrest, the end of the story. Right? NO - NEVER! The judgments were still unsatisfied and good for another eighteen years. I didn't get anything this time, but I did get Midnite to pay a buck and quarter for the subway on his return trip to the City … maybe.

The next day I was back in my office writing letters and shooting off fax's with more energy that could be found in

Midnite's bandana. I had to call the Marshal fast, to get the motorcycle. I had to call the Hudson Grill and demand compliance with the wage garnishment, and I had to subpoena the mysterious Bennett Pulaski, the superintendent at 71 Varick Street. So much to do! And so, the story continues.

XXXVI.   A Letter to the Debtor

My first letter was written to the judgment debtor himself at his "home" address. It read as follows:

Dear Mr. Michaels,

Thank you for participating at the supplementary proceeding which took place at Queens County Court yesterday.

I was surprised to learn that you were not aware of the other Notice of Judgment, Index 4189/92, since the court had mailed a copy of the decision to you. As a courtesy, I am faxing you a copy at the Hudson Grill so you will be sure to get it.

You should contact the City Marshal immediately concerning this. If you are not heard from within seven days, I will proceed to have you arrested again. You are advised that a second arrest will entail jail time.

Also, at the proceeding yesterday, you inquired of the judge how to take action against me. Of course, it is your privilege as a resident alien, but you will have to do so at Suffolk County District Court, Riverhead, NY. I shall look forward to meeting with you again.

If you have any questions concerning the above, please call me.

Sincerely,
Jonah Cohen,
Judgment Creditor

XXXVII. The Girl with the Red Camaro

As I recall it then, it was back in April, after I had had Midnite arrested, that I made arrangements with the Marshal's Office to levy on the motorcycle. Marshals in general do not like to levy on motorcycles; it's messy, and they don't usually bring in enough revenue, but my Marshal would. It's all about money.

The problem here was that it was inside the building, in the basement, and behind locked doors. The people from the towing company wouldn't be able to get in. In the real world, they don't break down doors, shoot out locks, or blow up buildings. In the real world, they are afraid of lawsuits resulting from the destruction of property, trespassing, violation of rights - all rights - civil, constitutional, human, privacy - but the judgment creditor has no rights. And so, as it turned out, the Marshal was unsuccessful concerning the attempted seizure of the motorcycle. I had to discuss things with the Marshal.

"What do you mean they couldn't get into the building? Just go in and take it!"

"Mr. Cohen, the door was locked and we are not authorized to ..."

"Mick, please don't give up!"

"Mr. Cohen, we're closing the case ..."

"Mick, PLEASE! You can't believe all the work that went into this ... Look, I'll tell you what. I will go down there personally. I will get into the building. I will look for the motorcycle, and if it's there, I will call you, and I will open the door. All you will have to do is take it."

The Marshal agreed.

I had never done anything like this before, but it's amazing what you can do when there is motivation. On a whim, I had gotten a process server's license from the City. Tired of paying process servers, I figured I could make a few bucks on the receiving end of the business. Anyway, the process server license ID came in handy.

I had lived in an apartment building, and so I knew a tenant's probable reaction to the stranger intruding upon private property. I had been in that situation many times myself. You may be opening the front door, you have the key in the lock, and you are turning it. The intruder approaches from behind and you give him the *"Who the hell are you?"* look. You might say to him, *"Who are you looking for?"* or *"Can I help you?"* Whatever the response, the reply is, *"See the super."* But in the end, you want to be helpful, and you let them convince you. You hold the door open for him, pray that you are doing the right thing, and you assure yourself that he's ok.

And so it was here. I waited outside for about a minute, followed a tenant into the building, and got the strange look. I showed the tenant my process server's ID, assured her that it was ok, and that I was there to make a delivery to a certain Neville Michaels. She held open the door for me and let me in. I was ok.

"Do you know what apartment Mr. Michaels is in?"

"I'm sorry, no."

Nobody knew Mr. Michaels. Nobody anywhere knew Mr. Michaels.

But now once in the building, I found myself in an unfamiliar environment. I was lost. In order to avoid arousing suspicion, I tried to walk fast and deliberate, as one familiar with his surroundings and as one who knew where he was going. It didn't work. I was approached by another tenant in the building, a pleasant but inquisitive young man.

"Can I help you?"

"Yes, I'm looking for apartment 1G, Mr. Michaels."

"Sorry, you should see the super."

"Well, I tried, but the super isn't in."

"Do you live here? Why are you here?"

The useless conversation continued for a few minutes until the tenant tired of it, went out, and left me alone, thank goodness. I checked out the configuration of the building and found the mailboxes. His name wasn't there, of course. I found myself walking toward two elevator doors at the far end of the lobby. The left one, going down, opened first. I got in and descended to the basement. Once in the basement, I was led into strange passageways, a maze leading to unmarked doors. I tried them all, but they were all locked. After the doors, I passed by the laundry room. The appearance of a tall black man stood in front of me. The inevitable confrontation between creditor and debtor had come to fruition. Surely the released prisoner would wreak his revenge! Holy Hell would surely break out! My heart began to race as our eyes met. No, it wasn't him. He was nothing more than another tenant doing his laundry, but once again, I got the strange look.

I continued on looking for the motorcycle. I ascended a stairwell and found myself back in the lobby. I went back down into the basement, passed by the same black man doing his wash, and I got the same strange look. I walked faster, still looking for the motorcycle, but it could have been anywhere. I knew that there was a gym in the building, but I didn't know how to get to it. It probably was behind one of the locked doors. And how does one get to the garage - the most probable place to look for a motorcycle? But now, somebody else saw me, and I was beginning to look very, very suspicious. Perhaps the real Neville Michaels a/k/a Midnite, complete with boots, gold earrings, and bandana would appear at any time from behind a door or a passageway. Panic set in. I went into a cold sweat. I had to get out. I quickly fled the catacombs of the apartment building basement and escaped into the bright sunlight and safety of the outside world. I didn't find the motorcycle, and so, I didn't get to call the Marshal. The mission was a failure.

Once outside, I got back into the Dodge and parked it on Grand Street, opposite the garage entrance and the two unmarked gray painted doors. There I waited, pondering over the futility of this wild goose chase. I couldn't even be sure that he lived there, but I was prepared to wait it out, however long it would take. Waiting for what, I didn't exactly know, maybe just waiting out of frustration.

As it turned out, I didn't have to wait long. Not three minutes went by when a late model red Chevy Camaro pulled up next to the building and parked. I looked on with curiosity. A good-looking, tall, blond girl got out, walked over toward the two little gray, unmarked painted doors, and rang one of the bells. I continued to watch from across the street and directly opposite. My view was unobstructed. She was standing near the doors and facing me, but not looking at me. Her stance was casual, her keys were in her hand, and she was shaking them gently while waiting. She turned around, rang the bell again, and waited a short while longer. One of the doors opened suddenly, and then, out of the darkness and into the bright sunlight emerged the dark alien - Midnite - in full and unmistakable view. The black alien spirit had surfaced. It was like Dracula in the sun. It was like the Creature from the Lagoon. Like an event taking place with less frequency than Haley's comet, so was the appearance of the strange and elusive Captain Midnite. He was happy to see her. They talked for a while, but did not kiss or embrace, nor did he invite her inside. They talked a while longer, and then walked together toward the Camaro and got in. She drove.

Old Faithful - don't fail me now, PLEASE!! But the old Dodge started right up, as if it too had a spirit and wanted to see the matter through. I quickly wrote down the license plate number, F57-2SC, for later tracing with the DMV. The Camaro pulled off, and Old Faithful and I followed in hot pursuit. They sped up Grand Street, turned north on Broadway, continued along Broadway, and then came to an abrupt stop. Why did they stop? I nearly panicked. I thought to myself, why the hell did they stop?

"SHIT! THEY'RE ONTO ME!"

I passed them and drove on. I hung a quick right at the next block, and then another right, and then another right so that I was now facing Broadway and I could see the Camaro. No. They didn't know that I was following them after all. Apparently, they had just stopped for cigarettes, or a soda or something. I crossed the intersection and waited. The Camaro took off again making a sharp U-turn heading toward Canal Street, and then west on Canal. It seemed that they were heading into the Holland Tunnel into New Jersey. I turned left, hoping to head them off. Yes, they were heading into the tunnel, but the heavy traffic was impossible. Damn!! I lost them.

It was just as well. The pursuit into New Jersey probably

wouldn't have accomplished anything anyway. I already had the plate number of the Camaro. The day was well spent. And so, the girl with the red Camaro, whoever she was, would be traceable.

XXXVIII. Whitey

The next day, back at the office, I called Mick at the Marshal's Office to let him know where we were with regard to seizing the motorcycle. I was supposed to find the motorcycle, and they were supposed to come and pick it up.

"How did you make out?"

"Well ... I couldn't find it..., but PLEASE DON'T CLOSE THE CASE! I'm still working on it."

"Well, Mr. Cohen, you know we're not making any money on this, and we've invested far too much already. Do you have any idea of what it cost us to send the tow trucks into Brooklyn?"

"Brooklyn? Who told you to send the tow trucks into Brooklyn? I could have told you right away that he's not in Brooklyn. He's in Manhattan. He moved, and you were supposed to pick up the motorcycle at the Varick Street address."

"Well ... I'll have to talk to the Marshal and see what he says."

So again, it was all about money. Right, wrong, justice - none of that mattered. The Marshal had to make some money. I called Mick again, but he wasn't in. I left a message for him to call back, but he didn't call me back. As a matter of fact, nobody calls back. Everybody gives up. I had to call again.

"Mick, please don't close me out!"

"Look, I spoke with the Marshal, and he said that he would levy on the motorcycle on condition that you get your own towing company."

"Ok. It's a deal."

I went searching through the Yellow Pages of the phone book, but it was hard to find a towing company that would pick up a motorcycle. One of them suggested a certain towing company in Queens, Cycle Care, and I got to speak with the owner. I conjured up in my own mind this mean looking Hells Angels type on the other end of the line, complete with tattoos, chains, Nazi helmet ... the works. I thought that Cycle Care would be perfect. But what I got was a wimpy,

"Gee, we've never done this before."

"Look, I'll get into the building and I'll open the door. All you have to do is pick up the motorcycle and store it until the Marshal picks it up for auction."

Cycle Care agreed. Yes, it's always up to the judgment creditor to initiate things and keep it going. Otherwise, it all stops.

"How much does it cost?"

"$125.00 for the tow and $10.00 per day storage."

It would be more money pissed away, but we had to keep things going.

"What kind of a bike is it?"

"A '74 BMW."

"It ain't worth shit."

"Well, maybe I just want to take it away from him. Will you do it?

"Sure."

"Great! And when I call you, if I can get into the building and find the motorcycle, who shall I ask for?"

"Ask for ... Whitey."

"Whitey?"

"Yup, that's what they call me, Whitey."

226

And so, it was creditor vs. debtor, matter vs. anti-matter, white vs. black, and Whitey vs. Midnite.

XXXIX. NationsBank

I never did lay claim to Midnite's motorcycle, or maybe did lay claim, but not possession. I wasn't able to find it. Whitey would have been great, but that's the way it goes. I had my last conversation with Mick at the Marshal's Office - they were sending me bills. For their totally inept collection attempts, I was now being charged. It truly pays to be a deadbeat. I tried ignoring them at first, but they kept coming. Things needed to be straightened out with the Marshal's Office. I called them the first thing in the morning.

"Good morning, Marshal's Office."

"Good morning. This is Jonah Cohen, Marshal's Case No. G-093. I'm calling about an invoice that I received …"

"Hold on, Sir."

I did a lot of holding on in those days, but soon the same familiar voice came on. It was Mick.

"Hello, Mr. Cohen. What can I do for you?"

"Hi Mick. This is in reference to Cohen vs. Michaels, Marshal's Case G-093 …"

"Yes! Yes! I'm very familiar with the case."

"What are these invoices that I keep getting? I already paid my marshal fees, and I'M NOT PAYING ANYMORE!"

Without conscious effort, it began to build into a crescendo.

"WHAT YOU DID WAS TOTALLY, TOTALLY, USELESS! YOU GOT THE DEFENDANT'S NAME WRONG - IT'S NEVILLE MICHAELS, NOT NEVILLE

MARCIANO! AND YOU GOT HIS ADDRESS WRONG!
HE HASN'T LIVED AT THAT BROOKLYN ADDRESS
FOR OVER THREE YEARS! AND YOU EXPECT ME
TO PAY FOR THIS? HE WAS AT VARICK STREET,
BUT HE MOVED …"

"Please Mr. Cohen. Please. Ok. You don't have to pay the invoice, but we are now closing the case. Effective December 31, 1995, this case is closed!"

"But I may be able to get you his new address. I just need a little more time."

"Mr. Cohen, the case is closed."

"You don't want his new address?"

"NO! THE … CASE … IS … CLOSED!"

"Ok, so long, Mick."

The conversation ended abruptly, unresolved, and on an odd note, but my association with Marshal Badge No. 53 had ended. I had to be content without my having to pay additional marshal fees. I supposed that if there were ever anything to collect, they would gladly reopen it, and of course I would always be able to start again with another Marshal and pay more marshal fees.

And as has been the case with this entire misadventure, one road would close and another would open. I read the note that was left on my desk. It was a message from Albert at Wyman Associates. Albert hardly ever called, but if he called, it meant that they had something. I liked Albert. His free flowing, ebullient manner of speech made him a pleasure to talk with at any time, but now there was substance in the effervescence. I could hardly punch the numbers on the telephone fast enough. The generic greeting was deliberate.

"Good afternoon."

This information services company operates in nearly total secrecy. I read about these companies, the information revolution, and the invasion of privacy. The big ones are of course TRW and Equifax, but there are many smaller ones. They share information, not just credit, but all kinds of information obtained from the same or different computer data bases. Some of it is legal, and maybe some of it isn't, and exactly from where it comes, nobody could be sure. Anytime you give your name to someone, or fill out a form, or subscribe to a magazine, turn on your electric power, or for anything at all, it's likely to wind up in a computer data base for easy tapping. Social Security numbers are dynamite, and I had his.

"Good afternoon. Albert please."

"Who's calling?"

"Jonah Cohen, Cohen vs. Michaels."

"One moment please."

The wait was short.

"Hello, can I help you?"

It was Albert's friendly voice, but I had to make sure.

"Albert?"

"Y ..e..e..sssssss. How are ya Jon?"

Without giving me a chance to respond as to my health and well being, he went right into it.

"We haven't come up with anything on the employment search yet, but we're still trying. We have a new guy here, very good, very conscientious, very good worker, and he's still checking it out. Something very interesting turned up. It seems this Captain Midnite character is living with a certain Vincent Marcus ... that's Vincent Marcus in Larchmont, New York. He turned up on a credit report with a Shel ..."

It all began to click and the bells rang. I paid Wyman on a contingency fee basis. That is I pay only if they find something, and thus far, I hadn't paid anything, and certainly didn't want to pay for information that I already had. And so, I stopped Albert, lest I felt an obligation to pay. The pieces fitted together. The connection was made. I continued the sentence for Albert.

"Shelly D. Carpenter, 22 Apple Terrace, Staten Island?"

I related to Albert how I came to know the girl with the red Camaro, and how I was able to get the DMV report using the license plate number. But the big news, the bombshell, was the credit report! I tried to fish for some more free information. Albert paused for a few seconds. Albert didn't pause often, but this meant he had something and it was big. Albert continued.

"Look Jon, I'm on your side. I want to get this Captain Midnite too. I don't like this guy. I really don't like him. There's an account here. The account was opened in '93. It's a joint credit card account in the name of Shelly D. Carpenter and N. Midnite Michaels. The social security number here is … wait, I see two numbers. It looks like he's trying to change his name too."

Albert was on a roll, and I had to milk it for all it was worth.

"Who's the bank?"

"Ha! Ha! You want the bank? We'll give you the bank! It's National Associates or something. Wait a minute. Here it is. NationsBank. It's a NationsBank visa card, credit limit $5,000, debit balance $3,815. The account is current with a "1" rating, the best. What can you do with this?"

Albert was really interested in my case. I related to him the Information Subpoena that I had sent to Shelly and the

"N/A -Unknown" responses that I received. If I could prove a financial association between Neville and Shelly, with the aim of bringing her into court on contempt charges, then possibly I would be able to collect the judgments from her. Albert liked it.

"She's in trouble!"

"Got anything else?"

"Come on Jon ... ok, ok, we've got a phone number here, (972) 583-3548. Want to have some fun with it? Go ahead. Look Jon, that's all we have, honest. Good talking with you. Good luck. Gotta go."

Albert had given me the address of the credit card company. It was NationsBank, N.A. of Delaware with offices in Virginia and Delaware, but what I needed was a New York address for service of process, and Virginia and Delaware do not have reciprocity agreements with the New York courts. America is a strange place indeed. An Information Subpoena would have to be served at a New York address. There was a NationsBank listed in the Manhattan telephone directory. It was the office at 767 5th Avenue. It wasn't the credit card company, but it was a NationsBank office. I wasn't sure what it was, but it was NationsBank and it would have to be ok. If I could get NationsBank served with an Information Subpoena, I would have the proof I needed to put Shelly, the girl with the red Camaro, in contempt of court, fined, and possibly collect the judgments from her. The answers from the bank would prove a financial relationship between her and Midnite, as well as provide me with his new address, telephone number, employment, assets, and who knows what else. There had to be something!

And so the crucial next step was to take out an

Information Subpoena and have it served on NationsBank. It was next summer, one of the hottest days on record that I found myself back at my old hangout, Queens County Civil Court, Small Claims Part, but as usual, there was a problem. There's always a problem.

"I'm sorry Sir. You have to have a name. A subpoena must be served on an individual, not a corporation. You need a name."

I wasn't sure about that, maybe so, but there was no point in arguing. The clerk would hold my papers, and I would go back to the lobby, call the bank, and get a name. Simple, right? We used pay phones in those days. I dropped in my quarter and I called the bank.

"Good afternoon, NationsBank. Denise speaking."

"Good afternoon. I'm a judgment creditor from the Small Claims Court and I need a name of a person who handles Information Subpoenas."

"And what is this in reference to sir?"

"A small claims case."

"And what does this have to do with the bank?"

The heat was awful, the beads of sweat were dripping off my forehead, and the operator wanted more money. Further delay and I would lose my place on line. Besides, the court was now getting ready to close. I pleaded.

"Please, I just need someone's name, any name."

"I'm sorry Sir, there's no one here to handle that."

"WELL, WHAT'S YOUR NAME?"

"Denise."

"DENISE WHAT?"

"Click."

I had to call back.

"Good afternoon, NationsBank. Denise speaking."

"Good afternoon. We were just cut off. I needed the name of someone who works at the bank."

The young lady, most likely sitting in her plush, air-conditioned office at the bank in perfect comfort, was extremely annoyed with me. I was obviously getting nowhere. The seconds were ticking away, the heat continued to build, and I was running out of bodily fluids faster than I was running out of quarters.

"Who would you like to speak with?"

"Anybody! Anybody at all! Give me the president of the bank!"

"Sir! I'm trying to help you! One moment Sir."

And as the precious seconds ticked by, our call was about to be terminated by the phone company.

"Please deposit five cents, or your call will be interrupted. This is a recording."

But then,

"Stanley Smyth, Sr. Vice President. Can I help you?

Thank goodness! I was finally able to get a name. I tried to explain to him what it was about, that it concerned a customer of NationsBank - not the bank itself, that he would receive a set of questions with an Information Subpoena.

"I never heard of an Information Subpoena!"

"Is that Smith, or is that Smyth, with a 'y'?"

"Click."

Now this was supposed to be a bank, and I was talking to the bank's vice president at the fourth biggest bank in the country, not one of Midnite's sleazy friends. Nevertheless, I did get the information that I needed, a name for service of process. And now quarter poor and drained of bodily fluids,

I stumbled back to Small Claims, paid the two dollars, and finally got my Information Subpoena. That was the easy part.

The subpoena was mailed by certified mail and signed for by a P. Yardi. Banks always sign for certified mail, so service on a bank is assured. Compliance is something else. I wasn't able to get to talk to Mr. Smyth anymore. He was either conveniently at a meeting or out of town, and did not return my calls. Nobody else at the bank seemed to know anything about my subpoena. I did get to talk to this P. Yardi, but she was just a low level clerk and wasn't able to give me any information. I guess I was just supposed to go away and stop making a pest of myself. The business of banking was more important. Eventually though, I did receive a letter from NationsBank at their North Carolina headquarters stating that there were no accounts in the name of Neville M. Michaels, or even N. Midnite Michaels.

I called the person who signed the letter, Mary D. Lowe, explained to her that the account in question was a joint credit card account, not a savings or checking account. Bank officers are usually pleasant enough to talk to. I don't know what Mr. Smyth's problem was. Maybe he had just gotten out of an inauspicious executive meeting, had a fight with his wife, was being sued, or maybe he was just a tough, hardened New Yorker and I had been stuck out in the suburbs too long. Anyway, Ms. Lowe referred me to Rhonda Edwards who was in charge of records at NationsBank of Delaware, the credit card operation. Ms. Edwards referred me back to Ms. Lowe, who referred me back to Ms. Edwards, with numerous and varied telephone recorded and voice mail interruptions along the way. I finally faxed the subpoena to Ms. Edwards with the following message on the cover sheet:

"IMPORTANT! Compliance with attached Information Subpoena and Restraining Notice - now 30 days old - is requested."

A response came in the mail in a letter dated September 5, 1995. NationsBank of Delaware, N.A. would not honor the subpoena. The claim was that they did not have offices nor did they do business in New York, and that therefore they were not required to comply with the subpoena. They said that I would have to domesticate the judgment in Virginia or Delaware, in a court of "proper jurisdiction," as they put it. They were deliberately making things difficult and I was being given the runaround. I was not about to stand in line at a Small Claims Court in Virginia or Delaware to find out how to domesticate the judgments.

I was referred back to NationsBank, North Carolina headquarters, Legal Department and got to speak with one of the bank's lawyers. I wasn't able to get his name when he answered the phone. I explained the situation to him and was told that the bank would not comply with the Information Subpoena, nor were they required by law to do so. The learned esquire at NationsBank needed some post law school education and some gently prodding.

"Ok. Fine! There's something you need to understand here. Your Sr. Vice President, Mr. Stanley Smyth at your branch in New York City, on Fifth Avenue has been served with a subpoena which was required to be answered within seven days. The subpoena is now over thirty days old. If I do not get the answers to the questions that were served with the subpoena, I will require your Vice President to make a personal appearance at the Civil Court of the City of New York, County of Queens on contempt of court charges."

"Do what you have to do."

I don't make threats anymore. People don't respond to threats. I can't believe how many times I've been told to "do what I have to do." Kravitz told me to "do what I have to do," Midnite told me to "do what I have to do" - so now, no more threats. I just state the facts and do what I have to do, but first I needed the lawyer's identity.

"May I have your name, Sir?"

"Click."

And so it was clear that NationsBank, America's fourth largest bank was just to big to be bothered with an Information Subpoena from an out of state Small Claims Court. The Order to Show Cause to Punish for Contempt was signed by Judge Jennifer A. Thomas on September 19, 1995 and the hearing scheduled for October 26, 1995. All that was left to do was to get the papers served. A liberal New York judge might have compassion on a poor black man, but perhaps not on a bank vice president.

I called my friend Morty. Morty had followed the case nearly from the beginning and was still interested in following it to its conclusion, if it ever happened. He agreed to do the service of process on the condition that I would go with him. Fine! I enjoy this! It would be a free lunch for him, a cheap service for me, and a day on the town. I try to schedule these things in order to make the most efficient use of my time, so we made the day of the service the same day as Bennet Pulaski's contempt hearing. If you remember, Bennet Pulaski was the superintendent at Midnite's building on Varick Street.

Not many people accept court papers these days and Pulaski was a master of evadence of process. He had no telephone, listed or unlisted, and he wouldn't answer his door bell. His name was on the directory, and he did sign the certified mail return receipt accepting service of the Information Subpoena, but compliance with it was something else. Pulaski also had to be served with the Order to Show Cause for Contempt.

Pulaski lived on the second floor, an apartment with huge windows facing out onto the corner of Grand and Varick. If the court papers were tied to a brick and thrown through the window, would that be a valid service? I think they would call that "conspicuous service," and its conspicuousness definitely could not be argued. My process server had to use conspicuous service, but not by my preferred method. I met Morty at Queens County Civil Court just before Pulaski's scheduled contempt hearing at 11:00 A.M. The time for the hearing approached, and the names were called out by the clerk.

"Michaels?"

I had to correct the clerk.

"No. The witness's name is Pulaski."

He wasn't there anyway, but at least he should have gotten the name right.

"Pulaski? Bennet Pulaski?"

There was no response. They gave him another fifteen minutes, and then defaulted him. The service of process was by conspicuous service, papers taped to the door, the so called "nail and mail" method. Nobody actually nails anymore. One can get sued or maybe even arrested for destroying private property. Nevertheless, I remembered the clerk's remark when I filed the papers with the court.

"You're gonna have trouble with this."

The service was proper, and should have been ok. I explained this to the clerk.

238

"The law provides for substitute or conspicuous service. There are some people in this world that just cannot be served."

"Counselor, I'm well aware of the statutes! I'm just telling you that you're going to have trouble with it."

As it turned out, the court clerk was right - the judge wouldn't sign a fining order for contempt. I would have to do the whole thing all over again, but now with in-hand service. I'm the only one who attends these hearings. I remembered reading a book on Small Claims, how service of process could be one of the most difficult things to do, and how some defendants have developed evadence of process into a fine, but silly art because "nail and mail" is now an accepted and recognized service. I guess evadence of process is not so silly after all. Only a fool should accept service of process.

And so, the service on the NationsBank VP had to be in-hand, proof-positive, absolute, and no screwups. Guaranteed in-hand!

We took the "F" train into the City on the Independent Line and got off at 50th Street at Fifth Avenue. We walked up plush Fifth Avenue looking for number 767. We passed Trump Tower. Donald lives on the top three floors. Now here's a man to sue - someone with assets! But I would imagine that service of process would be even more difficult here than on Mr. Pulaski. We walked past the expensive, upscale shops and boutiques, and then past some pathetic, aids infected homeless persons, until we came to what used to be the General Motors Building. I was familiar with the area because at one time I had worked at the DEA on the West Side, but that was a long time ago. The GM Building was the place we were looking for, 767 Fifth Avenue. The automobile showrooms had long since been converted into storefronts. We entered the building and tapped in Smyth on the computerized directory. Nothing came up. We tried Smith, but again, nothing. Smyth, the VP couldn't be that important. The security guard came over to investigate.

"We're looking for Stanley Smyth at NationsBank."

The security guard didn't know him, but suggested that we try NationsBank. It hit on the 14th floor. We ascended to the 14th floor, and as the elevator door opened, we were led into a plush, red carpeted lobby. The sign read in huge, golden letters, "NATIONSBANK CAPITAL MARKETS." This was the place for the super rich. I guessed that we should have worn our best suits for it, but then we didn't work for them and we certainly weren't clients. We continued to walk through the glass doors with great trepidation as if we were approaching the great and mighty Wizard of Oz, and then on toward the receptionist. I wondered if it was Denise. I asked for Stanley Smyth.

"And who shall I say wishes to see him?"

How do you answer that? Only a fool accepts service of process, remember? It was beginning to look like Morty and I were going to have to tear down doors and rip through offices to find this guy. I decided to play it straight.

"Jonah Cohen."

"Please have a seat."

Only a few minutes went by, when to my surprise and utter delight, appeared a blond haired, blue eyed gentleman coming out to greet us. He must have forgotten the subpoena and taken us for new clients ready to pour a few hundred thousand into the NationsBank coffers. I was out to screw this guy or maybe the bank anyway. I felt like slime. Smyth spoke first.

"I'm Stanley Smyth. Can I help you?"

I began my speech.

"Mr. Smyth, I'm Jonah Cohen. I have here an Order to Show Cause for failure to respond to an Information Subpoena."

I felt my voice beginning to quiver ever so slightly and wondered if it was noticed. He was after all a bank vice president, but Mr. Smyth was clearly more nervous than I was. I quickly regained composure, presented a strong front, and took the offensive.

"You are hereby required to appear in Queens County Civil Court on October 26th at 11:00 A.M. to show cause as to why you should not be punished for contempt."

Morty placed the Order in Smyth's left hand - guaranteed, proof positive, in-hand service. Smyth took it and held it. It was perfect. He opened the envelope, took less than a minute to read its contents, and began his own self-righteous speech.

"I came out here to help you. I don't know what you guys are trying to pull. This is NationsBank Capital Markets. We have nothing to do with a credit card company in Delaware. I will show this to our attorneys. You guys are making a big mistake, and be prepared ..."

Smyth went on like that for a while. It would be up to a Queens County Civil Court judge to decide the intricacies of the NationsBank corporate structure. I later found out that there were at least two different NationsBanks at this address. One was a corporate headquarters, which would have been more appropriate. We served the NationsBank Capital Markets, an investment company operating under the NationsBank corporate umbrella catering to the super rich people living in Trump Tower. Murphy's Law always works. And now here was insignificant little me challenging the NationsBank vice president with a ridiculous Small Claims Order, thereby interrupting all their million dollar deals. I wanted to use Kravitz's favorite expression, *"It's gonna cost!"* but I let Smyth ramble on. Our job was to serve the court papers and to get a good physical description of him, not to dissect and analyze the NationsBank corporate structure, or to worry about his threatened litigation. He talked for a long time, and so we were able to study him closely. The eyes were perhaps more green than blue, but blue would also be accurate; he was about 180 lbs., 5 feet and 11 inches or thereabout, blondish hair, good teeth, face slightly lined, about 38 or 39 years old ... and he was pissed off to no end.

"I will definitely show this to my lawyers!"

"Please do that, Mr. Smyth."

"And by the way... the spelling of my name, you spelled Smyth wrong. It's S. M. I. T. H.E."

The VP was steaming mad. He held the door open for us and in a very sarcastic way pretended to invite us downstairs for coffee. It was time to leave.

"Nice meeting you, Mr. Smithe. See you in court."

And so, service was accomplished, guaranteed, in-hand, proof positive, and no screwups. The outcome at this point could not be predicted, but what was certain to occur was a hearing at the Civil Court, or possibly a deal with the bank's lawyers. Sure enough, back at the job, I read the message that was left on my desk.

"David McGovern, NationsBank called. Wants you to call their attorney in New York, Theodore Hegarity."

I called Mr. Hegarity.

"Good afternoon, Law Offices of Myron and Allen."

"Good afternoon. Mr. Hegarity, please."

After the usual request for the identity of the calling party, and the inquiry as to what this was in reference to, what appeared to be a Mr. Hegarity came on the phone.

"Ah ... ah ... AH SHOO ...!!"

"Mr. Hegarity!?"

"Yes."

"G-d bless you ... I suppose it's ok to say, G-d bless you to an opposing attorney?"

The beginning of our conversation was, to say the least, unroutine, but the usual animosity and confrontation between litigating parties was clearly absent. After all, I wasn't suing the bank, and Mr. Hegarity, it turned out, worked for a private law firm which was hired by NationsBank to handle my Small Claims Case in order to protect the bank's interest. Yes, that's right! Because of me, the fourth largest banking institution in the country had to protect their interests and hired a private law firm to do it.

Hegarity laughed and thanked me. After the unusual introduction, he got right down to business.

"Look, the way I see it, the problem is simple. If I can get you a proper service of process address, or if I can find someone at the bank to answer your Information Subpoena, then you should have no reason to continue the contempt of court action."

I agreed.

"You know, banks have to be careful. Everybody wants to sue banks. That's where the money is, as they say. It's not that the bank doesn't want to help you. They are afraid of being sued by their customer, Mr. Michaels! So, if I can get you a good address at which to serve, then you would have no further claims against the bank?"

I had to think for a minute. Oh, would I have liked to have claims against NationsBank. That would even be better than claims against Donald Trump, and besides, the bank would be easier to serve. But there was little time for daydreaming. The lawyer was waiting for my answer, and so, I agreed again.

"I'm sure there is a proper service of process address in New York. Give me a few days. I'm not trying to put you off. I will get back to you. I promise. Let me have just a few days."

I could have really stuck it to Hegarity. I could have said something like, *"Come to court and explain it all to the judge. I don't have a few days,"* but I felt that Hegarity was really trying to be helpful, and after all, the objective here was to gain information, not to bring the bank's VP to court, although it might have been fun. Hegarity suggested that I call the New York State Department of State, Banking Department for a service of process address, which I did; but I got bounced around about a half dozen or so times and wound up talking with the U.S. Office of the Currency, and then bounced over to the NYS Department of State again, and finally got back to Myron and Allen.

"Hi, Jonah. How'd you make out?"

"Hi, Ted. Not so good."

The unspoken words were, *"We still have our hearing scheduled."*

"Ok, I'm sure I can get you an address. Just give me a few days. I promise I'll get back to you."

Mr. Hegarity, true to his word, did get back to me. Service of process would be accepted by a Gerald Brandon, Vice President, NationsBank of Delaware, N.A. I thanked Mr. Hegarity, and I signed the Stipulation of Dismissal of the

Hearing to Show Cause for Contempt.

The Information Subpoena was answered by Mr. Brandon. Unfortunately, but not unsurprisingly, there were no records of assets or employment, but I did have the proof that I needed to put the girl with the red Camaro in contempt of court. Here was the proof of the joint credit card account. Question No. 3 of the Information Subpoena was answered. It read as follows:

"Debtor has a credit card account #2435-0031-2010-4224 (no deposits held) in the name of Shelly D. Carpenter and debtor."

XL. Old Faithful

The old Honda Civic with its tiny four cylinder engine and twelve inch wheels was finished. The daily commute from Brooklyn to the job on eastern Long Island had done it in. The engine was burning oil so fast that I had to drive with a case of the stuff in the back seat. And it didn't always start up, a problem owing to low compression, probably due to worn cylinders and rings. The passenger door would no longer open, and the emergency brake had long since separated from its mounting. The many mornings of hard starting had also killed the starter motor.

Nevertheless, it was still barely drivable. Sadly, the decision had to be made to donate it to the Jewish Guild for the Blind. And so, it was with great skill, caution, and luck, that I was able to drive it into the junk yard and claim my tax receipt. But the end was, shall I say, unceremonious, not at all fitting for a car that had served me so well for so long. Having arrived at the junk yard, I had to keep the motor running because of the bad starter and low compression, and there was also no way to set the hand brake. I told myself that it would be all right. It would be just a few minutes while I took off the plates and attended to the business of transferring ownership in the office, but the car had begun to roll backwards, and continued to roll, finally crashing into a parked truck and knocking out the Honda's right tail light. Thank goodness that no one was hurt, the truck wasn't damaged, and amidst all the noise and confusion of the junk yard, nothing was seen or heard. It was destined for the crusher anyway. I wouldn't have wanted to stay to watch. I took my plates and receipt and walked quickly to the nearest subway. The old Honda was gone.

So, now without transportation, and in desperate need of a car, I happened to relate the story of the Honda to Bill, the QA manager at one of the companies that we serviced. His father had just passed away, and they had this 1973 Dodge Dart that they were looking to get rid of. It wasn't really the car that I wanted, but I was desperate, and at $600.00, the price was right. Bill didn't give me the sales pitch. He just told it like it was.

It's not really much to look at. Dad had a little accident with it - some fender damage at the right rear. It was his baby. He took care of it though - changed the oil every three thousand miles, kept it garaged. It just needs a little fine tuning - some TLC. If you want it, it's yours."

Of course, I jumped at it. The fender damage was pretty bad and the radiator was patched up, but everything else looked ok. There was only 65,000 miles on the odometer, and not a speck of rust. I wrote Bill a check, and it was a done deal.

And now, some 200,000 or so miles later, I found myself still driving the same car. It was supposed to be a temporary means of transportation, until I completed my move from Brooklyn to Long Island, but one gets used to things, so I kept it a little longer than originally planned.

Shelly Carpenter, the girl with the red Camaro and co-credit card holder with Midnite, had an address in Staten Island. I had her served with an Information Subpoena, but of course, and as expected, the answers came back with "No," "Unknown," and "N/A." Shelly had to be served with an Order to Show Cause for Contempt. I called my friend Morty from the office. Morty really didn't like process serving, but it was an adventure, another free meal, and a night out, so he agreed to go with me into Staten Island to do the service. I picked Morty up in Forest Hills with the Dodge Dart, a car I came to affectionately (but not always accurately) call Old Faithful.

Within seconds, Morty, I, and Old Faithful were barreling up the LIE, onto the BQE, over the Kosciusko Bridge, onto the Belt Parkway, over the Verazanno Narrows Bridge, and into Staten Island. I was surprised to find that there are actually some nice neighborhoods in Staten Island. It wasn't all garbage dumps and land fills for the Manhattanites.

We found Shelly's house without much trouble. It was a detached, single family home on a quiet, tree lined block. The lights in the house were on, but the red Camaro wasn't in sight. I gave Morty the papers.

"Why don't we just leave the papers in the mailbox and go? That should be ok."

Like I said, Morty didn't like process serving. We went up to the door together. Morty held the papers and I rang the bell. After a few seconds, an elderly woman, most likely Shelly's mother came to the door. I had to speak first.

"We have court papers for Shelly Carpenter!"

"Process servers?"

"Yes. Is she in?"

"Well, no. She'll be in later tonight. Shall I take the papers?"

Personal service was preferred, but this, substitute service had to be good enough. I could only hope that I "wouldn't have trouble with it." Morty handed her the papers and we proceeded to leave. We were almost a quarter of the way down the block when the Camaro pulled up in front of the house. The tall blond girl got out of the car, walked up the stairs, and was greeted by the elderly woman who handed her the papers. Morty walked faster down the block. I had to call out to him.

"Morty! Look! Did you see it? She took the papers! Look, Shelly took the papers!"

Morty looked quickly over his shoulder, and continued walking. Well, a more macho kind of service would have been nice, but this had to qualify for personal service. Success! We did it. We headed back home with the Dodge, but got caught in some terrible rush hour traffic on the BQE. It was bumper to bumper on all three lanes and traffic hardly moved. We were still high and relieved at the success of our process serving enterprise, when Old Faithful's oil pressure warning light began to flicker, and then lit up in steady red. Morty saw it also.

"STOP! You'll destroy the engine! You have to stop!"

But how do you stop in the middle of traffic on the BQE? There was no shoulder, no exit, and no place to go. DAMN! What luck! I kept going. It would be ok. If I could just make it to the next exit, it would be ok. Traffic inched along, the oil pressure light continued to stay red, and now the temperature gauge began to climb. It would be ok. The next exit was only a few hundred feet ahead. If I could just make it to the next exit, it would be ok. We got off the BQE and double parked, in what was not the greatest neighborhood. I checked the oil level. It was depleted. We weren't near any gas stations, and the auto parts store on the corner was closed. I had some used motor oil left over from the last oil change. I hated doing it, but used oil was certainly better than no oil. As repulsive as it was, I did it. I committed the great sin. I poured the contaminated, sludge laden slime into the engine. I started up Old Faithful, and she got us back home.

Of course, I changed the oil at the first opportunity when I got home. It was actually a week later, when coming home from work on the LIE that I heard the most excruciating sound coming from under the hood. It was like a chain saw hitting a nail or a thousand finger nails across a blackboard, but it was louder, deafeningly loud, and it was bad, very, very bad. What followed was a loud bang, bang, bang. The main bearings were shot. Still, she continued to run. She got me home, and I gently parked her away in my driveway. Old Faithful had made her last run.

XLI. More Supplementary Proceedings

I arrived at the Queens County Civil Court at exactly 9:30 A.M. for Shelly Carpenter's contempt hearing. Surely there would be some useful information coming, or at least some explanation with regard to the joint credit card account. I showed my papers to the court clerk and told him that I was the plaintiff.

"Mr. Cohen, your opposition has arrived."

The clerk pointed to the young lady seated behind me. It was the first time I was really able to get a good look at her. She must have been about 30 years old, tall, thin, with long wavy blond hair and blue eyes. Her skin was fair with a few light freckles. She was dressed appropriately for the court, and wore a dress just below the knee. What could possibly be the relationship between her and Midnite? They seemed to have come from different worlds.

We were led into Special Term, Part II for the hearing. Miss Carpenter was sworn in and the questions began.

"State the judgment debtor's full name …"

"Neville Michaels."

At least she didn't deny knowing him. She answered all of the remaining questions directly, calmly, and in a soft, feminine voice. The residence question came next.

"I don't know."

And there was the employment question.

"I don't know."

And there was the asset question.

"I don't know."

But then there was the banking question! There was no

way out of this one.

"I don't know of any bank accounts ... we did share a credit card account together, but the account has been closed."

The judge thanked the witness for coming, and ended the hearing. I should have expected it. In the end I got nothing. How is it possible for someone to share a joint credit card account with someone that they know nothing about? I followed the witness outside of Special Term, Part II and called out to her. Obviously, I wasn't satisfied with the answers.

"Oh, Miss Carpenter, you should know that we're going to do this again. You're going to have to come back here again!"

The witness turned to me, and then puzzled, looked over to the court clerk who explained it to her.

"The judgment creditor has two separate judgments. If he desires to do so, he can have you served with another Information Subpoena."

The young lady continued to walk outside of the court building. I followed her, and called out.

"Miss Carpenter, we will definitely be back here again, unless you decide to let me have some useful information."

I guess the young lady decided it wasn't worth it. It would be another trip from Staten Island and another day off from work. She opened up and gave me whatever she had.

"I really don't know where he's living now. He was in Larchmont, but he's not there anymore. He moves around a lot."

"Who are you to him? Are you a girlfriend?"

She paused, smiled, and answered the question.

"No. Just a friend, an acquaintance really. I met him in

the Hudson Grill after work. He seemed like a nice, friendly guy, just a little down on his luck. I felt sorry for him. I thought that maybe I could help him out. He was going through a pretty rough time ..."

She related the story of her acquaintance with Mr. Michaels. It reminded me of the sublet. I too felt sorry for him, as did Mr. Marciano, his friend from the band.

"Did he pay you anything for his card charges?"

"Yeah, actually he did, some of it anyway."

"Did you know that he was living in my apartment without paying rent, and that he now owes me quite a bit of money."

"Yeah, he did tell me a little about it. I told him that he should pay you."

"Where does he work?"

"Wherever he can - bars and clubs mostly. He was working at the Forest Hills Swim Club, and then at a place in Brooklyn called Indigo Blues, but I have no idea where or if he's working now. I haven't kept in touch with him. It's been several months now. That's all I know, honest."

I believed her. She told me everything that she knew. I had nothing to lose. Perhaps she would continue to help.

"Miss Carpenter, would it be ok if I called you once in a while, just in case you happen to hear from him again?"

She paused, thought about it for a few seconds, and then, surprisingly, gave me her business card. She was a vice president for a small Manhattan construction company. I took the card, studied it, and thanked her. She departed, walked quickly, and disappeared down into the subway.

XLII. The Ace Bar

I never did call Shelly again. There didn't seem to be much point to it. The Forest Hills Swim Club was no longer in existence, and Indigo Blues had closed and was now operating under a different name. Nobody there had ever heard of Midnite or Neville. I was right back to where I started - all paths blocked, all roads closed. Autumn turned into winter, and it was now January - the start of the new Gregorian year.

NYNEX Directory Assistance was as good a place as any to start over again. I called the number.

"Listing, please."

"Neville Michaels, M. I. C. H. A. E. L. S."

"Do you have a street address?"

It was the same question and the same routine. If I had a street address, I wouldn't need Directory Assistance.

"No."

I was then switched over to the NYNEX automated directory service.

"At the customer's request, the number is non-published. Again, at the customer's request, the number is non-published."

SUCCESS! Once again it worked! Of course there was no way to know if this Neville Michaels was Midnite, but if it was, this was truly great news. It meant that Midnite had an address, and maybe even a job. It meant that the elusive alien was becoming more like a real person again. Midnite going legit! Well, maybe not completely, but it was a good sign. I went back to the Small Claims Court, paid the two bucks for another Information Subpoena, and had it served on NYNEX by certified mail.

The telephone company is one of the few places where the Information Subpoena can actually work. Generally, they are very good at it, and also cooperative, but the subpoena came back stamped "Information Not Available." The alien spirit seemed to have all the luck. Everything is work and debate. I called NYNEX Legal.

"Subpoena Group, please."

"One moment, Sir."

And soon, I was connected with the Subpoena Group. The telephone company actually has employees whose only job it is to answer Information Subpoenas - they call them Subpoena Clerks!

"Subpoena Group, Deborah Parker speaking. May I help you?"

I gave the telephone company all the information that they needed including the debtor's social security number. I explained that I had found out from Directory Assistance that the number was non-published, but that since there was a number, they should have been able to provide me with answers to the subpoena.

"Did Mr. Michaels recently move?"

Did Midnite move? Captain Midnite is always in a state of being recently moved. In fact, he even gets around faster than the Starship Enterprise! I gave her the simple answer to the question.

"Yes."

"One moment, Sir."

The Subpoena Clerk was back in a few minutes. She had

enlightened herself with knowledge, and speech streamed forth:

"Address: 513 Courtelyou Road, Brooklyn, NY
Phone number: (718) 541-9766
Landlord: Kathy Phillips (718) 541-7970
Employer: Ace Bar, 471 East 5th Street, New York, NY
Bank Account: None
Deposits held: None
Other assets: None"

Well, it wasn't the riches of Croesus, but it was something to work with - an address and a job. It was a return to the real world. The Spirit of Captain Midnite had touched down for landing and returned to port.

I had to sit on all this information for a while. I wasn't sure how to handle it all and I didn't want to make the same mistakes of the past. If I had gotten a Marshal and had him attempt to garnish the wages, he wouldn't have been able to collect because Midnite probably, no, definitely worked cash-off-the-books. If I had him served with an Information Subpoena, he would just ignore it and then we'd have another useless contempt of court hearing, and then maybe another pointless arrest. I called him once at his home from my office to check out the address and phone number. I immediately hung up without speaking. He called back. I didn't know that he had caller ID. I was more nervous then, than he was when I had him arrested and brought before the judge in chains - well, in handcuffs anyway. It was the receptionist at the company where I was stationed, who answered when he called back. They didn't know who he was, thank goodness! Anyway, the address and telephone number were confirmed.

The next step was to call his landlady, undercover of course. Certainly the landlady would have some information. I called the landlady.

"Mrs. Phillips?"

"Yes."

"This is John Oswald. I'm with JAMAR, Inc. I'm calling for a reference on Neville Michaels, one of your tenants on Courtelyou Road. He applied for a job with us."

The name was a variation of the arbitrator's name who originally tried the case. The company was a random name picked from the Yellow Pages. It just happened to be a janitorial service. It was perfect. I spoke in rapid-fire rhythm, fast, and meant to confuse the person on the other end of the line. If you say that you are a judgment creditor from the Small Claims Court, nobody wants to know you. You become an instant enemy. You're the bad guy. You're out to get somebody's money - to cut out your "pound of flesh." But if you pretend that you are helping them, that maybe you're giving them a job, you get answers. And so it was.

"Oh, sure. Mr. Michaels is a very nice, very hard working young man, very quiet. He's always out ..."

"Where does he work?

She knew! Of course she knew.

"I don't know."

"You're his landlady and you don't know where he works?"

"Well ... I think he drives a cab or something ..."

And then faster than my rapid-fire introduction came,

"But I don't really know."

"Does he pay you rent?"

257

"Oh yes. Always on the first of the month."

"Really???"

"Oh yes."

"And you're holding security?"

"One month."

"Any banks? Does he pay you by check?"

"No banks, cash."

I didn't believe her. There was more, and she hadn't even mentioned the Ace Bar. I had her served with an Information Subpoena, but the certified letter was returned, undeliverable. I had to get a process server. I found a guy who would do it cheap, $25.00, a bargain. Of course, if something looks too cheap, there's got to be something wrong with it, and there was. The papers weren't served - I got "sewer service" as the term is used. I had to report him to the NYC Department of Consumer Affairs and I sued him in Small Claims Court for the $25.00 plus court costs and interest. There's no end to this.

My own part time process service business had been slow, which was just as well, because with the job and Midnite, I really didn't have time for it. But I had to show the IRS some revenue in order to claim business use of the home. And so, when the phone rang, I was happy to get a job.

"New York Notary & Process Service. Can we help you?"

"Yes, I hope so. I need to have some papers served."

It was the voice of a young woman. The papers were child custody papers from Family Court. It had to be personal delivery.

"Ok."

"Do you go to Manhattan?"

I don't like these Manhattan jobs. I try to stay out of the Big Bad City, but like I said, business had been slow. I gave the young woman a quote of $49.00, cheap for a Manhattan job, personal service. It was a deal.

The young woman came to my house and I examined the papers. It was a copy of the Petition and Order to Show Cause that had to be served. We talked briefly. Mr. Martinez, the respondent, it appeared, was a wife beater and a drug user. He was six feet tall, exactly 180 pounds, had a tattoo on his left arm, was about 35 years of age, had a small scar over his right eye, Hispanic, dark brown eyes, black hair, and lived with his mother on the Lower East Side.

I couldn't understand it. She was young, pretty, intelligent, polite, refined, and got mixed up with this worthless trash. But a process server is not a social worker or a psychologist. My clients seem to like me (but not the respondents.) These people are going through a period of tremendous stress. I'm their knight in shining armor, the champion of their cause, and the hero who came to conquer - all five feet, six inches and 130 pounds of me, but I can run fast.

Mrs. Martinez took out a $50.00 bill and we talked some more. He was only violent with her, she told me. We shook hands, I wished her good luck, and I was on my case.

I borrowed Mom's car, a 1986 Dodge Aries, and made the long drive into Manhattan after work. I took the Williamsburg Bridge into the City. The apartment was in one of the projects at the east end of East Houston Street near the FDR Drive. The job seemed to go smoothly. I found a place to park, found the building, got in without any trouble, ascended in the urine stenched elevator, and found the apartment. I knocked.

"Who eez it?"

"Is Manuel in?"

"No. Manuel, he not here."

"When do you expect him in?"

You don't give up. You have to be persistent, and don't blow your cover. Nobody wants to talk to a process server. Also, you should talk in a low voice. If they can't hear you, they'll open the door to hear better. The voice was that of Manuel's mother. It was very heavily accented in Spanish. As planned, the door was opened and the would be intruder was investigated. Once the door is opened, the process server is now able to move ever so slightly beyond the threshold, near the door hinge. I invaded, gaining the small, but important fraction of an inch of territory. I pretended to be a neighbor with some of Manuel's mail.

"I have some mail for Manuel."

"But he not here."

So now what? We went on like that for a while, but I was getting no place. I had to blow my cover. Sometimes it works. I played it straight.

"I'm a process server. I have some family court papers for Manuel Martinez. If he cares anything about his kids, he should take the papers and come to court. Otherwise, he may never see them again."

The elder Mrs. Martinez showed some concern. She asked to see the papers. I didn't want to give the papers to her. Service had to be personal, on Manuel.

"But he doesn't leeve here!"

"Where is he?"

"I leeve alone. Trust me!"

If someone ever says "Trust me," don't. But then the woman surprisingly opened the door wide open and invited me in to look around. I remembered the training that I was given at the NYC Department of Consumer Affairs for the process server license. If they invite you in - DON'T GO IN! Mrs. Martinez continued.

"I really don't know where he eez ... but he may be leeving with a girlfriend in Queens."

I had to believe Mrs. Martinez. I thanked her for her time and cooperation and left.

DAMN! I failed in my mission, and what would I tell the younger Mrs. Martinez? I really wanted to help her. I would have to do this again. I had wasted my time and made the forty-nine mile trip into the City for nothing. But wait! East 5th Street was only a few blocks away. It was the address of the Ace Bar - Midnite's employer as was given to me by NYNEX.

I decided to drive over to check it out. East 5th Street is a small residential side street in the East Village. There are mainly nineteenth century brick apartment row houses on each side of the street. I found the Ace Bar with some difficulty, and double parked. There was some construction going on next to it. Above the bar entrance was hand printed in black lettering on a white background, *"ACE BAR."*

The Ace is a small, quaint, inconspicuous kind of place, maybe more like a club. It looked clean and safe. I was able to look inside through the glass doors and widows. There was a brick wall and wood paneling, wooden floors, mirrors, and chrome and glass fixtures. There were pin ball machines, pool tables, and lots of memorabilia from the fifties and sixties, as well as a nice selection of international beers. In all, a pleasant place to pass some time.

Everything looked to be in order, and all was quiet. It was now about 6:40 P.M. I got out of my car to take a closer look. I ascended the three steps and peered into the bar. I read the signs taped to the window, looking for names, a clue, an owner - perhaps someone on which to serve an Information Subpoena if I needed to, or anything that might be useful. I saw the names of performers in a band or something, but I didn't see "Midnite" or "Michaels," or anything that was recognizable, or anything at all that could serve some purpose. As I read, the entrance door to the bar suddenly opened. A tall young man, dressed in blue jeans with very long blond hair came out and descended the stairs.

Should I have asked him? I felt like an idiot asking for someone named "Midnite." I remembered the second time around in Small Claims Court when the arbitrator inquired of me, "How can anyone rent an apartment to anyone named 'Midnite?'" But here we weren't in court. We were at a bar, Midnite's bar. Yes, I would give it a go.

"Excuse me. ... uh ... would you happen to know a guy named 'Midnite?'"

The man with the long blond hair turned to me and answered in a deep, resonant voice.

"Yeah, yeah."

"And, uh ... does he work here?"

"Yeah ... Tuesday, Wednesday, Friday, and Saturday."

Unbelievable! I asked a simple question and I got his whole work schedule. No Information Subpoena ever worked this well. I figured I might as well try for all I could.

"Uh ... Is he in the band?"

"Naa ... He's a doorman. As a matter of fact, he's gonna be here any minute."

"??#!!??#!"

I struggled to maintain my cool, regained my composure, and answered with an indifferent, even bored,

"Thanks."

The tall blond man continued on his way, disappearing down the block. I watched until only the blond hair was still visible. I looked at my watch. It was now exactly 6:44 P.M. I quickly got back into the car and waited. I watched the bar, and the people coming in and going out. There was a chalk board sign outside. It read,

"PRIVATE PARTY,
7:00 P.M. TO 9:00 P.M."

At exactly 6:45 P.M. I heard a low pitched and barely audible rumble which became progressively louder and louder. It was the sound of an approaching motorcycle, the sound gradually becoming even louder until deafeningly loud, and now reverberating up and down East 5th Street until finally reaching its destination at the Ace, and then suddenly going silent. The motorcycle and its rider were now visible. The rider dismounted in front of the bar. He wore a black helmet, a black leather jacket, tight black leather pants, and black boots. In the dark of the night, he was very nearly invisible, but he appeared as a faint silhouette in the dim light cast from the bar. The face and features could not be seen, but the shape of the silhouette was unmistakably that of the alien, the phantom from Trinidad. It was Midnite!

He removed his helmet. The long hair was wrapped in a black bandana. It had now been almost five years since it all started, three years since I had had him arrested, and about two years since I had seen him on Varick Street, but I recognized the shape and the walk. It was definitely Midnite. I watched as he walked the bike to the front of the bar, and while Midnite was exactly the same, the motorcycle

was different. He locked it up, and then went inside. I
decided to wait a while longer. I was parked in a dark spot,
safe, and could not be seen, but I kept my head facing
straight ahead, as one who was ... just waiting. I was
unnoticed, inconspicuous, and very safe. Would I go out
now and investigate? No, not yet. But then, Midnite
suddenly came back out, apparently remembering to take in
the helmet, and then returned inside. Now!

Courtesy of Piaggio

I got out of the car and walked quickly to the bike to
study it closely. It certainly wasn't the old beat up '74
BMW. I took down the license plate number - F771V - and
the make - Moto Guzzi. It was big, very big, and very
powerful. It was new, maybe brand new. And it was

expensive, extremely expensive. It was beautiful, clean, and shiny; its chromium was blinding, even in the dim light cast by the bar. I had never seen such a huge and powerful bike. And it was Midnite's. And it was an asset!

And so it was that I never did find Manuel Martinez … but I did find Midnite.

XLIII. Get the Guzzi

And so, after nearly six years of chasing the elusive alien through the streets, courts, and sewers of New York - in Brooklyn, and then into Queens, then Manhattan, and again back into Brooklyn, the sole asset, the Moto Guzzi motorcycle, had been located at the Ace Bar in Manhattan's East Village. The DMV records checked out. Midnite was indeed the titled owner and registrant of the motorcycle. How he managed to do it, I could only guess, but if you're not paying rent, well … that's how you do it.

City Marshals generally do not, or will not, seize motorcycles. The judgment creditor has to get a Sheriff to do it. Things began to get slightly complicated because Sheriffs are assigned to counties. Now with the motorcycle seen in Manhattan (New York County) and the residence in Brooklyn (King's County), which Sheriff would I be using? I decided to use the services of a New York County Sheriff. That's where the bike was seen. I called the Sheriff's Office and explained that I was a judgment creditor from the Small Claims Court, that I had located an asset to satisfy the judgments, and that although the judgment debtor lived in Brooklyn, he worked in Manhattan. It turned out that yes, they would be able to do it.

I was assigned a certain Deputy with the unlikely name of Stephen Schatzer. I explained to him the situation and what had to be done. The Deputy seemed to be light, carefree, friendly … maybe even a little comical, but beneath the façade, here was someone who took his job seriously, someone who was committed to getting the job done. Here was someone tough, fearless, maybe even reckless ... and the Deputy was also from one of the twelve tribes. I decided that I liked Deputy Schatzer. I was just about completing my introductory speech.

"... and he hasn't paid me any rent money. The judgments are now over $4,000.00. He works at the Ace Bar on East 5th Street between Avenues A and B. I saw him there with the Moto Guzzi motorcycle at exactly 6:45 P.M. last January on a Tuesday. I have the title and registration record from the DMV - he owns it outright - no lien holders. And now I need a Sheriff to seize it, and ..."

"And you're pissed off - I can tell! What kind of a guy is he?"

"What kind of a guy?"

"Yeah, you know. What does he look like? Is he dangerous? Let's see ... Neville. Is he an Englishman?"

Well, here we go again. I had to describe Midnite. I could only hope my description of Midnite wouldn't deter the fearless Deputy Schatzer from performing his sworn duty.

"Well, he's black, an alien - here legally though - from Trinidad and Tobago, dark complexion, about six feet - two inches tall, long black hair - sometimes tied up in a bandana, 180 pounds, and may be wearing gold earrings."

The Deputy continued to listen with interest, but I was quick to add,

"But no criminal record! I had him checked out. He comes off as a likeable, friendly kind of guy ... I don't think he's dangerous."

"Yeah, but you don't know! And you don't know what he'll be like when we take his motorcycle away from him."

I didn't want to lose Deputy Schatzer. He needed just a little encouragement.

"Oh, you guys can handle it. As a matter of fact, I had him arrested a few years ago. Yeah, that's right. He was arrested by a Deputy from the New York City Sheriff's Office. Maybe you know him? A short Spanish guy - Ramirez, Rivera or something ... or was it Desoto?"

"Bumpy?? You mean Bumpy?!! Yeah, he works here. And you say this Midnite guy isn't dangerous, huh?"

I really couldn't be sure. I just didn't know. Maybe he was dangerous, but there was no point in intimidating the Deputy, if that were possible.

"Look, he's not dangerous and he's not a criminal. He's just a low life deadbeat, off the books, doesn't pay taxes ... but he's not dangerous, just a very slick kind of character."

"Slick, huh? Maybe we should pour some Italian olive oil over his slick Italian bike? Ok, let's get going on this. It's $15.00 for an execution, two executions for two judgments is $30.00, plus $600.00 for us to seize the bike and sell it at an auction."

My immediate response took the Deputy by surprise.

"Ok, ok, to whom do I make the check out?"

And in the background, over the telephone receiver, the Sheriff's Office was buzzing, maybe like it hadn't buzzed in years.

"Hey guys, guys! We're going in on a job! Yeah, yeah ... he's got the money, he's got the title record ... yeah, we're going in!"

"Oh, make the check out to NYC Sheriff. Now you also have to get your own towing and storage company and

268

contract with them to pick up the bike after we seize it."

"What?! What was the $600.00 for?"

There was no point in debating it. Whatever it took. Anything in the pursuit of justice. I agreed.

"Ok."

The seizure of the motorcycle was becoming a major investment on my part. I had to find out what the bike was really worth. I called around and found a Moto Guzzi dealer in Brooklyn. I wasn't sure of the model, but was told that a new Guzzi in the 600 pound weight class could run anywhere from $11,000.00 to $14,000.00. I could sense the dealer's mouth watering with delight (and so was mine) at this prospect of yet another Guzzi customer. So if a new Guzzi was $14,000.00, and a slightly used one say $12,000.00, and a slightly used one at a sheriff's auction, maybe $6,000, the investment would be justified. I could even go to the auction myself and bid, just to get the bidding up, or maybe even buy it for myself!

But as might be expected, the Sheriff's Execution Requisition Request to seize the motorcycle got delayed at the Small Claims Court in Queens. I inquired of the Deputy as to the reason for the delay, but he assured me that the execution request was indeed sent out, that it was sent out promptly, and that it had to be sitting on some civil servant's desk at the Small Claims Court. I had to call Small Claims, but they insisted that the execution request was not received. We were getting nowhere. I called Deputy Schatzer.

"Good morning, Deputy Schatzer?"

"Yeah, yeah! Cohen wit da motorcycle. Come on, come on!! We gotta get goin' on dis guy - befaw he sells da modacycle. Let's go, let's go!!"

Schatzer had sunk into the deep, undisguised Brooklyn

vernacular. It meant that he was serious. The Deputy was insistent that the Execution Requisition Request really was processed, but rather than delay any further, he would put in a second request and then send it to me directly rather than to the court.

"And what am I supposed to do with it? Bring it over to Small Claims, to the clerk at the window?"

"Yeah. See if you can get them to give it to you right away. Convince them of how important this is. Give them your best act. Bring an onion."

"For tears? Maybe some garlic also, to ward off the evil spirits. Now exactly what am I supposed to do? Yell, scream, and jump up and down?"

"You got it. Do your best 'dog and pony show.'"

Well, the Small Claims Court wasn't able to give me the executions right away, but one was sent to the Sheriff's Office within about a week, enough to get started. The second one came a few days later which was pretty good for Small Claims, but then things got tied up in the Sheriff's Office. They couldn't act on it until I had contracted with a towing and storage company, which was another problem. Most towing companies didn't tow motorcycles, and the Guzzi would have to be stored in New York County, Manhattan, the Sheriff's county. Also, the motorcycle would have to be picked up in Manhattan. I wasn't having much luck with the Yellow Pages, so I tried NYNEX Directory Assistance and they gave me George Chan Mopeds and Scooters. I called them with my request.

"I need someone to tow a motorcycle."

"We wepair - no tow."

"You don't tow?"

"What size mo-ta-cycle?"

"About 595 pounds."

"Too big - no can do."

"Can you recommend someone else who tows?"

"E. O. Paggas."

"And do you have their phone number?"

"No. E. O. Paggas!"

"E. O. Paggas tows? Where are they?"

"No! E ... O ... Paggas!!"

"Oh! Yellow Pages! Well, thank you very much for that information."

So much for NYNEX Directory Assistance and the now infuriated Mr. Chan. That and a buck and quarter would get me on the New York City subway.

And then there was Anglo and American Cycles on East 4th Street. I'm sure I must have been talking with another Hell's Angels type, or maybe even the real thing. I had to explain to them that I needed a motorcycle towed, but that I didn't know when, that I wasn't the owner, and that I had a Sheriff who would perform the actual seizure. The response wasn't enthusiastic.

"Hey, what's up man? What gives?"

They couldn't do it, but they referred me to Paul - not Paul's Garage or Paul's Cycles - just "Paul." It turned out that Paul owned a garage called The Village Motorcycles. He said that he might have space, but he wasn't sure. I had to explain to him about the Sheriff, and then he definitely wasn't sure. He needed some coaxing.

"Look, this is all under the direction of a NYC Sheriff. All you have to do is pick it up and store it until the auction, about ten days, but surely under a month."

It turned out that Paul wasn't licensed to tow and didn't want to get involved with a Sheriff, but I did get a reluctant maybe.

"Call me back. We'll see."

And a few days later,

"I'm sorry. I really can't get involved in this."

The Sheriff's Office recommended Ron Globe, uptown. Of course he'd do it ... but for his price - $250.00 for the tow per attempt, and $60.00 per month for storage. It would all be added on to the judgment, but then it would all also be out of pocket expense, and who could be sure if the seizure would actually happen, and what would the motorcycle actually bring in at a sheriff's auction? And then there was no guarantee that Midnite would be at the bar with the Guzzi at any specific time or day.

"You mean he may be working at the bar, or he may not be working ... and he may take the motorcycle to work, or maybe not, and who knows how many trips I'm going to have to make ..."

And then there was Mountain Motorcycle Service. Yes! They would do it, or so they said. I signed the agreement with them, but they didn't fax it back. Three weeks went by before I got them to send back a fax written in broken English.

"Can't do because of problem we having in store. Sorry we caused you loss of time."

Don't worry about it. I have lots of time. The judgments were now six years old, another three weeks wouldn't matter. Out of frustration, I tried calling a couple of moving companies. I would have to crate the motorcycle myself before they would take it. Right! I could only imagine myself in front of the Ace Bar at eleven o'clock at night with saw, hammer, and nails crating up the motorcycle for "moving" - with Midnite and the bar patrons watching on in disbelief. I decided against the moving company - good for dramatic effect, but not very practical.

But then I found Cycle O. G. (Cute! Get it? A pun on psychology.) Yes! They would do it. And not only that; it turned out that they were having a "Spring Sale" - $35.00 for the tow and $65.00 per month storage. Such a bargain, who could refuse? The clerk who took the call was a little hazy on all this sheriff business, or maybe he just didn't care, but nevertheless, he agreed to it. Anyway, I got my contract.

And so now, with the property executions in effect and in the hands of the NYC Sheriff, all fees paid by the judgment creditor, and the contract with the motorcycle towing and storage company signed, we were ready to go on with the seizure. But one week became two weeks, and two weeks became three weeks, and nothing was happening at the Sheriff's Office.

"We'll do it next week - for sure! We're just too busy this week, too much happening. We have a couple of arrests and a heliport eviction going on ..."

I could only imagine what happens at a heliport eviction. Is it like a tenant eviction? Do they remove the helicopters? Whatever it was, it was more important than Midnite's motorcycle, but if the Deputy said next week, then it would be next week. I had never seen a seizure in progress. I had to ask the question.

"Do Sheriff Deputies wear uniforms? Do they carry guns?"

"We can't shoot him!"

"No! Don't shoot him! I have to collect some money from him first."

But the Deputy assured me that it would definitely be some time next week.

"When? Can I be there?"

I wanted to be in on the action.

"Well, you know, it's always the innocent bystander that gets hurt."

I wasn't an innocent bystander. I was the sole entity that was making this all happen, the driving force behind this entire enterprise. I was the judgment creditor! The Deputy assured me that it would all be ok.

"Look, don't worry about it. We'll call you. We may have the NYPD there, and we'll be in an unmarked van. We're coming in with helicopters and police. We'll be taking aerial photos, setting up air and ground communications, logistics … radar … whatever it takes."

The Deputy had to be joking, but something was definitely going to happen.

"Don't worry. We'll call you. Some time next week."

XLIV. Courtelyou Road

Midnite lived in the Kensington section of Brooklyn on Courtelyou Road, off Ocean Parkway. It was a lower middle class, kind of run down part of Brooklyn inhabited mostly by Blacks, Hispanics, and Lubavitcher Hassidic Jews, the overflow from Crown Heights where real estate prices had soared. It was a neighborhood where people generally don't want to be known.   Doors are sometimes unmarked; addresses are wrong or missing - the inhabitants thereby avoiding certified mail, process servers, debt collectors, Marshals, Sheriffs, the IRS, the INS … or worse.

And so, on my first visit, I really couldn't be sure exactly where Midnite lived. I thought that it might have been the old, run down apartment building on the corner. The bar that used to be on the ground floor had long since closed down, its entrance door now padlocked and covered with graffiti. A rusted steel door to the apartment building on Courtelyou Road was unmarked, had no bells or door knockers, and looked to be permanently locked. Next to the steel door was another steel door. This door was also unmarked, but there was a *mezuzah* nailed to the door post. That had to be the home of a Lubavitcher, but I couldn't even be sure of that. Would Midnite nail it up there just to throw me off, or even to perhaps protect the motorcycle from the Sheriff? In back of the apartment building was a garage with a thirty degree sloping roof leaning toward the apartment building.   The garage was also covered with graffiti and was apparently (yes, apparently - who knew?) unused and uninhabited. It was surrounded by trash cans and garbage. Where was 513?

And next to the garage and the garbage was a semi-detached house in a sorry state of disrepair and neglect. The western half of the house seemed to have "511" in barely visible, painted over numbers. The eastern half had "5 3." The middle number was missing. That had to be it! Next to the house was a narrow alleyway, just wide enough for a motorcycle. The front of the alley was protected by a five foot high wrought iron gate with a rusted pad lock, forbidding entrance to all unwanted intruders. At the end of the alley, in back of the house had to be where he parked the motorcycle. And on the other side of the alley was Schwartz's Shomorah Matzo Factory at 515 Courtelyou Road. So, Midnite lived next door to a matzo factory!

And it was nearly midnight at the simple, dilapidated one room apartment on the second floor of the house, facing Courtelyou Road. Plaster had fallen from a water stained ceiling, the result of a leaking roof that its owner hadn't bothered to repair in years. The window frames were rotted at the bottom, letting the cold winter wind into a barely heated apartment. Its sole inhabitant was a black man, a descendant of the Yoruba people of Nigeria. The black man was greatly troubled of spirit on this night. Something was amiss, something not right. The vibrations were wrong. What it was he was not able to discern. He walked toward the ivory statuette carved in the image of an African female, a goddess. It was the image of Ifa, the Oracle. It was considered "bad medicine" to offend the gods with too frequent, or too unworthy a request, but this night was special. Help was urgently needed. He recalled the ancient African prayer which was taught to him as a child in Trinidad. And so, the black man began the prayer

276

and called on Ifa, the Oracle, the spirit sent to earth by Orunmila. It was a time of great crisis, danger, and impending disaster. The black man continued on to the next stage of the ceremony. He carefully removed the palm nuts from the box held in the hands of the African female figurine, the image of Ifa. The palm nuts were used in the Ifa system of divination. He carefully counted out sixteen, held them in his huge black hands, and uttered another prayer to Ifa, the Oracle. He prayed that she would deal kindly with him, and reveal to him the things that were to be. The palm nuts were placed in a small dish, carried over to the center of the room, and the dish placed on the worn, faded red, thread-bare rug. Next, the divination board was removed from the eastern wall of the apartment and placed to the right of the dish of palm nuts. The divination board had along its circumference carved images of the gods, and of various animals. At the top center, at the twelve o'clock position, was the image of the face of a goddess, the image of Ifa. The black man next unlocked a worn, torn, old leather suitcase. He removed a small leather pouch containing the fine, white sand from the beaches of Tobago. He unzipped the pouch and poured the sand at the center of the divination board. Candles were lit on each side of the divination board and the incense burner near the door of the apartment was lit. The electric lights were turned off. The black man then took his place at the center of the room by the divination board. He was naked from the waist up, except for a white bandana that covered his head and draped down his back. He sat in the middle of the room with his legs crossed in deep meditation, murmuring prayers and chants inviting the spirits to be present to hear his supplication.

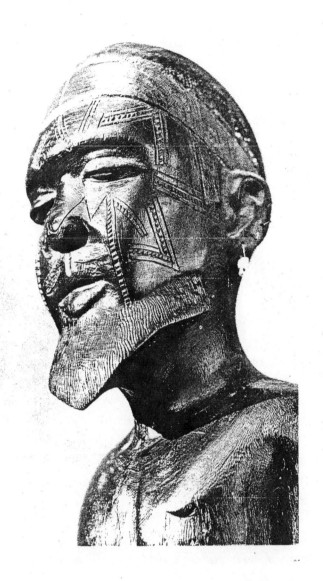

After an hour of prayers, chants, and meditation, the time was right. He took the palm nuts in combinations of four, tossing them from one hand to the other making several exchanges, and then casting the palm nuts on the divination board. Grotesque, shadowy images of the Yoruban descendant with his wild hand motions and flying palm nuts were cast on the apartment walls. He then traced the pattern of the palm nuts on the sand with his finger, the pattern pointing to the images of the antelope, the bird, and the scorpion. But Ifa was not yet with him. He chanted, prayed, and tossed the palm nuts again, now with greater speed, and in similar manner now traced out the antelope, the armadillo, and the bird. He continued again, tossing the palm nuts, and then tracing, and praying, and chanting into the early hours of the morning. And the palm nut tosses were becoming faster and faster, and the praying more fervent, and the chanting louder and louder, continuing throughout the night, and growing into a wild frenzy until the palm nuts began to glow a dull red. Smoke even emanated from them, and the chanting became yet even louder, and the palm nut tosses even faster, now seemingly to approach even the speed of light. The candle flames had now reached the end of their wicks and gave off a brilliant yellow light, like a star becoming a super nova. The African man chanted even louder, so that now the tiny apartment vibrated, even quaked as he made the final toss. And traced out on the divination board was the pattern pointing to the image of the goddess, even of Ifa herself!

A Lubavitcher, dressed in the usual black and white Hassidic garb was on his way to the morning minyan for morning prayers at the local Chabad House. He stopped and looked up at the spectacle on the second floor apartment of the house on Courtelyou Road. The windows glowed red and smoke poured out. The noise coming from the house was like thunder. A sudden bolt of lightning hit the building. The passerby did not know what to make of the event. Surely this had to be a sign of the coming of the long awaited Messiah. Should he call the police, or the fire department? He made the blessing: Blessed art thou O Lord our G-d who has created all things at the beginning.

The African man inscribed the pattern on a piece of calabash, and then gathered up the sand and placed it and the piece of calabash inside a small cloth bag. All concerns quieted, all apprehensions pacified, all anxieties tranquilled, the Yoruban descendant fell into a long, deep, and restful sleep.

Dawn had already broken on Courtelyou Road in Brooklyn. Schwartz's Matzo Factory had opened, as did the Puerto Rican bodega across the street, and Kosherland Supermarket on the corner.

XLV. Process Serving

The seizure would have to be on a Tuesday or Wednesday. Sheriffs do not work on Saturdays, and they don't like Friday nights, especially at bars. But Friday would have been a good time, a time when a bar is busy, and most likely to need a doorman, or a bouncer, but the Sheriff didn't like it. It was Sheriff Abrams, a man with a strong, deep, authoritative, and penetrating voice who spoke.

"Look, if we have to, we have to, but I would rather do this on a weekday. Friday night is dangerous. It'll probably be crowded, too many people, someone may get hurt ... and who knows, this Midnite guy may be hyped up on cocaine or something."

It would have to be on a weekday, which meant only Tuesday or Wednesday, his working days, assuming of course that he still worked there.

Things began to get very hectic on the job that Monday, the Monday before the seizure. Tests had to be run, reports had to be written up and completed, a hundred odds and ends had to be wrapped up, and lastly, my early out retirement papers filled out and sent in, but then the call came from a certain woman who needed to have papers served. The Yellow Pages listing for my new process service business was already getting results. Like I needed this ... now! The woman was clearly very nervous, confused, and obviously needed help.

"Are you a process server? Do you serve eviction papers?"

"Yes. When do they have to be served?"

"Well, I don't have the papers yet. I still have to go to court. I don't know what I'm supposed to do. Do you have the forms? And can you help me fill them out? Do I have to have a lawyer?"

"I might be able to help you. Suppose we start at the beginning."

"Well, you see, I have these two tenants living in my apartment, two girls, school teachers, and they seemed so nice at the beginning, and they gave me references ... and then they stopped paying their rent! Just like that! They stopped paying their rent ..."

As the poor landlady continued on with her tale of woe and impending disaster, I listened compassionately as I began to see it all happening again.

"How much do they owe you?"

"This month will be three months! And I have no money to pay the mortgage, or the taxes. I don't know what I am going to do ..."

The woman went on to describe the apartment. It was an apartment built on the top floor of a garage, with all plumbing, heating, and electricity. There was a long staircase leading down to a carport at the front yard ... but it didn't sound kosher. Still, I had to ask.

"And this apartment ... eh ... is it ... legal?"

As the landlady went on with the legality or illegality of her real estate nightmare, I thought for a minute of a court scene that would surely follow that would not be my own. And what I didn't tell her was that her miserable tenants would probably be living there for quite awhile, would not have to pay the back rent owed, would not have to pay any additional rent, and might be able to sue for the rent already paid. Nor did I tell her that she could also be reported to the town building inspectors for renting an apartment without a certificate of compliance, resulting in a stack of violations and summonses. And I certainly didn't tell her that the town inspectors might also come with sledge hammers to demolish the illegal apartment, thereby putting a permanent end to her apartment, and also to her real estate career.

There was also a problem with a shared electric meter, and an unpaid electric bill. LILCO was supposed to install a separate meter for the tenant, and had to turn the power off. (Or did the landlady turn the power off herself?) At any rate, there were police on the scene. An emergency call was made to LILCO, and the power got turned back on.

The unfortunate landlady went on with a long speech about her American rights, why there was nothing wrong with what she did, that the apartment was clean, modern, and well kept, and so on ... and then,

"Everybody does it!"

"Ok, look. You have to understand that I'm not a lawyer, and I can't give you any legal advice, but I can show you a sample form and I can help you fill it out."

"Oh, that would be great, and ... thank you. Thank you so much! And how much do you charge?"

"$47.00."

"Two papers have to be served."

"Same location?"

"Yes."

"47.00."

I remembered my own papers. It went something like Kravitz vs. Jonah Cohen, Neville Midnite Michaels, John Doe, Jane Doe, et al.

"But check with the court. To get a money judgment, we could do personal service on one of them, and the other can be by substitute or conspicuous service."

The landlady showed up at my house on that same day. We went into my office and we talked at length. She was a woman in her forties, brown hair, petite, hazel eyes ... and very, very nervous and confused over the legal mess she had gotten herself into. And as I was at the start of my own real estate misadventure, she was very nearly sick to her stomach. She told me that she had seen a lawyer, and that it costs $750.00 in court costs to do an eviction, and additional appearances could cost thousands of dollars more. She had asked me to confirm it.

"Is that true?"

"Yeah, but that's what you're paying your lawyer! That's his fee. Court costs in the State of New York are $35.00, and you may have to pay a Sheriff to do the actual eviction, but it nearly never comes to that. They just leave on their own, usually just before the Sheriff comes. And then of course, there's my fee, $47.00 to do the service of process. But no, it doesn't have to cost thousands of dollars to do an eviction."

The landlady was relieved and she was gaining confidence.

"You know, you're the first person to tell me that."

And then about her own lawyer she added,

"Why that lying so and so, that greedy no good ..."

"But tell me. If these two girls were so nice ... well, what happened?"

"Well, they had these two boyfriends... now I don't mind an occasional visit, but they were living there, and I rented the apartment to only two people, and ... Well, I happened to mention it to them and they really got nasty. I couldn't believe it! And then the rent stopped, and there were four people living there, and …"

I felt compelled to give her the capsulated version of the Midnite story. I felt that I should have started some sort of screwed landlord's club. And so, I told her the story of the so called illegal sublet in Brooklyn, the evil landlord, how Midnite came in, and the endless pursuit through the streets, courts, bars, and sewers of New York …

"… and right now, as we speak, I have a NYC Sheriff ready to seize Midnite's motorcycle in front of the Ace Bar! As a matter of fact, it should happen tomorrow night!"

The woman listened intently, not missing a word, and staring wide eyed throughout the whole story.

"Oh, I do hope they get it!"

We decided that we would serve Laura, the younger, gentler girl by personal service. She would be the one to go after.

"She leaves for school at exactly 8:45 A.M., is about 110 pounds, has long curly brown hair, and is about 24 years old."

I helped the woman with her forms and wished her good luck. She said that she would return the next day with the court papers, signed and sealed by the court clerk, and ready to be served by me.

"And if there is anything I can do for you, to help you with this Midnite character … Please, please! … Let me know. Ok?"

"Well, maybe just a telephone call to the bar, or something like that, to see if he's there. We'll see."

Tuesday morning, the day of the seizure, was pouring rain. Heavy storm clouds were moving in from the west, and rain was threatening into the evening. It didn't look good. Too many things had to happen. It had to stop raining, the motorcycle towing and storage company had to be ready, the Sheriff had to be there, and of course Midnite had to show up at work with the motorcycle.

Sheriff Abrams called me at home Tuesday night, at about 7:00 P.M. He was on the scene at the Ace Bar with Deputy Schatzer and two other Deputies, and they were waiting for Midnite and the Guzzi.

"Mr. Cohen?"

"Yes!"

"Sheriff Abrams here in front of the bar. He hasn't come yet, but we're all set up and we're waiting …"

XLVI. The Seizure

And so now, after six years of frustration and perseverance, the gem, the prize, the debtor's sole asset - the Moto Guzzi motorcycle - was so close, so very, very close. This was the night, and it was happening. The Sheriff and his Deputies were on the scene. Sheriff Abrams called me.

"Well, we got here at 6:30, no sign of him or the bike yet. What time did you say you saw him here?"

"6:45 P.M. exactly, but that was way back in January. I can't be sure of exactly what his hours are now, but he does work there!"

"Ok, ok. We'll hang out for a while. Will you be by the phone?"

Of course I would be by the phone! Did he think that I would abandon my station at a time like this?

"Yes, I'll be here."

I hadn't eaten supper yet. I was much too nervous. And the following morning I had the process service to do for the landlady, and then I had to miraculously be at work at the same time. The house remained absolutely quiet that night except for the loud ticking of the Halifax clock over the fireplace, along with its chimes on the hour and on the half hour. I sat by my desk in nervous anticipation, waiting for the next call which came in less than ten minutes.

"Abrams here. What's going on with this Cycle O. G. Towing? Are we set up with them or what?"

"What do you mean? Did you call the pager, (917) 273-7844?"

"Yeah, they're not answering. We can't seize the bike if there's no one here to tow it away. Do they know about this?"

"Of course! I have a contract with them. They said that they would be ready. I can't understand it. Let me try them. What's your number over there?"

"We're calling from a cell phone. We'll get back to you."

I didn't like it. When someone says they'll get back to you, they usually don't. There were too many people involved, too many things had to happen, and there were too many things to go wrong. And where the hell was Cycle O. G.? I was about to give up all hope on them. I called Alex, the night manager, to see what was happening. To my amazement, they answered. It was Alex's friendly voice.

"Cycle O. G. Towing, Alex speaking."

"Hi Alex. It's me, Jonah with the Guzzi. What's happening?"

"Yeah, yeah, we're waiting and ready. We got the call from the Sheriff. He must have a different cellular phone than ours, a different manufacturer. Maybe they're not compatible or something. When we called him back, we got some medical office somewhere."

"Ok, the Sheriff is going to call me in a few minutes. We're still waiting for the motorcycle's owner to come to work. When he does, the Sheriff will call me, and then I'll call you."

"Right! Gotcha!"

And almost immediately, the phone rang again.

"Abrams here."

"Hi Sheriff. I called Cycle O. G. - some problem with the cellular phone, but they're ready, so call me when he comes."

And now with the lines of communication re-established, albeit in a somewhat circuitous way, the seizure was on again. I waited nervously in the deathly silence of the room for something to happen. The Halifax chimed eight times, shattering the silence of the room like glass, and then that was followed by more silence. And in the silence I began to think, becoming engulfed in deep, dark thoughts. What if my judgment debtor really were dangerous? What would he be like after they had taken away his motorcycle, his only asset, and probably the only thing of value that he had ever owned in his life? And what was going on at the Ace Bar at this very moment? Was this a wise thing that I was doing? I would be his first target! What was my life worth? Perhaps I should have given it up years ago, perhaps it really wasn't worth it; but the deep dark thoughts were thankfully interrupted with the sound of the telephone ripping through the silence.

"Sheriff Abrams here. Well, it's about a quarter to nine now, and no sign of him or the bike. There are a few bikes here, and their riders look like his kind of crowd. We can check out an expensive Yamaha, just a shot. Maybe he moved up or changed ..."

"No! It's a Moto Guzzi! We're looking for the Guzzi!"

"Well, no sign of him or the Guzzi. You know, we can't wait here all night! Our job is to come, seize the bike, and leave. And it's your job to give us reliable information. The City's overtime budget is tight. How much longer is it going to be?"

"Well, I don't know. He's supposed to be there. I saw him last January, on a Tuesday, at exactly 6:45 P.M. Anyway, I did tell you to call the bar before you set this up, to make sure that he would be there! He's not working a nine to five kind of job here. My instructions were to call the bar first! He comes when he wants, if he wants!"

"Ok, ok. We'll hang out a while longer."

"Let me call the bar and see what's going on. Call me back in five minutes." And as I hung up, the Halifax had now struck out nine chimes. I called the Ace Bar. A man's voice answered.

"Ace Bar."

And now, still worried about arousing suspicion and having one of Midnite's buddies at the bar inform him that maybe something was going on, I had to bury my deep, dark thoughts. I had to put on an act even better than he did before the judge when I had him arrested. Anything unusual would certainly blow the deal. I had to act slightly inebriated, free-flowing, happy, and slightly high. I tried my best.

"Hello...o...o...o Ace Bar. Hey, uh … is Midnite there?"

"Not … as … yet."

"Well … ha, ha, ha. Do you, uh … ha, ha, do you expect him in tonight?"

"Yeah, he said he's coming. He should be here before ten … I hope."

"Oh … ok, man, thanks … ha, ha, thanks a lot."

But with the end of that brief conversation, and my drunk act concluded, the deep dark thoughts returned. The long minutes and hours of waiting in nervous anticipation were almost unbearable. My mother had died nearly a year ago now, and I thought about the many hospital visits, and the cancer that killed her. And then I thought of the funeral and the eulogy that I delivered. Besides the usual motherly accolades, I managed to work in a small part of my own special case. It went something like this:

"... and some of you may have heard a little of my legal problems concerning a certain alien from Trinidad and Tobago, and how he lived in my apartment as a squatter, and how I was being cheated out of many months of rent ... , and all the expenses and court appearances ...

They would all say, 'You're wasting your time.' And they would say, 'You're never going to find this guy.' And they would say, 'Why don't you give up!'

But Mom would say, 'Tell me about your case.' And she would say, 'When are you going to find this guy and collect?' And she would say, 'What is the next step?'"

But now, what would my own life be worth after the Sheriff's seizure. This was a dangerous thing I was doing. Perhaps I really should have given it up years ago, and moved on. Perhaps we should have abandoned the seizure ... but then the silence, and the deep, dark, thoughts were again thankfully interrupted by the Sheriff's call. It was time to move on. It was back to business, fast! This was the next step!

"Abrams here."

"Hi Stan. Ok, I called the Ace. He's coming. I think I spoke with the bartender. He said, 'Before ten, I hope.'"

"WE CAN'T WAIT ALL NIGHT! Look, I have a boss too. And I have to explain all this overtime money!"

"Well, I'm sorry! I just didn't figure on the City's overtime budget. I wish I had known before that this would be a problem. Maybe I should have transferred the case to Brooklyn and had a Brooklyn Sheriff do this in the daytime. Then I wouldn't have to worry about the City's damned overtime budget!"

"Ok, ok. We'll stay until ten, but that's it!"

And now, the Halifax struck out a single bell for 9:30 P.M. Its loud ticking seemed to build to a crescendo in the silence of the room, and then the phone rang again. It was Alex at Cycle O. G. Towing.

"Hi Jon. What's going on?"

"We're still waiting for him to come to work."

"I'm coming from Queens. Do you want me to start out now?"

"No, not yet. I'll call you."

"I'm waiting here in the truck. Call me, ok?"

"Yeah, thanks a lot, Alex."

I couldn't have asked for a more reliable towing company, but there was no point in having Alex make the trip for nothing. And at that, even I began to have my doubts. It was as if the alien from Trinidad knew. How did he know? He was supposed to have been there. Where the hell was he?

The minutes were ticking off, and still no call from the Sheriff. And now, the Halifax chimed out ten bells. Maybe now! After all, the bartender did say, "Before ten, I hope." "*I hope*," but perhaps after ten also, but then …

"RING … RING … RING"

Here it was! The call from the Sheriff!

"Sheriff Abrams - He's not here."

"???"

"Hello?"

"Yeah, I'm here. I don't know what to tell you."

"Well, I don't either."

"Let's give it to ten after, ok? Just ten after."

"Ok, but then we have to call it a night."

We waited while the Halifax ticked off another ten minutes, as if it too were possessed of the alien spirit from Trinidad. I had to call Alex and tell him to go home. It was off. Alex said that he would wait until twenty after, and even the Sheriff gave it another twenty minutes, but no Midnite, and no Guzzi. I found myself debating with the Sheriff - they wanted another $600.00 fee for a second attempt.

"Sheriff, I paid $600.00 for this. So, it didn't happen the first time, but I do expect another attempt. He works there, and he has the bike!"

"Well, I have to be able to justify this to my superiors ... hello?"

"Yeah, yeah, I'm here. I'm thinking. Well, suppose I stake out the bar myself, and when he comes, I'll give you a call?"

"We are not a 911 service! We can't do it that way."

"Then you're wasting your time, my time, Cycle O. G.'s time, and you're also wasting the City's precious overtime budget!"

After a brief silence, the Sheriff relented. The job was unfinished. He wanted to see it through.

"Ok, look. We'll make one more attempt at this, but you have to do some more work. Find out when he starts, when he finishes, and what days. I have to have something to go on. If you say that you saw him there with the bike at such and such time, then I can go to my superiors and say yes, we have something to go on. But first, you have to do some investigative work."

There was no point in arguing with the Sheriff. That's the way it had to be. I would do the investigative work, and they would make a second attempt. It was a deal.

"Sheriff, I will do that … and thanks for all your efforts."

The Deputy called me very late that night, after it was all over. He too was determined to follow the job through to its completion. He spoke slowly with words of encouragement and consolation.

"Hi Jon, Schatzy here."

"Hi Steve, thanks for trying. You guys were great. You gave it your best."

"Look, Stan is going to set this up again, but we need more … It could have worked. It really could have worked. We were there, Cycle O. G. Towing was ready … and we had you at the control panel coordinating this whole thing."

"We even had the Ace Bar cooperating! They gave me his schedule!"

"Yeah, how about that."

"I know that he works there. I know that for a fact. I can't understand why he didn't show up. Maybe it was some voodoo magic from Trinidad that got in the way?"

"Well, who knows? Stan still has to make it back to the Island. He's got a long trip ahead of him. He'll have about two hours of sleep tonight … but do your investigative thing and we'll be in touch, ok?"

"Right! Will do!"

"Good luck and be well, ok?"

"Thanks Steve, and you too."

XLVII. Undercover

The next morning I had to do the process service for that poor landlady who got herself into all that trouble with her dear tenants. I arrived at her house at 7:30 A.M. exactly, a time when I should have already started out for work. I waited in front of the house for the hapless tenant who was about to exit the apartment that was on top of the garage, descend the wooden staircase to the carport, enter her car, and drive out the driveway.

It is amazing how one's senses are sharpened in such a situation. Even the slightest sound or movement of a bird or insect, or the rustle of the leaves, or the gentle wave of a flag in the morning spring breeze does not escape notice. But it was now 8:15 A.M., I was already fifteen minutes late for work, and still no Laura. Well, maybe she just took some more time in the shower, or more time drying her hair, or couldn't find her keys ... or was this going to be another bust.

But then at 8:50 A.M. the front door opened. A young woman in her early twenties wearing sunglasses, her long brown hair blowing in the wind, descended the stairs, entered into her car, and started the engine. Almost simultaneously, the process server, dressed in a sweatshirt, jeans, and sneakers, started his engine. The young school teacher backed out of the driveway moving slowly toward the road. The process server then inched up so that his car was now half blocking the driveway. He exited the car, leaving the door open and the engine running, and taking his precious court papers with him. The tenant, the targeted would be recipient of the Petition and the Notice of Petition, the papers that would begin the process of her removal, was now trapped, confused and rendered immobile. She rolled down her window, only an inch or so to see what it was all about, just enough for delivery of her papers.

"Laura Christian? I'm a process server. I have court papers for you. You are hereby served."

I showed her my NYC Process Server ID for effect and officialdom, but it wasn't necessary. The hapless tenant now realized her error, and without any other alternative, accepted them, and responded,

"Thank you."

I was over forty-five minutes late for work that day, but I was on an important mission. It had to be done. And so it was that I got Laura, but the Sheriff didn't get Midnite, or the Guzzi.

Now, if Midnite wasn't working on Tuesday, a day that he was scheduled to work, maybe he would be working on Thursday, a day that he wasn't scheduled. Sometimes reverse logic works. I got to the bar around 11:00 P.M. The neighborhood was quiet and peaceful. It was a pleasant and warm night. A young Puerto Rican kid was dribbling a basketball and asked me if I wanted to play. A white guy was the bouncer-doorman at the Ace, but there was no Midnite, and there was no Guzzi.

But Tuesday…Tuesday was the day when he was supposed to work, not Thursday, and again, I had made the trip into Manhattan for nothing. I had already made too many calls to the bar. Surely, they were on to me! Now back in my office, I tried calling the bar one more time. It was in the afternoon, on a Tuesday, and luckily, I got someone else on the P.M. shift. I played it straight this time.

"Hello, Ace Bar."

"Hi, is Midnite there?"

"No. The bouncers start after ten. Try calling the bartender after ten."

Well, that was simple enough! So, he still worked there, he was a "bouncer," and he starts after ten! There absolutely could be no more calls to the Ace. I ate supper and left my house at about a quarter to ten.

The Ace Bar is on East 5th Street, between Avenues A and B, accessible only from Avenue B. East 5th ends on B, picks up again east of Loisaida, and goes one way west. As many times as I've been there, I still get lost. Midnite was a master of the art of staying well hidden. I arrived in the City a little after eleven, and parked on a street somewhere near the bar, not because I was afraid of blowing my cover - it was because I was lost. But the night air was warm and mild, the walk safe and pleasant, and upon arriving at the bar, to my utter joy and delight, there it was - the Moto Guzzi!

It was parked on the sidewalk, just as I had seen it last January. It sparkled, it shined, it was big, and it was beautiful! Its leather seat and trim were jet black, its gas tank and fenders were creamy white, and its exhaust pipes and shocks were gleaming chromium. Black leather streamers flowed from the handle bars. Everything was exactly as before - that is, everything except for one minor detail - the license plate was different! It was an Illinois plate, number 401-952. But the bike was his! It had to be his! And it was the same bike that I saw last January, but what was this deal with the Illinois license plate? It had to be stolen, or borrowed, or something like that in order to avoid parking tickets. Or could it actually be another Guzzi, with another owner? Or the same Guzzi with a different owner? And where the hell was Midnite anyway? A white guy was taking care of the door, but this was supposed to be Midnite's night. Here was the Guzzi, and some white guy was the bouncer at the door! I couldn't go into the bar to investigate. Midnite knew me too well - we were in court together too many times.

I went back to the car, drove it to East 5th Street, and double parked on the opposite side of the street, diagonally in front of the bar. I repositioned the rear view mirror so that it was now reflecting the bar door and the two motorcycles parked in front of the bar - the Guzzi (my Guzzi), and a Harley Davidson. I had to make the connection between Midnite and the Moto Guzzi motorcycle with the Illinois plate. I had to actually see him on the bike. It would be a long night, but it had to be done, and I was prepared to do it - whatever it took.

The night air had turned quite chilly. The dark blue sweatshirt that I wore and lightweight leather jacket, black of course, besides keeping me warm, afforded perfect camouflage. I pulled the black nylon hood over my head, slouched back, and watched the show from the rear view mirror. I'm sure that I was perfectly invisible. It was now nearly midnight and nothing had changed. The Harley and the Guzzi were still parked outside on the sidewalk. The same white guy was taking care of the door. He would stand outside for a while, take a drag on a cigarette, go inside for a while to warm up, and then repeat the same routine. Assorted East Village types, neighborhood folk, and passersby would go into the bar, stay for a while, and then leave. Two guys and a girl were sitting on the stoop of a brownstone opposite the bar, sometimes talking loudly, and then softly at various other times, so that I could only pick up small pieces of conversation.

"...each to his own. Hey, you can do it your way. I'll do it mine...but, I am no sexual pervert ..."

And then the conversation softened, so that I really didn't know what they were talking about except that it didn't seem to have anything to do with Midnite or the Guzzi. At a little past one, the two guys and the girl went into the bar. There was still no sign of Midnite. And as the night rolled on, I observed the night people of the East Village. The street lighting began to seem as bright as day. Various young people rode bicycles or roller skated up and down East 5th Street. Actually, I was really impressed with it all. Mayor Guilliani did a fantastic job of cleaning up the City - no disturbances, no crime, and no incidents. Some drunken teens got a little rowdy and did some shouting, but that was all. I was amazed at how many people are up at night. I wondered what they all did for a living. Who were these night people? Did they go to school, or a job, or do anything? It was now moving on to past 2:00 A.M., and I had to be at my own job at 8:00 A.M. The bar traffic had slowed down, and the same Harley and Guzzi were still in my rear view mirror. I tried to catnap, but kept waking up to the sounds of heels on the pavement, or a car or truck passing by, or by bits and pieces of conversation ...

"I gave you food stamps, and you go and lose them. I have no more food stamps to give you ..."

The garbage trucks came at about 3:00 A.M. and were

barely able to pass with my car being double parked. Anyway, the police didn't bother me, but then everybody double parked. The Harley and the Guzzi were still parked in the same place on the sidewalk in front of the bar, unmoved and unclaimed. Surprisingly, bar traffic started to pick up again. I had to think to myself,

"DON'T THESE PEOPLE EVER WORK? And doesn't this bar ever close?"

I catnapped for a while longer and woke up at about 3:30 A.M. If I had left then, I could have been home by about 4:30 A.M., gotten about two hours of sleep, and been at my job by 8:00 A.M. A Pechter's bakery delivery truck was making the morning rounds, and that was followed by a New York Times delivery truck, and now more people were leaving the bar than were going in.

"COME ON, MIDNITE! GET ON THE DAMNED BIKE ALREADY AND GO HOME."

But now my bladder was filling up something awful, and the only open bar, in fact, the only open anything, was the Ace. Well, this became an emergency situation. It was going to be the Ace Bar, or East 5th Street, and East 5th Street won out.

3:30 A.M. soon became 4:00 A.M., and now the entrance to the bar began to resemble a Marx Brothers movie. Hoards of people, bar patrons, all nearly falling out the door. Where did they all come from? I had been there the whole night, and I didn't see that many people go in! But amongst the hoards, Captain Midnite was not to be found. At 4:15 A.M., a tall white man with good straight features left the bar. He was carrying a motorcycle helmet. He descended the three steps to the sidewalk, and looked toward the Guzzi. He began to put on his helmet while studying the Guzzi, and while studying the Guzzi, I was studying him through my rear view mirror. I remained absolutely still and scarcely able to breath. The white motorcyclist took a step closer toward the Guzzi, and I began to go into a cold sweat. My entire body was now consumed with fear, hopelessness and disappointment. In short, I crashed. I don't know if it was a prayer, or mindless murmuring, but the words came out …

"PLEASE!!! LET IT NOT BE HIS! And after five years, let it not end like this!"

The white motorcyclist finished tightening up his helmet strap. He turned toward the Harley, walked towards it, and then mounted. The street lights had already been turned off. In seconds, the deep roar of the powerful Harley engine was reverberating up and down East 5th Street, and soon both motorcycle and rider had disappeared into the intense darkness before dawn. It was the most beautiful sound that I had ever heard in my life!

At 4:30 A.M., the bar lights went out, finally, thank goodness! Three white men exited the bar, and they were talking loudly.

"Hey, don't forget guys.   Block watch meeting tomorrow."
"Right! Ok, see ya tomorrow …"

And while they were talking, there was still yet one

person, spirit, alien entity, or possibly Illinois resident who would exit the bar. It would be the rider of the Moto Guzzi motorcycle. It was now 4:45 A.M. The last bar inhabitant finally exited. He was a tall, thin, black man. His hair was wrapped in a bandana. He was carrying with him a white bucket and a rag. He spilled out the water on the sidewalk, quickly wiped down the bar door, and went back inside. Within seconds, and still beaming with alien energy, he returned outside, locked the front bar door, and pulled down the steel gate over the bar window, locking it too. He then walked over to the three men who were apparently owners or managers. There was a minute or two of soft conversation followed by a final,

"See ya tomorrow."

Dawn was breaking on East 5th Street. The night people had disappeared into their holes, crevices, or secret hiding places; the normal people were still asleep; and the only two remaining souls on East 5th were the alien and the investigator.

The alien walked over to the Guzzi. He seemed to be looking for something in its saddle bag. Perhaps he was getting ready to switch license plates, but that wasn't it, and he didn't mount and start! Instead, he turned and walked! Why was the black man walking? It wasn't enough. I had to see him on the bike - him on the Guzzi! But why the hell was he walking? And was this black man really Midnite? He walked west on East 5th Street and turned the corner. Where the hell was he going? And why didn't he get on the damned bike?

I got out of my car and took a long, close look at the

302

bike. Yes, it was the same Moto Guzzi that I had seen last January. There was absolutely no doubt about it. I got back into my car, drove to the corner, stopped, and stared up Avenue A in the direction of the walker. Where was he? Did I lose him? Did he duck and disappear into a subway? And why was the Guzzi left abandoned?

But the walker returned, turning the corner and walking in the direction of the motorcycle. But who was this walker? It was early dawn, and daylight was just beginning to break. There was something terribly unnatural about having stayed up all night, and yet, I had still not positively made the connection between Midnite and the Guzzi, the information that I needed to give to the Sheriff. My eyes remained fixed on this black man walking toward the motorcycle. I studied his features intensively, but through the car's tinted windows, the early dawn light, and the walker's very dark skin, I could not be absolutely sure who it was. But then the walker's eyes turned to mine, and as I sat there gawking into the black man's eyes, his eyes pierced mine with instant mutual recognition. And if the eyes are truly the windows of the soul, then I had truly seen the alien spirit. It was Midnite!

It had to be good enough. Here was the Guzzi, here was Midnite, the bar was closed, and there was no one else in sight. He continued to walk toward the motorcycle. I had to get out of there fast! I might have blown my cover, but maybe not. It was still early dawn, and with the car windows tinted, it was darker inside the car than outside. Also, I was looking for him, he wasn't looking for me. I could have been anybody. Black men with gold earrings and a bandana might get a stare or two from anybody, even in the East Village.

303

It was now a quarter to five. I could still beat the rush hour traffic, get home by a quarter to six, sleep for an hour, and be at work by 8:00 A.M. I found myself on Houston Street, hung a sharp right on Delancey, sped up Delancey making all the green lights, made it through some construction, and then onto the steel grating of the Williamsburg Bridge. I didn't think that I was in any danger, and perhaps I didn't blow my cover, but I really was very late for work. And so, it was "pedal-to-the-metal" with the single fuel injected Dodge Aries pumping hard on all four cylinders with everything she had.

I thought I caught it first in my side view mirror. There was a faint rumble coming up front behind, and then there was a flash of light followed by the dopplarized roar of a very powerful motorcycle...

"ZZZZZOOOOOOOOOOOooooooooommmmm"

Midnite on the Guzzi had just passed me. And so, here it was, the connection I needed, proof positive. I returned home by 6:00 A.M., slept for about two hours, and came in an hour late for work. The first thing I did was call in my attendance. This time I had to speak to my supervisor.

"Good morning, Ken. A little trouble on the road. I had to take a detour."

The second thing I did was call Deputy Schatzer.

"Sheriff's Office - Schatzer here."

"Good morning, Deputy Schatzer."

"Cohen?"

"Yeah, I was at the Ace Bar last night. He was there with the Guzzi. He starts at ten and works until four-thirty. He's there all night. The bike is on the sidewalk. Pick it up anytime. Oh, one thing - he's got an Illinois license plate on it."

"An Illinois plate? I hope that's not a problem."

"Nah. He probably uses it to avoid parking tickets. It's probably stolen. But the bike is his. We have the New York title. He owns it. He's there with the bike."

"This is the kind of information we're looking for. Nice work, Cohen."

XLVIII. The Illinois Owner

Days went by before anything further happened. The Sheriff's Office is a busy place. There were other, more important law enforcement needs requiring the services of the Sheriff. There was another eviction taking place, and then there was some training, followed by a couple of arrests, and then the call came from Deputy Schatzer.

"We did a DMV run on this Illinois plate number you gave us. The bike is registered in the name of a Martin C. Solarz, 5113 Rosefield Avenue, Chicago, Illinois. We can't do anything."

"??*#&???"

"Hello?"

"Yeah, yeah, I'm still here... uh ... registered, not titled?"

"Registered AND titled."

"But it can't be! He can't do that! There's a Restraining Order. There was a Restraining Order served on the debtor!"

"When?"

"About two or three years ago. It was just before I had the debtor arrested for contempt."

"So? A Restraining Order is only good for a year."

"??*&#???"

"Hello, hello?"

"Yeah, yeah, I'm here. Uh ... uh ... let me do a little investigating ... I have to check on a few things. I'll call you back. Thanks for your help, Steve."

And so, once again, my case had hit a snag. Things were

falling apart fast. In a panic, I called Chicago Directory Assistance to at least confirm the existence of a Martin Solar, or Solare, or Soler, but Directory Assistance came up zero. This Martin Solar might have been a completely fictitious person, and the title a complete fraud, thereby rendering the debtor "judgment proof." Was Martin Solar a real person and the titled owner? Directory Assistance needed more information.

"Is that the North Side of Chicago, or the South?"

I knew absolutely nothing about Chicago, nor did I know if the person that I was looking for was a real person. I could offer no help.

"How would I know? Try them all!"

We weren't able to find this Martin Solar, if he existed. I had better luck with the Restraining Notice. I read the back of the form containing CPLR Sec. 5222(b) over, and over again, lip reading every word:

"A judgment debtor served with a Restraining Notice is forbidden to make or suffer any sale, assignment, transfer ... until the judgment is satisfied or vacated."

I called the Deputy back at my first opportunity to let him know the results of my mini investigation.

"There's no such person as Martin Solar. I called Chicago Directory Assistance."

"That's Solarz, S .. O .. L .. A .. R .. Z, 5113 Rosefield Avenue."

"Oh."

"Gotta go. Call me back if you have something."

"Wait, wait! There's something else. The Restraining Order is good almost forever!"

I read the Restraining Notice to the Deputy who listened carefully to every word, giving it his complete attention. He then asked me to fax a copy of it to the City lawyers for their review. That very same afternoon, I got a call from the Sheriff. It was a good news and bad news situation. Yes, they could go ahead with the seizure, but since there was now a third party involved, things were beginning to get complicated. I listened to the Sheriff as he explained.

"In order for us to go ahead and take the bike, you, the judgment creditor, will have to put up a bond in order to indemnify us for any lawsuit arising out of a third party claim due to wrongful seizure of the motorcycle ..."

The Sheriff went on to explain all about third party claims, sheriff bonds, lawsuits, expenses, and finally, why I should perhaps forget about the whole thing! It wasn't worth it. Here it was again. They were telling me to give up. It was time to move on to the "next step!"

"So, how much is a bond?"

"Well, I'd have to check on it with the lawyers, but I'd say, in a case like this, a minimum of $50,000.00. We have to be bonded for at least fifty thousand."

"And what does it cost to get the bond?"

"About ten percent of the bond. That's $5,000.00."

"FIVE THOUSAND DOLLARS?!"

"Well, I'd have to check on it to be sure."

"Yeah, ok, Stan. Please do that."

So, now what? I had hit another major obstacle, but if I had to get a bond, then that's the way it would be. I'd have to find a way to get the bond. Expenses, even without the greedy paws of a lawyer in my precious judgments, were mounting up fast. And what about this Solarz character, the supposed new Guzzi owner? Was he a real person? I tried

Chicago Directory Assistance once again, this time giving them the correct spelling. They gave me the phone number without any problem. It was listed. But then I did something that was a little stupid - I called him. I just had to know. Was he some poor innocent fool who had just bought an out-of-state motorcycle from someone he didn't know? Was he a friend? How does an Illinois resident come to buy an expensive motorcycle from someone in New York? There were too many questions. I called him and played it very straight. A young man with a slight Midwestern accent answered.

"Hello?"

"Hello, Martin Solarz, please."

"Speaking."

"Did you just buy a 1996 Moto Guzzi motorcycle?"

"Uh, yes. Who is this? What is this about?"

Should I have told him? Perhaps I should have said,

> *"Hey idiot! Your blankety-blank motorcycle is about to be picked up by a New York City Sheriff. It was transferred in violation of a Restraining Order, you fool! You own nothing!"*

I played it straight.

"My name is Jonah Cohen. I'm a judgment creditor from the Small Claims Court."

"What kind of court?"

"Civil Court, Small Claims, Queens County in New York. What did you pay for the bike?"

Sometimes it's amazing what an opponent will tell you if you just play it straight.

"Uh ... oh, about $13,000, but I don't see how it's any of

your business."

"Well, there may be a problem with the title. Did you buy this bike from a Neville Michaels? Is he a friend of yours, or what?"

"A friend."

"Thanks. Have a nice day."

There was no point in continuing the conversation. He was obviously a real person and he told me what I needed to know, but it was probably a very stupid thing that I did. No doubt that he would now notify the debtor who would now take extra precautions and keep the motorcycle well hidden. Or perhaps he felt secure with the Illinois title, and I was just some nut from New York making a crank call. Anyway, I really had to make sure that this Martin Solarz was not some poor, innocent idiot who might have had his motorcycle taken away from him, and maybe sue the Sheriff, the City of New York ... and me!

The Illinois title was an obvious fraud. The supposed new owner was living in Illinois, but Midnite was using the motorcycle here in New York, with an Illinois license plate. Solarz would have had to register the bike in Illinois, and send Midnite the registration and plate. The Sheriff wouldn't go ahead with the seizure without a bond, and the cost of the bond with the Sheriff and towing fees would most likely be more than what the Guzzi would ever bring at a Sheriff's auction. But what was the objective at this point? Was it to get the money? Was it to get even ... or, was it to get the Guzzi?

XLIX. Cash into the Court

I agonized over the situation. A $50,000 bond in a Small Claims case was just plain ridiculous. The Sheriff did get back to me, as he said he would, with some more information on the bond.

"I checked it out with the City lawyers. I guess I was mistaken about that bond. It's only $25,000, not $50,000. You have to get a $25,000 bond to indemnify the Sheriff and the City of New York for wrongful seizure of the motorcycle."

"Oh, *only* $25,000, and ten percent of that would cost me *only* $2,500. Right?!"

"Look, I don't make the rules. What do you want to do?"

"Let me think about it, ok? Thanks, Stan."

It was an obvious fraud, a sale of an asset in violation of the Restraining Order. Why should I be required to piss away $2,500 because of the debtor's illegal act? But then I got a really crazy idea. I seem to come up with these brain storms when confronted with a crisis. It was like when the subletting nightmare broke, and it looked like this "person" Midnite was about to become homeless, possibly because of my doing. I would find a cheap apartment for him, and continue to be his landlord. It was a very bad idea. And when I couldn't rent the apartment because I wasn't able to get the landlord's permission, I had another idea. I was going to rent my new condo. I recalled the advice of my friend at work.

"Man, are you crazy? Rent your new condo? Not a good idea, man! Not a good idea! Don't do it!"

Well, now here was another one. My early-out retirement from the job had come through with the $25,000 buy out. I had found the perfect use for it. Why don't I just put up the $25,000 myself and save the $2,500 to be paid to the bonding company? I called the Sheriff the next day and told him what I proposed to do. There was big money involved. I listened carefully to the response.

"Oh ... well ... eh ...we never did it this way before. It always went through a bonding company."

"But it doesn't have to. Right? I could put up the bond using my own resources?"

"Well ... eh, yes ... I'll tell you what. Let me do some calling around, and either Deputy Schatzer or I will get back to you."

I sensed a new spark of energy in the Sheriff's voice. The case wasn't dead yet. The judgment creditor had the funds, and he would put up his own bond. We were on!

I returned home and played back the messages on my telephone answering machine. There was a message from the Sheriff's Office. I listened carefully to Deputy Shatzer's instructions.

"The money gets deposited with the New York City Department of Finance, Division of Trust Funds. That's Department of Finance, Division of Trust funds."

I called the clerk at the Department of Finance, who asked his supervisor, who asked his chief, who got back to his supervisor, who spoke directly to me. I had to explain that I wanted to post a cash undertaking to indemnify the Sheriff for wrongful seizure of a motor vehicle. The people at Finance weren't sure what to do. They suggested that perhaps I should call the cashier's office and ask them, but that it might also be a good idea to call the Legal

Department. I called the Legal Department and spoke to Mr. Moseley. By chance, it was the very same Mr. Moseley that I had spoken with four years earlier. It was when I had Midnite arrested and had to get the arrest warrant approved by the Legal Department before the Sheriff's Office would carry out the arrest.

I explained to Mr. Moseley the problem that I was having in getting the $25,000 cash bond to the City. I happened to mention the arrest warrant, and he seemed to remember it vaguely. There aren't many Small Claims civil arrests in New York, so they do tend to remember. Mr. Moseley spoke in the same self-assured, comforting, and soothing voice that he did as at the time of the arrest. Alas, although the City was equipped to make arrests, believe it or not, they were not equipped to take my money! The good lawyer spoke at length, but he didn't have an answer. I pleaded with him hopelessly.

"But there must be a way to get the money to the City!"

"I really don't know ..."

The pause was long, uncomfortable, and disappointing. Nobody wanted my money! I had to give up on the Legal Department. In a fit of frustration, I called the Sheriff's Office.

"Stan! This is insane! Here's what I'm going to do. I'm going to fill a paper bag with $25,000 in one dollar bills, and I'm going to drop it on a desk in the Sheriff's Office!"

"Ok, ok! Don't panic. There's an answer to this, and we'll find it. We'll get back to you soon."

Time was being wasted, and it was important to act quickly. Did Midnite still work at the bar? Did he still own the motorcycle? Did he manage not to wreck it in an accident? Did the Illinois resident obtain possession?

The answer to the question regarding the cash bond came back to me via a fax that same morning. It was in CPLR 2601 - Payment of Money or Securities into Court. The money would have to be paid into the court. But payment of money into the court presented other problems. There was no legal requirement for me to pay money into the court. No judge had ordered it, and no plaintiff had demanded it. There was no paperwork, no hearing, nor was there an index number assigned. I called the Small Claims Court for assistance, but the clerk didn't know. She referred me to her supervisor, who wasn't sure, but he thought that I might have to file a motion. It didn't sound right. How do you file a motion on something when there isn't even a case? I had to ask.

"And how do I go about doing that?"

"You have to get a lawyer. I'm not being paid to be your lawyer!"

The Small Claims clerks are not always the nicest people to deal with. Everybody hates you if you're pro se, but in Small Claims, they're supposed to help you. I had to answer him directly.

"You're being paid to answer my questions! And do you really expect me to pay a lawyer for the privilege of paying bond money into the court?"

"Click."

Perhaps I really should have given up years ago. There was no cheap way out of this. I would have to pay a lawyer, pay a bonding company, or give up. But wait! I had almost forgotten about the request for title record that I had sent to the NY DMV. The new title record had come in the mail that morning. I had the copy of the Illinois title. It looked legitimate, and probably was, but now I also had the latest

314

copy of the New York State title record, showing Michaels, Neville M. as the current owner! Also, the new title record was dated after the Illinois title date. I called the Sheriff's Office the next morning and the Deputy answered.

"Good morning, Deputy Schatzer. How can I help you?"

"Good morning, Deputy Schatzer. I HAVE THE TITLE RECORD!"

"Yeah, yeah. I know."

"No. This is a new title record. It's after the Illinois title record. It's dated June 11, 1997. Michaels still owns the bike!"

"Can you fax it to us?"

"It's on its way. Do you still need that bond?"

"No. We can go with this. We'll set this thing up for Tuesday, around 11:00 P.M. You said that he works Tuesday, right?"

"Yes, Tuesday."

"Ok, we'll make the seizure on Tuesday. Let me talk to Stan. We'll be in touch."

L. Seize the Guzzi

Here we were again, Act II of the seizure. It was Tuesday and we were set up for the seizure of the motorcycle at 11:00 P.M. And again, everything had to go exactly right. Midnite had to still be working at the bar. He had to own the motorcycle. He had to come to work with the motorcycle and park it in its usual place in front of the bar as before. And the weather had to cooperate. If it rained, maybe he wouldn't take the motorcycle to work. And what if, heaven forbid, Midnite had an accident and wrecked the Guzzi? There would be no way to collect. Also, the Sheriff and the Deputy had to be there, and of course, there had to be enough money in the City's precious overtime budget to pull it all off.

Cycle O. G. Towing wasn't available that night, they were booked solid and had no more storage room. I had to contract with another towing and storage company. I really wanted Cycle O. G. to do it, but luckily, I was able to find another company, City Boys Towing. I could only hope that they were as reliable as Cycle O. G. I spoke with the night duty clerk at City Boys to confirm that they would be ready to do the pick-up, and they said that they were ready and waiting.

And what voodoo black magic from the land of Trinidad might possess the alien to perhaps make him sleep for another couple of hours, thereby exhausting the City's overtime budget and putting an end to the seizure?

And then there was stupid me. Why did I make that call to Solarz, the other owner of the Guzzi. Surely he had called

Midnite and warned him that maybe something was about to happen, but then again, maybe not. Perhaps he believed himself to be the true owner with the Illinois title. The Guzzi would be safe and secure from seizure!

I wanted to go to the scene of the action and witness the spectacle first hand, but if there were a communications block like the other time, I'd be needed at home manning the telephone and coordinating the whole thing. This Midnite was a slick character. Too many things had to happen. Surely the mission would be doomed to failure. I couldn't worry about any of this. I could only wait it out until 11:00 P.M. to see what would happen. I tuned in Channel 5, Fox News and waited. If there were any action at the Ace Bar, Fox News would have it. At 10:15 P.M., the phone rang.

"Stan Abrams here. What kind of Moto Guzzi bike is that?"

The idiots! They were supposed to have had all this information! Why were they asking me now?

"I don't know. I didn't see a model name on it when I saw it."

"Was it the California model, like the Harley?"

"Well ... eh ..."

"You don't know bikes?"

"Well, it's a Moto Guzzi. It looks brand new, shiny. It's got a windshield, and it's big, with black leather seats. Its color is black and white ..."

"Like cream color on the gas tank?"

"Yeah!"

"We're gonna check something out. We'll call you back."

Check something out? Call me back? Check what out?

I went back to Fox News. There was something about

Whitewater, Bill Clinton and Paula Jones, the latest update on Roe vs. Wade, a new cure for AIDS, but there was nothing from the Ace Bar, and there were no more phone calls. What the hell was going on? I continued to listen to Fox News.

"Sadam Hussein has again defied the United Nations weapons team in its efforts to uncover suspected chemical or biological ... biological weapons ... biological weapons of mass destruction ... weapons ... mass destruction... weapons ...

"We have to interrupt our regular news program. We have a late breaking development. A major disturbance has just broken out at a bar on East 5th Street in Manhattan's East Village. Sounds of gunshot fire have been heard by area residents. The NYPD is on the scene and have blocked off the area between Avenue A and Avenue B. There are reports that an attempted motor vehicle seizure by a NYC Sheriff and his Deputy had sparked the incident leading to a confrontation with a dangerous alien from Trinidad, and an as yet unidentified man from Illinois. Stay tuned to Fox News for the latest developments."

And inside the bar lay the bloody carnage of three City lawyers. An unidentified Illinois resident took refuge behind the bar. The lawyers were apparently working late on overtime at their office at the New York City Department of Finance. They were working on a strange and difficult case involving the acceptance of a $25,000 cash bond that was mysteriously found on a desk at the Department of Finance in a paper bag containing twenty-five thousand one dollar bills. There was concern *that the case would not be completed due to the limited funds available in the City's overtime budget. The lawyers had stopped into the bar for a few cocktails and a late night supper after their hard work.*

A fourth lawyer, badly wounded, was slumped over the bar. He apparently worked at the NYC Sheriff's Office and was working on another difficult case involving the question of ownership of a Moto Guzzi motorcycle with two separate titles and two separate owners - one from New York, and one from Illinois.

A NYC Sheriff and his Deputy, in full uniform and with guns drawn, attempted to restore order and complete their mission in accordance with their sworn public duty to carry out the orders of the court. The judgment must be satisfied at any cost!

Suddenly, a shot rang out from behind the bar. The Sheriff took a hit and dropped to the floor. Instantly, and from out of nowhere, an alien appeared swinging on a rope from a tiffany chandelier. He wore a black cape and was dressed completely in black, except for the long white bandana tied to his head. He held, clenched between his teeth, a steak knife. He landed on top of the bar with supernatural agility. The Deputy took a stab to the chest, but still managed to get off three well aimed shots before he too dropped to the floor. The alien, with the tail of his bandana flying behind, ran for his life to the front door. Although bleeding profusely, it was as if he were somehow propelled by the supernatural energy force within the fabric of the bandana.

If he could just make it outside, descend the three steps, and hop onto the Guzzi; if he could only break through the police barriers; if he could just whip through

Delancey Street, and tear up the Williamsburg Bridge, he would be home free! But the motorcycle wasn't there. The alien stood still, defeated, helpless, and bleeding. The bandana hung lifelessly in a pool of blood. The Guzzi was gone!

Fox News had just issued another release:

"There's been another development related to tonight's shootout in the East Village. A flatbed truck carrying a Moto Guzzi motorcycle and heading east on the Long Island Expressway has been stopped at exit 58 by Suffolk County police. Its destination could not immediately be determined, but it is known that the judgment creditor in the case also resides on eastern Long Island. The driver, an employee of City Boys Towing Company of Manhattan is being held for questioning ..."

Fortunately, before they questioned the driver, the phone rang, piercing through the endless drone of the TV set. It was 11:29 P.M. I staggered to the phone still half asleep, dazed, and confused in reverie.

"Hello."

"Stan Abrams here. We have the bike."

"WHAT?!!"

"We have the bike."

It should have been mission accomplished, but the Sheriff's voice sounded down and tired. Something was wrong.

"He claims that the bike was sold in March. I guarantee he'll be in our office tomorrow morning to present whatever evidence he has to show that the bike was sold - a bill of sale, a title record ... You may have to get an attorney to sort this all out. If he can present evidence, we may have to release the bike to him. It may be that he never turned in his plate, so the DMV title record still shows him as the titled owner."

"But there's a Restraining Notice in effect! And it's good for the life of the judgment!"

"I know. I know, but that may not affect a third party claim from this Solarz guy. If Solarz bought the bike in good faith, unaware of the judgment or the restraint, he may have legal title. Oh ... Solarz's girlfriend is living in New York. She may somehow also be on the title... Look, it's late. Tomorrow is another day. We'll talk some more. We'll see what happens."

"Ok, thanks Sheriff. Thanks for everything."

Deputy Schatzer called me later that night. It was well after 1:00 A.M.

"Cohen! It's Schatzer."

"Hi Deputy Schatzer. Congratulations! I hear we pulled it off!"

"Yeah! We did it!"

"Stan is telling me that you may have to give it back to him."

"Well, tomorrow we'll show all our evidence to the City's lawyers and they'll decide who owns the bike."

"How did it all go tonight?"

"Well, it was pretty ugly, but we'll talk more tomorrow."

"How did Neville react when you seized the bike?"

"Neville? Neville is in a state of shock!"

"Couldn't believe it, huh? Let him stay in shock!"

"You know, those bozos at City Boys were completely

useless. They didn't know anything. They even asked <u>me</u> for money!"

"They were already paid! I paid them!"

"Well … it's very late and we're really tired. Stan still has to make it out to the Island. He'll be lucky to get an hour of sleep. Look … we'll talk tomorrow, ok? Call me. Be well!"

"Thanks for everything, Steve. Nice work!"

LI. Guzzi Blues

It started out as just another day at the office. I was finishing up the end-of-the-month reports to be faxed over to the main office. The numbers were right, I had the back up paperwork to support it, my reports were always neat, detailed, clean, and accurate - they'd love it. But all I really cared about was the Guzzi - my Guzzi! I worked long and hard for it, and now it was almost mine. Well, not quite yet, but almost. I would be hearing from the Deputy that morning, but it was now after 10:00 A.M. What was going on in the Sheriff's Office? Did the opposition have evidence of ownership? Did they have lawyers?

I could only imagine how many lawyers there were now at the Sheriff's Office: Midnite's lawyers vs. the City's lawyers, Solarz's lawyers vs. the City's lawyers, or even Solarz's lawyers vs. Midnite's lawyers! Or was the Ace Bar damaged during the seizure? Ace Bar lawyers vs. the City's lawyers? Yes! I could see it all happening. Armies of lawyers engaged in an unholy orgy of escalating arguing, debating, yelling and screaming, jumping up and down, and finally driving themselves into a climactic frenzy of proof and presentation to see who would ultimately claim final possession of, and title to the Moto Guzzi motorcycle!

I collected up my reports and started to walk to the fax machine when the phone rang. I was sure that it was the Deputy, and it was.

"DCMC Long Island - Cohen."

"Cohen - Schatzer, Schatzer - Cohen. I'm you, you're me. Neville - Solarz, Solarz - Neville ... Who knows who's who? Look, the bike is his!"

"HIS? Not mine?"

"Yeah, his. Neville is the titled owner, not Solarz."

And as pangs of fear and hopelessness turned into whatever hormones joy is made of, the Deputy continued on with his good news report.

"We can take it."

"Oh! So the seizure is final? I mean … you don't have to give it back to him?"

"No. I'd say it looks very good for you."

"FANTASTIC! GREAT!"

"Now things can still happen, but it looks good."

"Did they show up at the Sheriff's Office this morning … to prove their case?"

"Nah, nobody showed up. There is no case! The bike is his."

"And the bike is in the warehouse now?"

"Right, and we'll be contacting you in a few days about the auction."

"Do we have to send it to auction? I mean, can I accept the motorcycle as satisfaction of the judgment instead of cash?"

"No. It has to be cash. You can go to the auction though, and you can bid on it. I can't, but you can. That Guzzi is a nice piece of machinery. It'll fetch a few bucks; that is, if those idiots at City Boys didn't mess it up too much."

The Deputy didn't seem to be in too much of a hurry. The night before, the night of the seizure must have been quite an ordeal, so they were taking it easy that morning. Now would be a good time to ask. And so, now oozing with curiosity, I asked the question.

"Tell me, Steve - how did it go last night?"

"Well … it was pretty ugly. Pretty bad."

Bad? Ugly? How bad and ugly could it be if they got the bike? What happened? The Deputy continued on with his account of the events.

"Who are these bozos at City Boys? Where did you find them? The driver didn't know what he was supposed to do, he couldn't operate the equipment, he didn't know where to take the bike, and on top of all that, he wanted to get paid! Did you make arrangements with these guys so they would know exactly what this is all about and what they were supposed to do?"

"Yeah, sure. I spoke with Rhoda over there. I told her exactly what they were supposed to do … and of course, I paid them."

"Well … anyway, here's what happened. The bike was parked on the sidewalk. I was put into the very awkward position of having to ask Neville to help me take it off the sidewalk and put it on the street so that we could roll it up the ramp, and load it onto the flatbed. And so, in as nice a way as I could, I asked him."

"AND HE HELPED?"

"Yeah! Can you believe it?"

"Do you guys wear uniforms? Carry guns?"

"Oh, sure!"

"Tan uniforms?"

"No, dark blue, like the NYPD, but the arm shields are different."

"Wow! … How'd the seizure go?"

"Well, here's what we did. When we went into the bar, Neville was there sitting at the bar and eating a hamburger. Stan came into the bar first and sat down next to him at his

325

right. About a half of a minute later, I came in and sat down at his left. We moved very slowly, very casually, and we didn't say anything. And then, with Neville still seated between the two of us, the hamburger that he was eating suddenly fell out of the bun and rolled all the way down the bar! I guess we shook him up a little."

"YEAH! He must have been scared shitless!"

"Then we asked him about the bike. He said that he sold it in March, but he didn't have any papers - no insurance, no registration - nothing."

"Could you ticket him for that ... and for parking on the sidewalk?"

"Sure, but we didn't want to antagonize him and make the situation any worse than it already was. Anyway, I said to him, 'Come on, Neville. We know that this is your bike.' ... You wouldn't believe how many friends he's got at that bar - the whole Neville fan club is there. One girl came over to us and told us that it was her boyfriend's bike and not his. ... Nice place though, The Ace. Very quaint, old lunch boxes in a showcase, tiffany lamps ... and that neighborhood! A regular freak show! People walking around without their shirts, one guy walking around in pajama bottoms ..."

"Eh ... any violence?"

"The only violence is being saved up for you!"

"What?!"

"No, but seriously, the people there were pretty calm and cooperative. You know, everybody feels sorry for this guy. Even Stan was beginning to have second thoughts."

"The Sheriff!?"

"With me, it's just a job."

"Well, I don't feel sorry for him, not anymore. I've been

chasing this guy for six years. I lose him, I find him, I lose him, I find him. I pay Marshals, Sheriffs, court fees, process servers, towing companies ... I've chased him through the gutters and sewers of Brooklyn, Queens, Manhattan, ... in and out of Landlord-Tenant Court, Small Claims Court, Special Term Part II ... I lose days at work, I lose time, I lose sleep, and I lose money. I gave this homeless bastard a nice, cheap place to live, and he wound up living there for free, for five months, and yet, I'm the 'bad guy.' You know, everybody feels sorry for this guy - witnesses, judges, and now you tell me even the Sheriff! And he has friends, lots of friends, everybody likes him, but what about me? What about the guy who got screwed? I'm the American citizen - he's the alien! What about the guy who lost money? What about the guy who played by the rules. What about the judgment creditor - the guy who went to court and won? WHAT ABOUT ME?!"

I didn't mean to let it all out on the Deputy. I guess it was the Sheriff of all people feeling sorry for him that triggered it. But the Deputy responded directly to my rhetorical tirade of six years of pent up frustration.

"Well, if somebody is right, if he won a judgment, he should be paid. If he's right, he's right. Let all those people who feel sorry for him chip in and pay the judgment ... Look, I gotta run."

"Oh, Steve, if it's ok ... I mean if it's not against regulations or anything - and if the bike gets sold at auction - I'll buy you a beer ... and lunch too, at the Ace! Ok?"

"Well, I'm not looking for anything. We'll see. We'll be in touch about the auction. Take care, and be well."

"Thanks for everything, Steve. Nice job!"

Things were going too well, much too well. The Guzzi

was in storage at City Boys, under the care and direction of the Sheriff. The details of the auction were in progress. And now, my six year sublet misadventure was coming to a close. But what if anything was the opposition doing? I didn't know about Solarz, but Midnite would never abandon the only thing that he had ever owned in his life. What was going on? What was happening? And what late night telephone conversation might have taken place between the cities of New York and Chicago? ...

"Hello Martin? It's Midnite."

"Midnite? Neville, do you have any idea what time it is? It's after 2:00 A.M., Chicago time."

"I know, I know. How are you mun?"

"HOW AM I? Neville, what the hell is going on?"

"Well ... we been having leetle beet of a problem here, and ..."

"OH NO! YOU WRECKED THE BIKE!"

"No, no, no. Dee bike eez fine, mun ... and we goin' to get eet back. Trust me."

"What?!"

"Well, some yars back, I went and rented meself dees apartment, you see, an illegal sublet. Den dee landlo'd, and also dee guy I rented eet from wanted to keek me dee hell out. So I sez to meself, 'Neville, you ain't payin' nothin' to nobody.' And you know what, I got evicted, and sued, and den dey even arrested me! Can you imagine? And den dey found out about dee motorcycle and den dee Sheriff ..."

"AND THE SHERIFF SEIZED THE GUZZI? NEVILLE, YOU IDIOT! WHY DO I BOTHER WITH YOU? I'LL BE ON THE NEXT FLIGHT TO NEW

*YORK TO PERSONALLY BREAK YOUR LITTLE
BLACK ASS INTO A THOUSAND PIECES. WHEN I
GET DONE WITH YOU, YOU'LL NEVER RIDE
ANOTHER BIKE AGAIN! YOU WON'T EVEN BE
ABLE TO RIDE THE SUBWAY!!"*

*"Martin, pleeze! Try to relax yourself, mun. We're
goin' to get eet back. Trust me, mun. You know, I have
dee connections. I can do eet. Just trust me, mun. Ok?"*

It was already the beginning of July when Deputy
Schatzer finally got back to me, but it wasn't about the
auction.

"Just wanted to bring you up to date. Your buddy's got
himself a lawyer and she's on my back hot and heavy over
this thing. She wants to take a look at our files, and she's
ready to make trouble. Look, you're going to have to do
something about this! You're going to have to do something
fast! We may have to give the bike back to him ... Oh, and
we're going to need that bond ..."

LII. Bonded

It was now becoming clear that with a lawyer on the side of the debtor, my situation was becoming very precarious, to say the least. Should the judgment creditor have a lawyer to do battle with the lawyer for the judgment debtor? The cost would be prohibitive. No, not yet. But how was the debtor able to afford a lawyer?

And there was also the matter of the bond. If I didn't get the bond, or find some way to get the cash into the court, or the Sheriff's Office, or to wherever else it was supposed to go, the Sheriff would be forced to release the motorcycle to the debtor.

I continued my telephone conversation that morning with Deputy Schatzer. He wanted to know more about the Restraining Order.

"What's the date on that Restraining Order?"

"It was served back in April, 1994 ... BUT IT'S STILL GOOD!"

"Well, she's saying that assets coming into the possession of the judgment debtor after service of the Restraining Notice is exempt from restraint."

"NO! That's simply incorrect! It says in the CPLR, in Section 5222(b):

'This notice also covers all property, which may in the future come into your possession or custody, in which the judgment debtor has an interest ...'"

"Well, we'll have to run it by the lawyers. We may have to give the bike back. You're really going to have to do something ... and fast!"

"Wait! Ok, ok! ... She? That's the lawyer?"

"Yeah."

"And is she representing Neville or Solarz?"

"Neville."

"Even though he supposedly doesn't even own the bike anymore! If it doesn't belong to him, then let the other guy get a lawyer. Who is this lawyer anyway? What's her name?"

"Lorraine Callucci."

"Is she local?"

"Yeah."

"A free lawyer? Pro Bono?"

"Who knows? Probably ... a typical liberal do-gooder on the Lower East Side. She has her office on Ludlow Street... Look, she's trouble. You better start doing something fast!"

I wasn't just sitting on my hands. I related to the Deputy my latest legal strategy, the "next step."

"Well, here's what I did. I was in court yesterday, and I took out contempt papers on him for violation of the Restraining Order - transferring the motorcycle to this guy in Illinois."

"Good! You did it! Good!"

The Deputy's initial disappointment with the unfolding of events had turned to hope, encouragement, and even mild elation. The judgment creditor was fighting back! The seizure wasn't for nothing. With Schatzer, it wasn't "just a job," as he put it. Enforcement of the judgment of the court had meaning. I continued to explain my new legal offense to the Deputy.

"Now, a judge has to sign the Order to Show Cause and I have to call back tomorrow. The clerk took it, so I don't expect that there will be any problems with it."

"Good!"

"And then there'll be a hearing ..."

"With him?"

"Yeah."

"Ok, I'm glad to see that you're following this up."

"Do you still need that bond?"

"Yes!"

"Ok, ok, I'm working on it. Did you call that bonding company that the Sheriff suggested? Blaike, I think. You were supposed to call Annette at Blaike?"

"No. Stan's away today, so we have a reprieve. It'll buy us a few days before we have to release the bike. But I've got this lawyer on my back and she's getting to be a real nuisance. She wants to see our files. NO WAY! They're not public domain. It becomes public domain only after the case is completed."

"Ok, we'll work on getting the bond ... Now getting back to this contempt thing, when the judge signs the papers, I'll have to get them served. Do you guys do that?"

"Yeah, sure ... and we're cheap too! Twenty-seven bucks."

"Twenty-seven dollars? You mean I get the uniform, the guns, and everything else for my twenty-seven dollars?"

"Yup."

Midnite wasn't finished with me yet. He was about to get yet another visit from an armed and uniformed Sheriff's Deputy, and all for only twenty-seven bucks. And then there would be another hearing in Civil Court, Special Term Part II back in Queens, the scene of the arrest.

And while I was gaining new hope and confidence in my case, I saw my newly formed process service business going down the drain. How could little me possibly compete with a NYC Sheriff? They blew me away on price, to say nothing of the guns and uniform. I had to ask the question.

"Well, why would anyone use a private professional process server?"

"They're just assholes, I guess."

I admired the Deputy for his bluntness and honesty, but of course, there was more to it. A Sheriff or Deputy might be tied up with a case, have to make court appearances, meet with lawyers, or take care of any number of law enforcement efforts, with resulting long delays. But to help a client with certain types of situations, perhaps even one like mine, yes, they would serve. The Deputy went on.

"… and the word of a Deputy Sheriff would hold more credibility in court than that of a so called professional process server where too often, you might just get 'sewer service.'"

The Deputy found it necessary to add quickly,

"Not you, of course …"

"Steve, do you know how I got into this business? This case! Him! I figured why should it be only me paying process servers? I could serve papers for others and get paid. At the start of this fiasco, I knew nothing. Now I'm an expert in this and all legal matters. But you know something, as I learned, he learned. We're both experts …"

"Look, we'll be talking, ok? I'll talk to Stan, and you see what you can do to get going on the bond. Will you be in today?"

Maybe the Deputy thought that I would be out running papers all day, but there was no business.

"Yeah, I'll be in most of the day, and thanks for your help, Steve. We'll be in touch."

Late that afternoon, I cut out early from work to pick up my contempt papers at Special Term Part II in Queens. Yes, the paper was signed by a judge, but my request for night hours service was completely ignored. I tried to explain to the clerk that the debtor slept all day and worked at night starting after 11:00 P.M. In order for a successful service to occur, it would have to take place at the bar, and at night. Personal service was required, and written by the judge on the contempt paper was "In Hand." The papers had to be placed in his hand. I was dealing with the impossible. The pro se receives no respect. Perhaps a lawyer could have done better. Images of the Deputy Sheriff in full uniform with guns and bullets, and an Order to Show Cause began to fade. The clerk would only shrug. I pleaded.

"But the debtor works at night! Why can't I have him served at night? Wouldn't that be ok?"

"Probably not."

I thanked the clerk and left. Thanking the clerk does not entail any additional fee. Defeated, I mailed a copy of the Contempt Order to the Sheriff's Office, together with my check for $27.00, hoping that it would somehow happen.

The next day, and now working against time, I went to work at getting the bond. I called several bonding companies that I found in the Yellow Pages. Most of them didn't know what I was talking about, or they just didn't deal with that type of bond. All the others only dealt with lawyers. There is no justice for the pro se plaintiff. Unless I got the bond, or got cash into the court, I would lose the motorcycle, and still be stuck with the expenses. Against my better instincts, but without any viable alternatives, I called

Small Claims and explained about the seizure, and the need for a bond. The response was as expected.

"We don't do that here."

"Let me speak to the supervisor, please."

It was Mr. Halsey, the same person who had hung up on me before. Of course he remembered. How many people want to pay $25,000 into the court? As politely and respectfully as I could manage it, I asked him what to do.

"Please, I need your kind cooperation on this matter. How can I possibly get $25,000 into the court?"

"Well, I don't know. You're probably going to have to file a motion."

"And how do I go about doing that?"

"Sir, you're going to have to get a lawyer. I'm not even sure this court is equipped to handle it. You may have to go to Supreme Court with this."

"Supreme Court?! This is supposed to be Small Claims."

"Sir, if these debates are going to continue, I'm going to have to hang up."

"Look, I'm not getting a lawyer so that I can give you money, and I'm not going to Supreme Court!"

"Click."

In just a matter of days, the motorcycle would be released and I was getting nowhere. Then I remembered my friend Jerry from the *shul*. There was some justice in this world. Jerry was a lawyer, but I wasn't sure exactly what kind of a lawyer Jerry was. I think he did matrimonial stuff, among other things, but he knew the basics. Yes, Jerry would help. Here was a pro bono lawyer for the judgment creditor. I had spoken to him previously about the case, and he knew all about the motorcycle and the seizure. I was proud of my work, but now my fax must have landed in his office like a bomb.

"Jerry - URGENT!!! They want to release the motorcycle. PLEASE HELP!"

Jerry called back and suggested that I serve the Sheriff with a Restraining Order.

"SERVE THE SHERIFF!?"

"Yes, that will at least give us more time to get the bond."

I didn't like the idea of serving the Sheriff with a Restraining Order. I knew it was just legal papers and nothing personal. Maybe it would have worked. I didn't know. I'd have to write it up, have it signed by a judge, have it served ...

"Jerry, these guys have gone all out for me. I don't know if we should do that. Besides, it might take too long. If I could just find a way to get money into the court, or get a bond ... These bonding companies only deal with lawyers, no pro se."

"Use my name, but of course, the bonding company will still have to agree to the undertaking."

The solution was simple, and the problem immediately solved. So now, thanks to the good lawyer, hopefully there wouldn't be any trouble with getting the bond. Still, there would be no guarantee on its approval.

I asked Jerry about posting a cash undertaking, and I told him of the trouble that I had with the Small Claims clerk. He said that the clerk might have been right about that. It might have to be done in Supreme Court after all. He said that Small Claims was a court of very limited facilities, but I could try. I typed up the Motion to Post a Cash Undertaking on the computer. It was neat and it looked perfect. I had it notarized and mailed it in. And while I was at it, I also typed up my own personal bond. It was stunningly beautiful and read as follows:

KNOW ALL MEN BY THESE PRESENTS:

That Jonah Cohen, a resident of the State of New York, herein called the principal, is held and is firmly bound unto the Office of the Sheriff of the City of New York, hereinafter called the Obligee, in the sum of twenty-five thousand and 00/100 dollars for the payment whereof to the Obligee ...

Whatever it took! Nobody was giving back the Guzzi! The Sheriff called me the next day. He had spoken to Annette at Blaike about the bond. I would be receiving forms shortly, and as long as I would cooperate with them in getting the bond, the Guzzi would be safe. I told them that I would be using my lawyer friend's name and that it shouldn't be a problem. It turned out that the fee to the bonding company was only two percent of the bond value or five hundred dollars. Not too bad, but if I could get money into the Small Claims Court, I would be able to save the bond fee. Anyway, I received the forms, filled them out, mailed it with my check for $500.00, and waited anxiously for the bond application to be approved.

My Motion to Post a Cash Undertaking with the court unfortunately came back in the mail. Irreverently scribbled at the bottom of this work of art was the following message:

"Incorrect Form ... See CPLR ..."

I called Small Claims for the last time. It was Mr.

Halsey, the supervisor who answered. I pleaded,

"What's wrong with the Motion?"

"It's not in accordance with the CPLR. Look, I refuse to continue these debates, and I'm going to ..."

"No, no, no! Please don't hang up. Just tell me what's wrong with it. All I'm trying to do is deposit $25,000 into the court."

"If you want to deposit the cash, if you want to try dumping $25,000 at the cashier's window, then go ahead."

"Would it work?"

"Probably not."

"Let me speak to the Chief Clerk ... or maybe the cashier."

"Click."

My frustrations with Small Claims were somewhat alleviated by the call that soon came back from the bonding company.

"Mr. Cohen?"

"Yes?"

"It's Annette from Blaike. Your bond is approved."

LIII. Service on the Server

It was a hot, humid night in July. I had just returned home from Brooklyn where I was finishing up on some long delayed dental work. My uncle-dentist had put a gold crown an a third molar. It was truly a work of art, even more so than my Motion to Post a Cash Undertaking. It was a quiet night. The sound of the traffic had died down. There was a gentle breeze blowing and a slight rustling of the trees. I opened the front door and lit the porch lights. A few minutes later, there was a gentle knock at the front screened storm door. It was a neatly dressed, young black man. It was 9:50 P.M.

"Jonah Cohen?"

"Yes."

"Court papers. You are hereby served."

As I nervously read the papers, the process server disappeared into the night darkness. It was an Order to Show Cause with an Affidavit in Support of a Motion for Preliminary Injunction. There would be a hearing at the Supreme Court, County of New York. The plaintiff was Neville Michaels. The defendants were the Sheriff of the City of New York, and Jonah Cohen.

The process server might have been waiting for me for hours. After 10:00 P.M., the service might have been deemed invalid, only another ten minutes! If only the dental work could have taken ten minutes longer, if only I could have hit some heavy traffic, or if only I could have stopped off somewhere for a six-pack of beer, but such was not the case.

And so, the server had been served, the plaintiff was the defendant, the defendant had become the plaintiff, and we were all on for July 25th.

LIV. Preliminary Injunction

Supreme Court was out of my league. This was strictly lawyer stuff. It looked like I would have to get a lawyer for this, but first I sat down and slowly began to read the papers with which I had just been served. It read:

"The Sherriff of the City of New York and Jonah Cohen,"

in that order.

I had immediately noticed that Ms. Callucci, the attorney for the plaintiff had misspelled "sheriff." Apparently, the lawyer had far less experience with sheriffs than I had. I thought it was a good sign. And although nervous, I continued to read the Order to Show Cause with some amusement.

"On the annexed affidavit of Neville M. Michaels ..."

AFFIDAVIT? HA! He even swore to it! I continued to read.

"Ordered that the defendants above named or their attorneys show cause at a motion term room to be held at the county courthouse of New York County, in the City of New York ... why an order should not be entered to restrain the sheriff from the sale of the Motoguzzi motorcycle registered in the name of Martin T. Solarz ..."

Ms. Callucci had also misspelled Moto Guzzi.

Obviously, she didn't know any more about bikes than she knew about sheriffs. I finished reading the Order to Show Cause.

"... and to prevent all acts and proceedings on behalf of the sheriff's department to dispose of the motorcycle, pending a hearing and determination on the title of the motorcycle."

There was also a Notice of Motion. It was carelessly made up, containing several blank spaces, and it was unsigned. How do they get away with this stuff? My neatly typed, complete, and professional looking Motion got rejected in Small Claims, and now this! Handwritten in the lower left hand corner were place of service addresses. They were the addresses of the Office of the Sheriff, Corporation Council, and me. The Corporation Council was the entire battery of New York City government lawyers. And finally, there was Midnite's sworn, notarized affidavit.

I read Midnite's affidavit with even more amusement. It was really quite entertaining.

SUPREME COURT STATE OF NEW YORK
COUNTY OF NEW YORK
---*x*

| *Neville M. Michaels, plaintiff* | **Affidavit** |
| *vs.* | **Index No. 9999 97** |

The Sheriff of the City of New York
and Jonah Cohen, defendants
---*x*

STATE OF NEW YORK
COUNTY OF NEW YORK   ss.:

Neville M. Michaels, being duly sworn, deposes and says:

1)   That he is the plaintiff in this action and makes this affidavit in support of its application for a preliminary injunction, pursuant to CPLR Article 63.

2)   That he has standing to pursue the application because he was holding the motorcycle for the titled owner, Martin Solarz, who expected delivery ...

The affidavit went on at great length. Apparently, Martin had purchased the Guzzi on March 21, 1997 and Neville was merely holding it for him, which of course explains why Neville titled the bike in his own name, and not in the name of the alleged owner. If I could have gotten the Sheriff and the Small Claims Court to move faster on the property execution, or if the original execution hadn't gotten lost, or if I could have checked out the bar sooner, maybe we could have beaten the alleged sale of the bike to Solarz, and then the Guzzi would have been sold at the Sheriff's auction without a problem. Anyway, we were now in Supreme Court. Supreme Court, of course, is not the highest court in New York State - the Court of Appeals is - but for me it was pretty big - gargantuan, in fact, when compared to Small Claims.

I continued to read Neville's fabricated affidavit. He claimed that he was never served with a Restraining Notice. He must have forgotten that he was fined and arrested for contempt for failure to comply with the Information Subpoena and Restraining Notice. I remembered when he was led away, handcuffed, under the escort of a Deputy Sheriff, into a private room, before the hearing took place. He had claimed that he was never served with the second judgment, which was the default judgment, the one used to seize the bike. But a defendant is not *served* with a judgment - he gets it in the mail. Ms. Callucci must have been as confused between summonses and judgments, as she was confused between Sherriffs and Sheriffs, as well as Motoguzzis and Moto Guzzis. Anyway, Midnite was always on the move, and he never had his mail forwarded. Why should he want bills and summonses forwarded? So, maybe he never really did get it, which didn't mean anything anyway. And Midnite never really did understand about the default judgment. Even though it had a different index number, different dates, different amounts, and a claim for a different time period, he thought it was a duplicate of the trail judgment.

I laughed as I finished reading the affidavit.

That the sale of the subject matter will cause irreparable harm and damage, because of the custom nature of the motor vehicle and its unique character, and that he will be liable to the titled owner of the motorcycle ... for the replacement cost ... which is indeterminable, given the custom nature ...

Did Midnite ever worry about being liable for his rent? Or his judgments? HA! SEND THE DAMNED THING TO AUCTION!

I had to call Deputy Schatzer to see what was happening on their end. Was the Sheriff served? Corporation Counsel -

the City lawyers? And did I need my own lawyer? But it was getting very late. It was already after midnight … that is, I mean it was after 12:00 A.M.

I called the Sheriff's Office at exactly 8:00 A.M. that morning. There was not a minute to lose. I spoke with the Deputy. Yes, the Sheriff of the City of New York had been served, along with Corporation Counsel. It looked big, very big; and I must have sounded nervous, very nervous. The Deputy, a rock of invincibility, listened calmly as I excitedly fired away my questions.

"And the Sheriff was served?"

"Yes."

"And the City lawyers were served?"

"Yes, yes."

"And we're on for the, the … I can't read it. It's illegible on my copy … the 23rd of July, I think. It's all crossed out and scribbled in. It's like she doesn't want me to know when to come. Maybe I should just ignore the papers, like Midnite ignored all my papers …"

"DON'T DO THAT!"

"Ok, the 23rd. Will you be there?"

"Probably. I'll try, but I can't be sure what else I'll have going that day."

"And the City lawyers? Will they be there?"

"Well, I don't know. I'll have to talk to Corporation Counsel to see if they want to be represented. But I'd say yes. There should be some representation."

"Should be? You don't know? What about me? Do I need a lawyer? Am I supposed to go into Supreme Court by myself? They'll destroy me! I can't go in there by myself! SEND LAWYERS! PLEASE SEND SOME LAWYERS!"

"Cohen! Get a hold of yourself! I never heard you talk

like this before. All along it was 'Get the bike! Get the bike no matter what!' Now you're falling apart on me. I thought you were an expert!"

"Yeah! With Small Claims, maybe. But this is Supreme Court! I've never been to Supreme Court!"

"Don't worry about it. You'll do fine. Look, gotta go.

We'll be talking, ok?"

Midnite's case was absurd. The Deputy was right. Maybe I really didn't have anything to worry about. He worked at the bar in the City and he rode the motorcycle to work. He kept it in back of his apartment in Brooklyn, and he held the New York title, current and legal. And there was the coincidence and timing of the transfer which occurred in April, 1997, about the same time as the Sheriff's execution was being prepared. Midnite must somehow have known. Was it via West Indies black magic, a friend and informer at the bar, or was it a screw up on my part? The transfer, at any rate was in clear violation of the Restraining Notice. No, there was nothing to worry about. And best of all, there would most likely be representation by Corporation Counsel - a team of tough City lawyers - the meanest sons-of-bitches the City had to offer - Gotham's worst - and they would all be fighting for me, and for the Guzzi, in the pursuit of justice.

LV. Supreme Court, Part I

The night before the hearing, I made sure to prepare my case to the best of my ability, anticipating the questions that might be asked, and verbalizing the answers out loud. I had, after all, decided to go-it-alone, without hiring my own lawyer. I was assured that the City lawyers would be there. We were all named co-defendants. It was enough. I carefully read through all the papers and meticulously clipped together the two judgments, the very precious Information Subpoena and Restraining Notice upon which my entire case rested, the even more precious Affidavit of Service, the Order to Show Cause to punish the debtor for contempt for non-compliance with the Information Subpoena and Restraining Notice, and finally, the Affidavit of Service of the Order.

I neatly placed all my important papers in a vinyl legal folder, and placed the folder into my new leather portfolio briefcase that I had been given at my retirement. It would perhaps be my lucky briefcase. This was going to be one of the most important days of my life. Protect the Guzzi! Nothing should go wrong.

I arose early the next morning, the day of the hearing. As was my habit on very important occasions, I planned on arriving at my destination at least an hour or two early. It was a little after 10:00 A.M. when I got off the subway at Spring Street. The hearing was scheduled to take place at 11:30 A.M. There was still plenty of time. Not sure exactly where 250 Centre Street was, I walked down Lafayette to the northern end of Centre Street, and then walked down Centre Street. On either side of the street were mostly tenement buildings with stores and small shops below. It wasn't an area where one would be likely to find a courthouse. Where was Supreme Court? It was as if I had entered into a bizarre Kafkaesque universe, where it can be inferred that there is a close association between the Law and Guilt, from which it would follow that Supreme Court would be at any particular path or entrance I might choose. Somewhere near here, I would find my way to *The Trial,* my trial!

I eventually came to number 250, but it wasn't a courthouse. It was a red brick tenement building with a shop on the street level. I stopped, opened up my briefcase, and took out the Notice of Motion. Perhaps I had the wrong address, but the paper said 250 Centre Street. There had to be a mistake. I knew downtown Manhattan well - the courts were much further downtown, but yet I was standing in front of number 250. Perhaps it was the building directly opposite. Here was an impressive looking structure with granite blocks, arched windows, and columns at the front. Two bronze lions on each side of the short granite staircase guarded the entrance. Perhaps this was Supreme Court, or an adjunct to it, but there was no name on the building, and there were no people. This obviously wasn't Supreme Court, and yet it had to be. I ascended the stairs and entered the building. The guard gave me a strange look, and I stupidly had to ask,

"Is this Supreme Court?"

Of course it wasn't! I showed the guard the paper with 250 Centre Street on it. The address was wrong, absolutely and perhaps deliberately wrong. The plaintiff's lawyer had tricked me! So this was Ms. Callucci's legal strategy. Send the pro se idiot on a wild goose chase. Maybe he would get lost, or wouldn't show, or maybe he would come in late, and then they'd get the bike released!

It was already nearing 11:00 A.M. There was still enough time to get to the hearing by 11:30 A.M., but I had to walk quickly. I made it to the Supreme Court by 11:05 A.M. Supreme Court looked like Supreme Court, or at least a temple of Zeus. Anyhow, in big, bold, Roman style letters chiseled in stone read,

"THE TRVE ADMINISTRATION OF JVSTICE IS THE FIRMEST PILLAR OF GOOD GOVERNMENT"

And above the entrance, atop huge, intimidating stairs leading to the entrance where only the boldest of the pro se dare to venture, read, in gold lettering,

"SUPREME COURT"

This was the place! But I wasted another ten minutes at the metal detector, and then I didn't know where to go. I showed the guard my papers, I was directed to a room, waited on line, and then I was asked,

"Where are your papers?"

Of course, I didn't have the right papers. I first had to go to another room on the second floor and wait on line again. It was now 11:16 A.M. Oh, Lorraine! You smart-assed lawyer! Is this the best you can come up with? I agonized as I waited, and as the precious minutes ticked off, the line hardly moved. I studied the people on line as I waited, nearly all of them most likely lawyers engaged in petty, trite, useless conversation, and they were holding up the line.

Come on! Move it!

It came my turn to see the clerk at the window. Was I waiting in the right place? Did they have the case file? Would I again get the strange look? Yes! They had it! The clerk wrote something down on a slip of paper. It was another building.

"Rm. 278, 80 Centre Street."

It was now 11:25 A.M. I didn't wait for the elevator, but ran down the stairs, passed the metal detectors, and with my leather briefcase flying behind, pushed through the revolving doors, propelling them with such force that Zeus's Temple nearly left the firmest pillars of good government, flying straight up to the heavens.

Fortunately, 80 Centre Street was right nearby, and there were no metal detectors. I walked into room 278 at exactly 11:30 A.M., thereby managing to make it through all of Ms. Callucci's mine fields.

The room was filled with litigants and lawyers, plaintiffs and defendants, claimants and respondents, all waiting for their cases to be heard. I scanned all the people in the room. I was sure Neville would be there, and he was. The Spirit of Captain Midnite had once again touched down for landing. He was in fully re-molecularized form, his essence was of physical substance, and his presence was of more or less human form. He was there, and he was real!

He wasn't hard to find. The hairdo was different. The long hair was now done up in braided pig tails. The bandana was also gone. He wore a solid color, dark pull-over shirt, open at the neck. And around the neck he wore a large gold medallion. (Another asset?) He was sitting next to a young, thin woman with thin features and dark hair. It had to be the Solarz girlfriend. And while studying my opposition, I was approached by a young, short, plump woman with shoulder length blond hair and blue eyes. She wore eye glasses with large, round lenses set in a thin plastic frame, perhaps making her look a lot smarter than she really was.

"Mr. Cohen?"

"Yes."

"Lorraine Callucci, Mr. Michaels' attorney."

Mr. Michaels' attorney! It had such a strange and funny ring to it that I had to try hard to keep from laughing. But this was really very serious business. The lawyer extended her hand in greeting. I took an instant dislike to Mr. Michaels' counsel. Nevertheless, I reluctantly reached out, and we shook hands. The hand was clearly a woman's hand. It was warm, soft - and it was also very sweaty. I wiped off the sweat that she had deposited on my hands, onto my pants in disgust. This was the enemy! I was sure she must have been quite surprised to see me there, on time and in the right place, in spite of all her ill found efforts. I continued to scan the room for the other named defendants, the Sheriff's Deputy, and the City lawyers, but they were not there yet.

It wasn't long before the case was called. I followed the plump, sweaty, little Ms. Callucci and the clerk into the judge's chamber, and the hearing began. It was an informal hearing. The only people present in the room were the judge, the lawyer, and the judgment creditor. Introductions began.

"I'm Judge Amanda Grossinger."

The judge then looked at the lawyer.

"Lorraine Callucci, attorney for Mr. Michaels."

And then the judge's eyes turned to me.

"Jonah Cohen, judgment creditor, pro se."

The judge then gave a brief summary as to why we were

there, a description of the Preliminary Injunction that had been started by the debtor, and instructions as to how the hearing would be conducted.

"Mr. Cohen."

"Yes, Your Honor."

"Did you file opposition papers?"   What? Opposition papers? Pangs of fear ripped through my very soul. We hadn't even started yet, and already it was going wrong. Nobody ever said anything about opposition papers.   I thought of all the records that I kept at home, neatly arranged in manila file folders by year beginning in 1991. It now measured over two feet high, each folder being neatly labeled with the year and titled, "Cohen vs. Midnite." Wasn't this enough?   Was I supposed to file yet more papers? I had not yet grasped what was happening, or what I was supposed to do or have done.   But then I remembered the contempt papers that I filed in Queens County Civil Court. Surely these were papers in opposition! Was this what Her Honor was referring to? With confusion and hope, I responded,

"Not in this court!?"

This was not the correct answer. It was only later that I learned that when one is served with papers, one must answer with papers. My answer might have sounded cocky or stupid, but the truth was, without any instructions as to how to proceed, I didn't know what I was supposed to do.

Anyway, where the hell were the damned City lawyers? They should already have been there by then. Didn't they file opposition papers? It looked like I would be on my own again, as usual. Fortunately, the judge was forgiving to the uninitiated and unrepresented lay person.

"Well, Mr. Cohen is not an attorney. Opposition papers

should have been filed, but we'll forgive him. Ms. Callucci, you begin."

And Ms. Callucci certainly did begin. It was a long winded tirade of everything her client had suffered since the time that he had rented the Brooklyn apartment. It began with how he had entered into the lease agreement in good faith, how he was asked to leave after he had moved in, the harassment he received, how he was evicted from his apartment in January, the coldest month, and made homeless, and eventually arrested …

"… for something as ridiculous as an ILLEGAL SUBLET!"

The words echoed off the walls of the small hearing room, rising far above the rumble of the air conditioner. The judge turned angrily to me without speaking. It wasn't easy being a landlord. I felt smaller that Neville's bank account, but responded stoically and without hesitation.

"The case was tried in Small Claims Court and I won. I have two judgments, Your Hon …"

Ms. Callucci's eloquent remarks began even before I could finish addressing Her Honor. The plumb, little lawyer popped up from her seat like a poison mushroom and screamed,

"BULLSHIT!! My client was ARRESTED! He was led away in HANDCUFFS for not paying rent on an ILLEGAL SUBLET!!!"

Ms. Callucci delighted in emphasizing, even screaming the right words. The opening expletive that prefaced her legal argument was readily recognized by the judge, as well as the self-represented judgment creditor. It occurred to me that Blumfield, my closing attorney on the condo, had used the same legal terminology when he remarked,

"That's typical builder's BULLSHIT!"

But now the judge turned to me again.

"Is that what happened, Mr. Cohen?"

"No, Your Honor."

"Please go ahead and tell us what happened."

"Mr. Michaels was arrested for not complying with an Information Subpoena. He was properly served with the subpoena, which he ignored; then he was served with a Show Cause Order for Contempt, which he ignored; and then he was fined, and finally, a warrant was issued for his arrest."

The plump, little Ms. Callucci, now red with obviously elevated blood pressure, continued to scream and fight for her client.

"Your Honor, the warrant was issued against the default judgment. My client didn't know about the default judgment. The default judgment is a duplicate of the trial judgment. THE ARREST WAS IMPROPER! The warrant was issued against a phantom judgment. IT'S THE SAME THING! My client should be entitled to monetary damages for the improper arrest, which occurred without due process of law, violating my client's civil rights, my client's constitutional …"

"Is that true Mr. Cohen?"

"No, Your Honor. They're separate judgments for different rental periods. Mr. Michaels chose not to be present at the second trial, so an inquest was held and I was awarded a default judgment."

The little lawyer wouldn't concede even an inch, and now kept it up with even more fervor than before.

"MY CLIENT was never properly served with a Notice of Claim for either of these judgments. HE NEVER

KNEW!"

It is a standard legal defense to knock down a case right at the beginning, at the service of process. At this point, I tried to explain to the seemingly ignorant lawyer that service of process in Small Claims is by first class mail, and by certified mail, return-receipt-requested. But Ms. Callucci didn't want to hear what I had to say, and apparently, I blundered again by violating courtroom procedure. The response to my correct and honest explanation was,

"WHY ARE YOU TALKING TO ME!?"

But the judge allowed it.

"Ms. Callucci, he can talk to you."

The little lawyer continued, now directing her words to the judge.

"BUT HE NEVER KNEW! I move to dismiss both judgments due to improper service of claims."

And now it was the judge who directed her anger at the lawyer.

"BUT MS. CALLUCCI! HE WAS THERE! I put little value in a default judgment, but there was also a trial judgment. There was a trial! HE WAS THERE! HE WAS THERE!! MS. CALLUCCI, THERE WAS A TRIAL! HE WAS THERE!!"

The tension was broken when the other defendant, the sole representative from Corporation Counsel, representing the Sheriff's Office, entered meekly through the door. He was thirty minutes late. He looked young, much too young to be a lawyer. His beard was not yet fully grown in. He had the slightly nervous, slightly bewildered look of inexperience. His handshake was loose and insincere. He was soft-spoken and barely audible above the hum of the air conditioner, and found it necessary to clear his throat each time before speaking. Was this one of the tough, mean sons-of-bitches from the pack of rabid City lawyers? Was this the best the Sheriff's Office could do? Was this Gotham's worst? Yes, this was Supreme Court, and I was entirely on my own.

"Achem ... achem ... Dan Shimmel, Corporation Counsel. I'm sorry I'm late."

LVI. Supreme Court, Part II

The sole representative from Corporation Counsel quietly took his seat beside me. Mr. Michaels' two named defendants now sat opposite the little but loud Ms. Callucci. After the usual introductions, the Sheriff's lawyer began his opening remarks.

"The Sheriff's Office has no financial interest, or any other interest, in these proceedings. I am here merely as an observer, and to assist in providing any needed information."

Mr. Shimmel would have been completely useless anyway. His opening remarks were unnecessary. As the hearing continued, Ms. Callucci now attempted an alternative argument. It was clear that the burden and the success in the cause of the defense, now rested entirely upon my own shoulders. The attorney for the plaintiff began.

"Your Honor, we have here a judgment awarded in Queens County. The Sheriff's seizure of the *bicycle* occurred in New York County."

Ms. Callucci's discussion of jurisdiction would have sounded silly enough, but she also erred in confusing a monster motorcycle like the Guzzi to a mere child's bicycle. She was apparently trying to demonstrate that the seizure was improper because a judgment from a Queens County court would not have effect in other counties within the City of New York, which of course was ridiculous. The lawyer read from a law book of unknown identity, and which was several inches thick. And as she read on, the judge became first confused, then impatient, and then infuriated.

"MS. CALLUCCI! WHAT HAS THAT TO DO WITH

ANYTHING? QUEENS COUNTY SMALL CLAIMS HAS JURISDICTION OVER THE ENTIRE CITY!!"

And if that were not enough, Her Honor let loose with more.

"Ms. Callucci, I am singularly UNIMPRESSED with this presentation! I am TOTALLY UNIMPRESSED!!"

The plump little lawyer stopped, blushed, and looked up at the judge in bewildered silence. It was the look of defeat, but Ms. Callucci wasn't finished yet. She saved the best for last. It was the question of title. Who really did own the Guzzi, and if it was sold, when? The mystery of the Moto Guzzi's ownership was about to enter into the light of justice. Ms. Callucci attempted to recover and continued.

"Your Honor, the seizure was improper because at the time of the seizure, Mr. Michaels was not the titled owner. Mr. Solarz was the titled owner. Title had been previously transferred to Mr. Solarz."

Ms. Callucci produced the Illinois title, and showed it to the judge who examined it closely and responded,

"Where is the bill of sale?"

But there was no bill of sale. Instead, Ms. Callucci produced an affidavit signed by Mr. Solarz stating that the transfer did indeed take place. In addition, a receipt for twenty-five dollars from the Illinois Department of Motor Vehicles for the transfer of title was presented. The judge continued with her line of questioning.

"Did he pay anything for the motorcycle?"

"Mr. Michaels owed money to Mr. Solarz. So, Mr. Michaels sold Mr. Solarz the motorcycle for the value of the loan."

The strange transaction was confusing and steeped in mystery. Maybe it did happen the way they claimed, or maybe it didn't. It was, however, clearly in violation of the Restraining Notice, and it occurred at about the same time as the sheriff's execution.

"Ms. Callucci, I don't see consideration here. There was no money exchanged. I am not impressed with this affidavit! Should Mr. Solarz receive payment for a debt before Mr. Cohen? Your client has a judgment against him … two judgments. Is that right, Mr. Cohen? Or is this for the same thing as Mr. Michaels and Ms. Callucci claim?"

I was beaming. The chubby little Ms. Callucci was being cut to pieces - her fat flesh an offering on the alter! Her Honor was on my side, and I played my part well. I answered directly and confidently.

"They're two separate items, Your Honor. Two different index numbers. One was a trial and one was an inquest."

"Ms. Callucci, your client has two judgments against him! He has a legal obligation to pay! He must make some attempt to pay …"

It was going well, much too well. The judge had clearly taken up my cause. Ms. Callucci had proved herself to be a highly incompetent attorney. The case for the defense was well presented and documented. I had wished Her Honor would have wrapped it all up right there and had gotten rid of it. Things couldn't have gotten any better; they only could have gotten worse. Her Honor continued on with her speech about debts, judgments, obligations, and legal responsibilities, as the air conditioner compressor cycled on and off several times. The judge now completed her lecture, and it was left to Ms. Callucci to respond, but the little lawyer had run out of material. Nevertheless, she tried again.

"But Your Honor, he was never properly served. He had

no indication ..."

The judge was furious! She grabbed the paper of the trial judgment, and while shaking it violently in the air, she repeated her previous remarks, now nearly shouting.

"But he was there, Ms. Callucci. He was there! There was a trial! Mr. Cohen, did he pay you anything on these judgments?"

"No, Your Honor."

"In over six years, Ms. Callucci, Michaels has made no attempt to pay anything on these judgments ..."

Her Honor went on for at least another three or four cycles of the air conditioner compressor. It continued to go much too well. Oh! If she only would have ended it. I looked at my co-defendant, the lawyer from the Sheriff's Office who hinted a smile, a signal of victory, of complete and total victory. My enemy was crushed. At last, closing remarks were in sight and it was ending.

"... and based on the testimony and the evidence presented before me, and considering the fact that the plaintiff-judgment debtor has chosen not to be present ..."

It was absolutely incredible, but up until this time, nobody had seemed to notice the absence of the plaintiff, the elusive alien, the spirit of Captain Midnite! Ms. Callucci's abrupt interruption was a sharp and simple,

"But he's here!"

"Where?"

"Outside."

"Well, bring him in!"

And, like I said, it was all going much too well. Neville came into the hearing room, somewhat awkwardly and quietly. He was polite and humble before the court, and he took his place directly opposite me, and next to his attorney.

While still standing, he addressed the judge. He still wore the same dark green pull over shirt, ragged and torn as it was, with the medallion around his neck. Even this version of Midnite evoked sympathy, maybe even more than before. He stood quietly, facing Her Honor as she addressed him.

"Mr. Michaels, Ms. Callucci, your attorney, has been fighting valiantly on your behalf, and she has done a very commendable job, but I must say, it does not look good for you..."

Neville's head was slightly lowered. His eyes squinted as if he were suffering real physical pain as the judge spoke. It was like the crack of a master's whip on the bare back of his slave. As the judge finished addressing him, there were a few seconds of silence, but after he had digested the judge's remarks, he took a deep breath and exhaled slowly without saying anything further.

"Do you have anything to say before I rule against the release of the motorcycle and order it to be sold at auction?"

Neville's eyes were slightly red and watery. He sat down, paused, and began his story. He spoke clearly, audibly, and without the West Indies accent. He started at the very beginning with the sublet and how he answered an advertisement in The Voice for an apartment. He continued with how Kravitz and I conspired to evict him shortly after he had moved in. It was the whole messy and sordid sublet ordeal all over again. He continued his story with how he was thrown out of his apartment in January, became homeless ...

"... and I was harassed, and ... and I was arrested because I couldn't pay the rent. And I have been fired from jobs, and I have lost apartments, and now ... and now the motorcycle ..."

I listened to Neville's tale of despair and misfortune with a curious combination of embarrassment and delight. He wasn't after all the streetwise, all-knowing superman that I had once thought him to be. He was flesh and blood with all the usual human frailties, and he had suffered.

"Well, Mr. Michaels, unless you make some attempt to pay these judgments, these things are going to continue to happen to you."

"But Judge, the motorcycle isn't my property. It isn't mine! I was holding it for a friend, Mr. Solarz in Illinois. It was mine, but I sold it to him …"

"When?"

"Back in April. Here's the Illinois certificate of title."

"What do you have to say to that, Mr. Cohen?"

"Your Honor, I have here a certified copy of a New York State Certificate of Title dated June, 1997. Mr. Michaels was and is currently the titled owner of the Moto Guzzi motorcycle. In addition, the attempted transfer of title was in violation of the Restraining Notice."

The judge examined the New York State title, and then shook it in her hand and waved it in the air. And now screaming,

"THIS IS THE DOCUMENT THAT GIVES A NEW YORK CITY SHERIFF THE RIGHT TO SEIZE PROPERTY!! I put no value in the Illinois title! I recognize only the New York State title!"

"But Judge, I never received the Restraining Notice."

Ms. Callucci, awakened from the dead, came back and joined in, and with complete self-assurance and self-righteousness echoed the words of her seemingly more capable client.

"But Your Honor, he never received it!"

At this, the judge called a ten minute recess. We had been going at it for almost an hour and half. Ms. Callucci and the judge went into private conference. Private conference with the judge?!! Is that allowed? There was no way to know what was happening, and I could only fear what behind-the-scene deals might have been made. I was left in the hearing room with the useless Mr. Shimmel, the Sheriff's lawyer, and the plaintiff-judgment debtor, Neville. A very awkward minute or two of silence passed, but it was Neville who spoke first.

"Jonah, you know I wasn't served with the Restraining Notice."

I was enraged. Not only did my arch enemy for the last six years have the nerve, ... no, the *chutzpah* to call me by my first name, as if we were long lost friends, or brothers once again reunited, but he pretended not to know about the Restraining Notice! I immediately snapped back.

"Mr. Cohen to you!"

Neville looked up at the ceiling, paused, and as politely as possible tried again.

"Ok, Mr. Cohen, you know I wasn't served."

I thought back to the events leading up to the service of the Information Subpoena with Restraining Notice. The first service was attempted by certified mail which came back undelivered. I recalled how I had asked my friend John to do the service, how terribly cold it was that night, how he failed at the first attempt and wound up in the hospital with a stomach ulcer, and how he promised to do it again. I told him I needed the Affidavit of Service and that how he served the papers, was his business, and so I got my Affidavit of Service. But then Neville was served again, this time with an Order to Show Cause for Contempt, with all the related papers including the Information Subpoena with the Restraining Notice. I had a professional process server do the service. Unfortunately, it was by conspicuous service, so called "nail-and-mail," not personal. But then, of course there was the arrest! And with the Warrant of Arrest were all the related papers including the Restraining Notice! After the arrest, he was read the questions on the Information Subpoena by a judge. To make a claim that he was never served with the Restraining Notice was absolutely absurd! He had to know! He worked hard at it and he was good. As my frustration grew, I became even more enraged.

"Mr. Michaels! Service of a Restraining Notice is normally done by certified mail, but you don't accept certified mail, and you evade process servers. You move every six months or less, in and out of every rat hole and sewer in New York. You're on the run and you hide. So please, Mr. Michaels, don't tell me that you didn't know about the Restraining Notice!"

Before Neville could respond, the recess ended, and the judge and the plaintiff's attorney took their respective places. The hearing resumed with the judge's line of questioning still centering on the service of the Restraining Notice.

"Mr. Cohen, may I see the Affidavit of Service of the Restraining Notice?"

I reluctantly showed it to Her Honor. It was signed, dated, and notarized, but it was a crudely printed form of extremely poor quality. It was a standard form that I had been given in the Small Claims Court. It had been copied over perhaps thousands of times ... and it only said "Information Subpoena." There was nothing about "Restraining Notice."

"Mr. Cohen, this is an Affidavit of Service for an

Information Subpoena. Where is the Affidavit of Service for the Restraining Notice?"

And as I felt the gentle rumble of the subway below, I could also feel my entire case crumbling faster than the walls at the Battle of Jericho. I had been caught in a technical snag, and I struggled to get out.

"Your Honor, it's the same thing. In Small Claims it's the same form. It's the 'Information Subpoena with Restraining Notice.' It's the same thing, and here's a copy of the one that was served."

Her Honor pretended to puzzle over it, but there was a definite problem with the affidavit. I quickly remembered the "Order to Show Cause for Contempt," which was served with the "Information Subpoena and Restraining Notice," and produced the far more professional looking Affidavit of Service from a professional process service company. Unfortunately, that only said "Order to Show Cause." I was in trouble. Midnite had accomplished the impossible! The Guzzi would be released, and I had to think fast. I glanced over at the still useless Mr. Shimmel from the Sheriff's Office, and then tried again, almost pleading.

"But Your Honor, it's the SAME THING and it's on the same form. It's the SAME FORM! If he got one, then he got the other ..."

"Mr. Cohen, I can't recognize these affidavits ..."

Now I really had to think fast. It was almost over.

"Ok, ok, ... uh, ... May I request an adjournment, ... for the purpose of obtaining the original "Information Subpoena with Restraining Notice," from the Civil Court in Queens? Then we will be able to know the original paper, a copy of which was served on the debtor."

It was Neville's lawyer who answered, almost before I

366

had finished saying the word "debtor."

"But Your Honor, all the court records are here. I HAVE THEM, and IT'S NOT HERE!"

I blushed, I was confused, and it was all out of control. Did a lawyer have the right to walk off with original court papers, selectively, and deliberately losing or destroying whatever might be detrimental to her client's interest? I waited for Her Honor to challenge the lawyer's statement, but there was none. What exactly did Ms. Callucci have, and how did she get it? Perhaps I should have asked to see the papers, but one cannot see what is not there! I looked again toward the useless Mr. Shimmel for help, but none came. He sat smugly with the satisfied smile of a detached and amused spectator. There was certainly no help coming from him, and there was none from the judge. And at this point, I was totally sapped of energy. My mind became incoherent and lost in a hopeless morass of confusion. It was my turn to respond.

"Mr. Cohen?"

The absolute absurdity of the whole matter had a nightmarish quality to it from which I had not yet awakened. Slowly, I began to recover. I needed an adjournment badly, and I needed a response. I needed an answer. I had to think of something fast. The response came.

"Your Honor, may I suggest that I return to the process server who served the Order to Show Cause. It is possible that he would still have the records on file, and then he would be able to complete a new Affidavit of Service proving exactly what was served, namely, the Restraining Notice."

It was a risk. Process servers don't have to keep records for more than two years, and it was now over three years. I couldn't even be sure that this process service company was still in business, or if the individual process server who worked for this company and served the papers, still worked there.

Thankfully, the adjournment was granted. The judge summarized the proceedings of the hearing for the court stenographer.

"... and Mr. Cohen, the judgment creditor, has argued adamantly that the Restraining Notice was served on the debtor, and has cited all the reasons as to why the debtor's asset should not be released. Mr. Michaels and his attorney, Ms. Callucci, have argued with equal force as to why the asset should be released ... We are hereby adjourned for one week."

With a burst of renewed energy, I left the hearing room quickly, embarking on my new mission - get the new affidavit. I wouldn't waste a minute, but I was stopped by a voice from behind.

"Mr. Cohen!"

It was Neville. I looked back, but didn't answer. He stood humbly, and although his head was slightly bowed, he still towered more than six inches above me. He clasped his hands in front of him, and in a soft, but audible voice, politely began his speech.

"Mr. Cohen, I beg you ... please, please! If you have any goodness in your heart ... if you have any compassion in your heart, please ... Can we discuss this? ... Can we ... can we come to some kind of agreement?"

I looked up at Neville. He had the look of despair and desperation. Neville evoked sympathy and pity, but now it was not entirely an act. I had to fight hard against the natural inclinations of my soft heart, and struggle to suppress my compassion, for this too was part of the sublet disaster. I remembered the words of my first subtenant, Peter, when he said,

"Give the guy a break ..."

The horrors and frustrations of the past six years flashed through my mind in seconds. I thought of my landlord Kravitz and his threats, my introduction to Landlord and Tenant Court, the police raid on the Brooklyn apartment, Small Claims Court in Queens, the witnesses, subpoenas, orders, judges, marshals, sheriffs ... and then I thought of my own sorry financial situation when the disaster broke. And now, with the asset, the Moto Guzzi motorcycle, so close to the Sheriff's auction, Neville wanted to come to an agreement.

"I was paying my mortgage and your rent. For over four months, I was paying my mortgage, and your rent! Did you care about me?"

Neville didn't answer immediately, and there was another period of awkward silence before he continued.

"If you had only helped me to find another apartment ..."

We were right at the beginning of the real estate fiasco, and I had remembered every detail much too well. I had foolishly wasted time, money, and energy in my efforts to try to find Neville a place to live, and whenever I did find an apartment, the response always was,

"But I like it here!"

Of course he liked it! It was free! And at this my eyes widened, I was totally enraged, and I breathed hard, but still somehow managed to stay in control, and responded with a simple, but very effective,

"You didn't want the deal, remember?"

Neville backed off. Perhaps he didn't remember, but most likely, he didn't want to remember. I studied my opponent as he continued, all the time struggling to suppress any spark of compassion that might erupt.

"Please … do you have any idea of how many people's lives you've affected? … Do you know?"

No, I didn't know. There was Solarz in Illinois, but I had no idea as to how far the repercussions of the Guzzi seizure actually went. Did Shelly, the girl with the red Camaro have anything to do with it? Or Marciano, his friend from the band? And how Neville was able to buy a motorcycle as expensive as the Moto Guzzi remained a mystery. There had to be others involved, but as to why, how, or who, I could only guess, and I never found out.

Neville was in trouble, but I didn't know how much trouble. He had said at the hearing that he had lost his job, and I believed him. I had called the bar a few days earlier, and I was told that he no longer worked there. Sheriff's raids and motorcycle seizures are bad for business. Maybe he didn't have that many friends at the bar after all. And Neville's landlady had told the process server, the one that I had sent over there with the contempt papers, that he didn't live there anymore. Neville was homeless and jobless, again. With some people, it just repeats. His clothes were ragged and unlaundered, as if he might have been sleeping in them. He emitted the stench of unwashed flesh. Despite his downfall, he was still the enemy. It was my turn to respond.

"Where are you living?"

"With friends …"

He hesitated, and then continued.

"…on South 9th Street."

Neville had made the complete circle. It was the address that he had given to me before the sublet, and before the misadventure began.

"Brooklyn?"

"Yeah."

"What's your number?"

"233-8697"

I fumbled for a pen and then quickly wrote it down on the back of a copy of the Information Subpoena. I had no idea as to what I would do with this information, probably nothing.

"I'll call you. Let me think about it."

"I … I … I'll do what I have to do, but I can't … I just can't let you have that motorcycle."

He left walking quickly down the aisle, shaking his head, and throwing his hands in the air, and repeating,

"I can't let you have it. I'll do whatever I have to …"

This bizarre face-to-face meeting with my six year arch rival was unexpected, and not completely welcome. Why would he want to deal if there were a problem with the affidavit? What did Neville's lawyer discuss with the judge during the recess? And what did Neville mean by,

"I'll do whatever I have to do?"

And so, with Neville's last words still ringing in my head, and with all the pressures of Supreme Court temporarily relieved, I walked quickly to No. 3 Park Row, the address of National Process Servers, the process service company that I used to serve the contempt order on Neville, along with the Information Subpoena and Restraining Notice. It was a good shot that the process server still worked there, or at least could be located. Hopefully, they would still have the records in the file.

I walked down Broadway, passed City Hall, and looked across City Hall Park at the buildings on Park Row. With my eyes scanning excitedly in search of No. 3, I could see No. 17, No. 13, and No. 5. I crossed Broadway for a better look. Where was No. 3? But at the end of Park Row, a building demolishing project was in progress. I watched as the jaws of the huge crane took a bite of bricks, concrete, wood, and whatever else might have been in its way. No! No! This could not be No. 3! But Park Row ended. There were no more buildings. And as reality began to set in, I stared helplessly, watching as the crane's jaws took yet another bite of bricks, wood, and maybe even a certain file cabinet containing court papers with an Information Subpoena and Restraining Notice. I stood motionless for several minutes, staring in hopeless disbelief as my eyes began to well up with tears. I would lose my case ... and the Guzzi.

LVII. Wheels, Deals, and The Roadrunner

I gave a great deal of thought to my situation. It wasn't quite over yet. Even if I had lost the motorcycle in Supreme Court, I would have still had my judgments. The two of them were very much intact, and generating interest at the rate of nine percent simple interest. And my contempt action against Neville in Queens County Civil Court for violation of the Restraining Notice was still very much alive. The contempt action had to do with the transfer of the Moto Guzzi motorcycle. So now, even though the judge at Supreme Court might have ordered the release of the motorcycle, the question of violation of the Restraining Notice would again be debated in Queens. In short, we would do it all over again, but this time in Queens! In fact, we could have actually done it twice - once for each judgment! More Orders to Show Cause! More contempt proceedings! More fines! And more arrests! No, it wasn't quite over yet.

It was true that I might not have had the motorcycle anymore as hostage, and I would have had to find a way to get Midnite served, but at least I wouldn't have had to pay the motorcycle storage charges to City Boys anymore. At $10.00 per day with an uncertain end, the charges were beginning to add up.

I decided that I would seek to bury my opponent in paper. I would have Neville served again with another Information Subpoena and Restraining Notice, this time on the other one of my two judgments. I would give the pro bono Ms. Callucci a full time payless career. I would make

Neville and his lawyer commute out to Queens ... as often as possible. Perhaps I would even be able to subpoena the mysterious Mr. Solarz from Illinois, and have him testify as a witness concerning the illegal transfer of title. It would be hell on earth. No, it really wasn't over yet. The hard part would be getting the elusive Captain Midnite served, and the opportune time to do it would be while he was still here on planet earth, in Supreme Court.

I also thought about the strange disappearance of National Process Servers and the building demolition. Perhaps I had overreacted. Wasn't it possible that the company had simply moved to another location? I tried looking them up in the Yellow Pages. Yes! They were now on Vessey Street. I called them and spoke to the office manager. I explained that I needed a new Affidavit of Service concerning records that were now three years old. She wasn't sure. I would have to speak to Mr. Keller, the owner, who just happened to be away on vacation.

"ON VACATION?!"

"Yes, Sir."

"But ... but this is a very important case, and a great deal of money rests on this affidavit! When will he be back?"

And so now, the fate of my case, and the Moto Guzzi rested on Mr. Keller coming back from vacation - alive, healthy, of sound mind, and on time. He was scheduled to return on Monday. The hearing in Supreme Court would be Wednesday. It was close.

And then there was the matter of obtaining the original Information Subpoena and Restraining Notice from the Civil Court in Queens. If I could have obtained the original Affidavit of Service and the original Information Subpoena and Restraining Notice, and presented it at the hearing which

374

was to take place at Supreme Court, I would have been able to prove that the Restraining Notice was served, and thereby, have the judge rule that the Guzzi be sent to auction.

The question was how does one subpoena court records, assuming that it can be done at all? I was told at Small Claims that I needed a Subpoena Duces Tecum, but that meant subpoenaing another witness to bring the records. And I was told to do it through Supreme Court, but that was wrong. Then I was told first to go to Civil Court, who then told me to go to Supreme Court, who told me that I should get a lawyer.

I eventually found myself in the Pro Se Office of Supreme Court. I didn't know beforehand that Supreme Court had a Pro Se Office, but they did. It was my kind of place - no lawyers. I happened to be first on line and I was immediately directed to a young Chinese-American law clerk with bright penetrating eyes, and a quick mind. The young law clerk listened to my story with interest, and proved himself to be quite helpful. I showed him the court papers that the deceptive and incompetent Ms. Callucci had served upon me, including the one with the blank spaces, incorrect courthouse address, and unsigned signature block.

"A lawyer did this?!!"

I asked the law clerk if a lawyer could take original court records out of the courthouse for her own use, or for the benefit of her client. It was Ms. Callucci who said that she had all the original papers.

"NO! Of course not! I don't know what that lawyer might have taken to the hearing with her, but they were not original papers!"

Finally, I asked how to subpoena records from the court. I guess the request sounded unusual.

"Why would you want to subpoena original records?"

I explained the problem I had with the Affidavit of Service of the Restraining Notice, and the judge's unwillingness to recognize it. The young law clerk shook his head in disbelief. He suggested that he might go and inquire directly of the judge exactly what it was that would satisfy Her Honor. He did so and returned shortly.

"Go to the Civil Court and request certified copies."

It was all so simple. I thanked the young law clerk for his help.

"You're very welcome, Sir. Good luck!"

Wasting no time, I jumped on a subway to Queens and went to the Civil Court. I began at Special Term, Part II, was sent down to Small Claims, and was told that the records were archived, and that it would take two weeks to retrieve them. It would be after the hearing date.

"Two weeks!? The hearing is next week!"

It turned out that that wasn't the right answer either. This was a different Order to Show Cause. This was an Order to Show Cause for Contempt, which was on file in Special Term, Part II. The clerk retrieved the records without a problem. I carefully examined the file. All the original records were intact, even the original Information Subpoena and Restraining Notice. Nothing was missing. Why did the deceptive Ms. Callucci say that she had all the records, when in fact she did not? And at the hearing, why did she say, "It's not here?" Perhaps it was out of ignorance, but probably not. And why didn't Her Honor question it? At any rate, I made copies, paid the $5.00 certification fee, and thereby obtained the vital evidence that I needed to prevent the loss of the motorcycle.

On Monday, I called National Process Servers. Mr.

Keller was back from vacation, alive and well. Yes, they still had the file. Maybe the speech wasn't necessary, but I gave it to him anyway.

"Mr. Keller, a great deal of money rests on this affidavit. It has to say 'Order to Show Cause with Information Subpoena and Restraining Notice.' The judge wants to see 'Restraining Notice.' Can you do it?"

"Sure, no problem."

"Great!"

"Should we mail it, or will you pick it up?"

"NO! Don't mail it! I'll pick it up, and thank you for all your cooperation!"

And so, now I had the certified copy of the Information Subpoena and Restraining Notice, and a new Affidavit of Service from National. These were the two records that I needed to show proper service of the Restraining Notice.

My next step was to arrange service of the new Order to Show Cause for Contempt on Neville in Supreme Court, a place where he was sure to be, absolutely! I decided to use a professional process server rather than the Sheriff - the Sheriff's Office was just too busy and there would be long delays. I called Mr. Keller at National again. They were close to the court. It was only a ten minute walk. It would be an easy service, but it would have to be done on the day of the hearing, between 10:30 A.M. and 11:00 A.M. Service by the so called due diligence, and the usual three attempts would be useless; it had to be "in hand." The alien spirit was sure to re-molecularize during this rare window of opportunity. This was the time to do it. Mr. Keller's response was disappointing.

"That kind of service is v e r y e x p e n s i v e!"

"Oh, really?"

"Yes!"

"Well ... how much?"

"$150.00 ... and up."

I began to add up all my expenses. There was $630.00 in Sheriff fees, $92.00 for the towing charge, over $400.00 in storage charges, $500.00 for the Sheriff's indemnity bond, ... and now it would be another $150.00 for the in court process service, another piece of small change into the Midnite rat hole! I told Mr. Keller that I would think about it.

A strange piece of mail came a day or two later. It nearly got tossed into the dumpster with all the rest of my junk mail, but the name sparked my interest. The name on the envelope read,

"The Roadrunner - Legs for the Industry"

I opened the envelope, and with curiosity read the letter.

" ... DEPENDABLE, QUALITY, FULLY LICENSED, INDEPENDENT PROCESS SERVER ..."

As I continued to read, it looked better and better, but best of all, The Roadrunner was cheap, only $15.00 per subpoena, plus mileage. They were even cheaper than the Sheriff, but no guns or uniforms. I decided to use The Roadrunner. We would meet at Supreme Court at 10:30 A.M. on the day of the hearing.

I was gaining renewed confidence in seeing the successful outcome of my case. I had all the evidence that I needed for the Supreme Court hearing. It would be a short, simple hearing. I'd crush my opponent in Supreme Court, and then I'd bury him in Civil Court. I remembered Neville's last words, spoken to me at the hearing.

"I'll do what I have to ..."

And then I remembered that I was supposed to call him. He wanted to deal.

The experienced lawyer and litigant know that things can go wrong in court. Anything can happen. Air tight cases can leak or burst apart. Hard and sure evidence can be challenged and rendered inadmissible. A judge can, for whatever reason, or no reason, change sides. The wrong words, the wrong facial expression, the wrong timing ... anything can alter the whims of a judge's decision. A good and fair settlement was nearly always preferable to risking everything in court. And so it was, not out of fear of bodily harm, and certainly not out of compassion, that I called Neville. A familiar voice with a faint West Indies accent answered the phone.

"Hello?"

It was him. The number that he gave me worked. He really was living with friends on South 9th Street.

"Hello, Mr. Michaels. This is Mr. Cohen."

He spoke slowly, clearly, in a cool business-like manner, and with the accent of the Islands. I was resolved to say as little as possible and I let him do most of the talking. Neville got right to the point.

"Ok, look, mun. Dee best I can do is $3,000.00. That's everything I have, and I mean everything ... everything I own, everything I can hock ... everything I can borrow from friends ..."

As Neville continued his prepared statements pertaining to his financial condition and worldly assets (but without the benefit of certified accounting records prepared by a CPA), I thought about the six years of frustration, disappointment, expense, and relentless pursuits through the streets, courts, and bars of New York. It had all hardened my heart, and yet, I had to fight against the re-emergence of any bit of compassion. Neville had completed his speech, and I began mine.

"NO GOOD!"

"Look, Jonah ... honestly mun, $3,000.00 is really dee best I can do ..."

A long pause ensued. It was now up to the judgment creditor to negotiate. The very name "Midnite" still sent shivers up my spine, but now it also sounded silly. At any rate, progress was being made and the two old time adversaries were now at least on a first name basis. If Israel could negotiate with the PLO, perhaps I could negotiate with Midnite. Significant ground had been broken, and serious discussion was at hand, but I had to be firm and careful to avoid undue concessions.

"Well ... Midnite ... eh ... Neville, you know expenses have been building up, and it's going to cost!"

Subconsciously, I was beginning to sound like Kravitz, Jr., my landlord. (*"It's gonna cost!"*) I learned well. I continued.

"Together, the two judgments, including interest and expenses, now come to $7,772.07."

"WHAT!?"

"Well ... Do you want me to give you an itemization?"

Neville was interested, perhaps for the first time in nearly seven years. I complied, cleared my throat, and I read.

"Judgment 10/27/92, $2000.00; Small Claims Fee, $5.58; Interest through 8/6/97, $862.45; Judgment 12/1/92, $2000.00 ..."

I read through the entire list, for it was long.

"... Sheriff, City of New York, $630.00; City Marshal Fee, $25.00; Additional Marshal fee, $25.00; Contempt Fine, $260.00; Sheriff Bond, $500.00 ..."

Finally, I was coming to the end...

"... Towing Charge, $92.01; and Storage Charges to date, $476.30."

There was another long pause before Neville responded.

"You know, mun ... that second judgment ... I moved, I wasn't there ..."

"Well, you were there part of the time, and you did owe me some additional rent. You should have come to court ... I'll tell you what. I'll drop the second judgment. Give me $5,000.00 and we'll settle.

"Ah, hah!"

It might have been a tactical blunder, an admission on my part that maybe there was something wrong with the second judgment. Nevertheless, I held firm, decided that we had had enough negotiating, that I held the upper hand, that the Moto Guzzi motorcycle would surely cover the judgments and costs, and that I would end the call. I gave Neville my number.

"Neville, $5,000.00 - think about it. Call me back."

Neville did call back, but he was still stuck at the same $3,000.00 offer and wouldn't ... or perhaps couldn't budge. Perhaps it really was everything he had, and everything he could have hocked, or borrowed from friends. Or perhaps his strategy was not to negotiate, or to raise the offer, but to make it very expensive for the judgment creditor.

"Look mun, I can delay this. I know you're paying storage charges. I know it's costing. I can bring action after action. I can delay it indefinitely. I could make it very expensive for you. It would make sense for you to take the $3,000.00. It really would, mun ..."

Neville went on with his argument, and it did make sense, but he was also getting off cheap and easy. I didn't want to hear anymore, and I was financially and emotionally prepared to outlast him, whatever it took.

"Neville, $5,000.00, or I'll see you back in court, ok?"

The day of the hearing approached, but there was no further communication from the judgment debtor. Neville had made his first and only offer. I collected up my new evidence, the Affidavit of Service together with the certified copies of the originals of the papers served, and neatly placed everything in my black vinyl legal folder. I then called The Roadrunner and arranged for him to meet me at Supreme Court on the day of the hearing for service on Neville.

True to his word, and as he stated in his advertising circular, The Roadrunner met me in front of the judge's chamber at Supreme Court. He was tall, thin, had balding gray hair, and looked to be of advanced middle age. He was dressed in jeans, and while he wasn't exactly what one would call marathon material, he was honest and reliable. He was there at 10:30 A.M. exactly. But now where were Midnite and Ms. Callucci? 10:30 A.M. became 10:35 A.M., and 10:35 A.M. became 10:45 A.M. The Roadrunner looked at me with some concern. The imminent arrival of Captain Midnite was in doubt.

"Are you sure he'll be here?"

"Of course he'll be here."

The Roadrunner was becoming edgy. He had a stack of other papers to be served for other clients. I let The Roadrunner know the basics.

"You see, he has this motorcycle, a Moto Guzzi that I had the Sheriff seize. If he wants the bike back, he has to come to the hearing."

But 10:45 A.M. advanced quickly on to 10:50 A.M. and The Roadrunner was becoming even more impatient, and now I too began to wonder. With the hearing set for 11:00 A.M. sharp, where the hell were they?

"You know, I can't stay here all day. I have other work to do. I really have to ..."

"Ok, ok ... just stay until 11:00 A.M. Ok? He'll be here! I know he'll be here!"

I said it, but now I wasn't so sure anymore. I went over to the calendar clerk to make sure that I had the right date and time. I couldn't have made a mistake, but I had to check. I gave the clerk the case name.

"Michaels vs. Cohen?"

"Let's see, Michaels vs. Cohen ... hmmm ...Index number?

I gave the clerk the index number.

"Oh! I think there was a call on this one. Let me see. Yes, there was a call ... Was there also a Sheriff named as a defendant?"

"Yes! That's it! That's the one!"

"Yes, we had a call this morning. That case was settled."

"SETTLED?!"

LVIII. The Deal

There was no time to puzzle over the mysterious telephone call that the clerk might have received. Nor was I able at that time to understand the meaning of a possible one sided settlement. After inquiring as to the correct calendar date, the clerk addressed me.

"You're Cohen?"

"Yes!"

"Well, you're still on for eleven o'clock."

Whatever had been going on behind the scene, the important thing was that we were still on the calendar, and now it was only a few minutes before 11:00 A.M. Neville and his lawyer had not yet arrived. Where were they? I turned toward the door in nervous anticipation, and at that very instant, the tall, black, alien figure emerged. He was exactly as I had described him to The Roadrunner - black, wearing a large gold medallion around his neck, braided hair - only now, he had on designer, wrap-around sunglasses. Midnite looked cool, and he was smiling the smile of victory.

The Roadrunner was at the door, but facing me and wondering what was going on at the desk of the calendar clerk. With split second timing, I nodded ever so slightly. The Roadrunner turned a sharp, fast one hundred eighty degrees to his right, faced Neville eye to eye at point blank range, and placed the subpoena into Neville's right hand. It was a process server's dream. It was clean. It was beautiful.

It was the pinnacle of perfection and success at its summit. This was quite possibly the only time Midnite had ever been served personally in his entire life. And as The Roadrunner took the extra minute to explain the subpoena and show the original, Neville stood still, dumbfounded, and nearly crapping in his pants. The Roadrunner then looked up at me, and as I gave him the nod of approval for a job well done, he quickly departed. His mission having been accomplished, there was more work to be done in the pursuit of justice.

The short, slightly plump Ms. Callucci entered after Midnite, followed by the somewhat emaciated Solarz girlfriend. I was still standing at the desk of the calendar clerk, but I was able to follow the ensuing agitated animation with great interest. From across the crowded room, I was still able to hear,

"... but I don't live there anymore! I moved ..."

Neville was still looking for a way out. Never mind that the subpoena was placed directly into his hand by a professional process server, and that the identity of the recipient was certain, there just had to be something wrong with the process service. The concerned and curious little Ms. Callucci took the package of papers from Neville and excitedly went on looking for technical legal inconsistencies. She would have plenty of pro bono legal work ahead of her, but not now. Our case was coming up.

"MICHAELS VS. COHEN"

It was the judge's clerk, Mr. Ahrens who called the participants of the case to the bench.

"Are you Michaels?"

"No. I'm Cohen."

"I'm Michaels."

"And I'm Lorraine Callucci, Mr. Michaels' attorney."

"And Ms. Callucci, what are you proposing?"

"We have offered to settle the judgments for $3,000.00 by means of a certified check payable to the creditor within twenty-four hours."

"And Mr. Cohen - please step forward - you've agreed to this, correct?"

"WHAT!?"

"You haven't agreed to do this?"

"NO!"

"Mr. Cohen, the debtor has come forward with a reasonable offer of settlement that seems to me to be a fair and acceptable offer ..."

"And it seems to me that offers of settlement should come before the award of a judgment, not after. And certainly not after the seizure of an asset. Anyway, the judgments with interest and expenses are now close to $8,000.00."

It was Ms. Callucci who interjected herself, still fighting "valiantly" for her client, and of course still screaming the magic words.

"The judgments were erroneously awarded on an ILLEGAL SUBLET ..."

What Callucci lacked in vertical size, she more than made up for with the verbosity her mouth. Ms. Callucci kept it up. She wouldn't let it go away.

"... and my client was never served with the summons for the second judgment, a phantom judgment ..."

Ms. Callucci went on with it as if she were trying the entire Cohen vs. Michaels landlord-tenant case all over again. I saw no point in debating her. My judgments were intact. No one would be able to take them away from me. There were no appeals. I responded with a simple,

"The case was tried in Small Claims - I won."

"Mr. Cohen, I want you to write down on a sheet of paper all of your out-of-pocket expenses."

"Why?"

"Please, I'm asking you."

"But, I'm not prepared. This wasn't supposed to be a hearing to negotiate a settlement. I don't want a settlement! We were adjourned. I'm here to present evidence of service of a Restraining Notice. That was the problem! The service of the Restraining Notice."

I opened my legal folder to present the precious evidence that I had collected with so much difficulty in order to satisfy Her Honor.

"Please, Mr. Cohen. This is not a trial or a hearing!"

"But my evidence - you don't want to see my evidence?"

"Mr. Cohen, I don't have all day and the judge doesn't have all day. Again, I'm asking you to list all of your out-of-pocket expenses."

"Well, there were the two judgments ..."

"NO! Your expenses! What did you pay in rent?"

"Well ... eh, it was about $500 a month in rent ... maybe a little more, but what does that have to do with the motorcycle?"

"And when did Mr. Michaels move out?"

"Well ... eh, it was on January 6, 1991."

I remembered the exact day that he moved out. It was a day of great celebration.

"So, ok, he owes you about four months rent."

"NO! I was still responsible for the lease, and there were additional expenses incurred."

"Did you pay anything else on the lease?"

"No, but there were expenses."

"Mr. Cohen, we're not getting anywhere! I ask you again! What were your expenses? Please step forward and write them down on a sheet of paper!"

"And if I refuse?"

"Then we'll go straight to the hearing, and I don't think that the judge will be very sympathetic to your case."

"But, but … the affidavit, the new Affidavit of Service of the Restraining Notice …"

"It's from an event that happened over three years ago, and I don't think that it will carry much weight with the judge."

"But the transfer of title just happened now! You call this justice? Justice in America? I want an adjournment! I want a lawyer! I have a right to a lawyer! I'm not answering any more questions. I demand payment of my judgments! I WILL HAVE MY JUDGMENTS!"

> *"I'll have my bond; I will not hear thee speak;*
> *I'll have my bond; and therefore speak no more.*
> *I'll not be made a soft and dull-ey'd fool,*
> *To shake the head, relent, and sigh, and yield*
> *To Christian intercessors. Follow not;*
> *I'll have no speaking. I will have my bond."*

(Merchant of Venice, Act III, Sc. III - Wm. Shakespeare)

We were at an apparent impasse. The clerk had been given the nearly impossible assignment of effecting, or perhaps even imposing a settlement. I realized that an adjournment and further delay would only add to expenses. Storages charges were mounting up at $10.00 per day, and now I was asking for a lawyer with resulting major legal expenses. Perhaps I should have taken the deal. Perhaps I should have taken the $3,000.00. Or perhaps they would offer even more!

> *"What sum owes he the Jew?"*
> *"For me, three thousand ducats."*
> *"What! No more? Pay him six thousand, and deface the bond;*
> *Double six thousand, and then treble that ..."*

(Merchant of Venice, Act III, Sc. II - Wm. Shakespeare)

"Ms. Callucci, can your client do better that $3,000.00?"

"NO! My client will offer no more than $3,000.00 on a judgment awarded on an ILLEGAL SUBLET!"

Ms. Callucci and Mr. Michaels had been standing by the clerk at the bench. Mr. Michaels had placed his expensive designer sunglasses with his keys, on the ledge of the bench. Progress was slow. I wasn't being cooperative. The clerk was becoming exasperated, then angry, and then his anger was aimed directly at me.

"MR. COHEN! PLEASE!!"

I backed away in fear and confusion. What had I done wrong? I had only asked for more to satisfy the judgment. The clerk apologetically motioned me forward.

"Let's try again. Let's try going over these expenses. Maybe we can work something out."

I approached the bench again, laid down my legal folder, and not noticing them, nearly knocked down Neville's expensive designer sunglasses. Fortunately, he quickly came forward to retrieve them, perhaps saving me from another lawsuit. Neville and his attorney receded far back. The clerk continued.

"Ok, so we have about $2,000.00 that you paid in rent. What else?"

"Well, it was a little more … but I also paid the Sheriff's bond, $500.00."

"Can you get that back?"

"No. It's gone."

"What else?"

"Sheriff fees, about $600.00."

"You'll get back part of that."

He shouted over to Mr. Shimmel, the Sheriff's lawyer, who was seated at the far end of the room. Shimmel, who had both physically and mentally removed himself from the session, had craftily positioned himself to be the first one out the door at its conclusion. Now, brought back to life, Shimmel shouted back that seventy percent of the Sheriff fee would be refundable. It came to $420.00. The deal looked better, not good, just a little better.

"And there was $50.00 in Marshal fees."

"Marshal fees? You collected from a Marshal?!!"

"NO! I just paid fees."

"Ok, ok, we're making some progress. Make a list of all your expenses. Sit down over here. Take your time and make a list."

I hesitated, and then the clerk continued on in an undertone.

"Come on. Are you going to continue chasing this guy for the rest of your life? You know, you will never see an end to this. You'll be chasing him for ever …"

"Le loi, c'est le loi!"

390

The clerk's remark was true. I was weakening. I would be chasing Midnite's shadow for the rest of my life. Here was the chance to finally end it. I humbly sat down to compile my list.

It came as a shock, and in a flash. Her Honor unexpectedly exited her royal chambers to personally inspect the progress of the deal! The judgment creditor still needed a little more persuasion, some gentle prodding, and a bit of convincing. The episode happened quickly and in a fog. Was it an implied threat? Did it actually happen? Did I imagine it? Did my recollection of the events become so muddled and confused that imagination and reality had merged? The impropriety of her sudden appearance and the short episode that followed stunned me then, and had remained with me for many years thereafter. Now dressed in her black robe, swishing along, Her Honor found it necessary to stop at my desk. Without looking directly at me, and in a barely audible undertone, she inquired as to how we were doing. Her Glorious and Majestic Honor was addressing pro se little me!

"They offered $3,000.00."

I answered the obvious. Her Honor most certainly already knew beforehand. The deal had already been made behind closed doors! The one sided, perverted settlement had already become a fact! And then came some "advice" on the deal, words from the mouth of Her Honor, or the lack thereof, delivered silently, so that it was only the judgment creditor that could hear.

"That's a good deal ... and I think you should take it."

"But, but ... there's $2,000.00 in compound interest at nine percent, and my judgments are for $4,000.00 ... and there's about $2,000.00 in expenses, and there's the contempt fine $260.00 ..."

"Simple interest, but why so much ...? Take the $3,000.00."

> "A pound of that same merchant's flesh is thine;
> The court awards it and the law doth give it."
> "Most rightful judge!"
> "And you must cut this flesh from off his breast;
> The law allows it and the court awards it."
> "Most learned judge! - A sentence; come prepare."

(Merchant of Venice, Act IV, Sc. I - Wm. Shakespeare)

"Mr. Cohen?"

I hadn't yet finished my list. I had come close to $3,000.00, but there were the myriad of other expenses: gas and mileage to and from the courts - Landlord-Tenant, Small Claims, and Supreme; process server fees, photocopies; faxes; telephone calls -local and long distance; postage; legal forms - the list went on without end. The law said that I was entitled to nine percent interest per annum on the judgments, but I wasn't being given any at all. And what about the contempt fine? And could I put a cost value on my own time, or time off from work? And what would be the value of seven years of frustration and aggravation?

"Mr. Cohen, are you ready? Please approach the bench."

"Tarry a little; - there is something else. -
This bond doth give thee here no jot of blood;
The words expressly are a pound of flesh."

(Merchant of Venice, Act IV, Sc. I - Wm. Shakespeare)

But no, I wasn't ready. The seemingly endless barrage of badgering, questioning and coercion had seriously eroded my fighting will. My spirit had been crushed and broken. Mr. Ahrens, the judge's clerk had done his job well. The veneer of my role as "evil landlord" or "champion of judgment creditors," had worn thin. And would I want to be "chasing this guy for the rest of my life?" I wanted it to be over. I had gone up against the professionals - lawyers, and judges, together with their assistants. In my own mind, I had fought admirably, and without representation, but now fell victim to a brutal and corrupt system of feigned justice. The beautiful and impressive artwork on the ceiling above the rotunda of Supreme Court depicted the images of the great law-givers of ancient and modern times - Solon, Justinian, Blackstone, Marshall, Hammarabi, and Moses, all looking down at every lawyer and litigant, judgment debtor and judgment creditor, and at the judges and the judged. Oh, but if these great people could only know of the horrors of injustice within the chambers of Supreme Court, above which their awesome images presided!

"Take then thy bond, take thou thy pound of flesh;
But in the cutting, if thou dost shed
One drop of Christian blood, thy lands and goods
Are by the laws of Venice confiscate ..."

(Merchant of Venice, Act IV, Sc. I - Wm. Shakespeare)

The opposition had me cornered. To demand to have the hearing would have meant not only certain defeat, but also financial responsibility for all the expenses: sheriff, towing, storage, etc. I had been warned by Her Honor, and it was perhaps wise to heed the warning.

> *"When the signal is raised on the mountain, look!*
> *When the Shofar is sounded, listen!"*

(Isaiah, 18:3)

To demand the hearing would have been to demand entry into a medieval inquisition chamber! To demand representation by a lawyer would have meant certain expenses and uncertain results. The last alternative was the deal, the settlement. But now, was my objective to settle and collect some money; or was it to punish Midnite - to get the Moto Guzzi motorcycle sold at auction - at any cost! Where did justice lie?

"Mr. Cohen, what did you decide? Do you want the hearing or the settlement?"

"I don't know."

"Decide!"

"I'm being coerced!"

"YOU'RE NOT BEING COERCED! WHAT DO YOU WANT?"

"JUSTICE IN AMERICA!"

"Well, Mr. Cohen?"

"$4,000.00 - I'll settle for $4,000.00."

"No! We need an answer now. Decide!"

"Why can't I ask for $4,000.00?"

"Mr. Cohen, we need an answer right now! What did you decide? Do we settle, or do we go to a hearing? Decide! Decide now!"

"3,000.00?"

"When?"

"Ms. Callucci, when?"

"3,000.00 within twenty-four hours by certified check - no, we can do better. We can have it this afternoon. Tell us where."

"Mr. Cohen? Decide! Decide now! What are we doing? Well …?"

LIX. The Settlement

It was coming to an end. Suddenly and quickly, it was all coming to its own inevitable conclusion. As I sat in Supreme Court, I had become the focus of attention of everyone. It was all up to me. The pressure was intense. I had been totally sapped of energy, and drained of enthusiasm. I was, at this point, confused, cornered, and coerced. In short, I had been broken. But now, at last, here was the chance to end it, and to at least claim a partial victory. I had had enough of lawyers, judges, courts, and hearings. To continue would almost certainly have meant losing everything.

> *"...nay, if the scale do turn*
> *But in the estimation of a hair, -*
> *Thou diest, and all thy goods are confiscate."*

(Merchant of Venice, Act IV, Sc. I - Wm. Shakespeare)

"Mr. Cohen, what are we doing?"

If I had requested the hearing, and lost, I would be held responsible for all the expenses. All my efforts would have been for naught. Yet, here was a way out - It was really the only thing to do.

"Mr. Cohen, the hearing or the settlement?"

> *"Give me my principal, and let me go."*

(Merchant of Venice, Act IV, Sc. I - Wm. Shakespeare)
"Ok, let's do it."

"I understand that you had the plaintiff, Mr. Michaels, served with some papers this morning. That's finished. Right?"

I thought of the trips to the court, The Roadrunner, the impossible service performed with perfection … It was all for nothing.

"Yes, it's finished."

And with these fateful words, it was as if a bullet had pierced my heart. I became faint and only white appeared before my eyes. But the settlement was in motion, and things began to move quickly. Ms. Callucci began writing it all out at a feverish pace. Mr. Shimmel wrote out the Sheriff's acceptance of the settlement, as well as the partial refund of the Sheriff fees.

But the pain was not over. It was yet intensifying into a violent climax as the next question was darted at me.

"Mr. Cohen, where is the motorcycle?"

"What?"

"Mr. Cohen, the motorcycle - where is the motorcycle?"

I hesitated, but then I gave it all away.

"City Boys Towing, 11th Avenue at 14th Street."

I had remembered that Deputy Schatzer had warned me not to give away the Guzzi's location. And now, it was as if I had betrayed him … and myself.

> *"But tell the traitor, in the highest degree*
> *He hath abus'd your powers."*
> *"Traitor! - How now!"*
> *"Ay, traitor, Marcius …*
> *You lords and heads o' the state, perfidiously*

He has betray'd your business, and given up,
For certain drops of salt, your city Rome - ...
Breaking his oath and resolution, like
A twist of rotten silk ..."

(Coriolanus, Act V, Sc. VI - Wm. Shakespeare)

Yes, I had sold out, I had been broken, and now at last, the settlement papers were being handed to me. I took a seat in the jury box and read over the settlement very carefully, very slowly, and lip reading every word. Ms. Callucci had made me responsible for any damages which may have occurred during the period of time of the motorcycle's storage.

"Ms. Callucci, I will not agree to a settlement where I'm held responsible for damages. Take back your settlement!"

"My client has a right to receive the motorcycle in the condition that it was prior to the seizure!"

"I won't agree to it - TAKE IT BACK!"

The deal was falling apart, but the judge's clerk intervened to rescue it. He suggested that the matter of damages could be resolved if I would give the debtor permission to inspect the motorcycle. I reluctantly agreed.

"Mr. Cohen, please call the storage facility and arrange for the inspection. You can use the telephone in this room, and there's the phone book if you need it."

It wasn't what I wanted, but events were moving along on their own, being propelled by their own momentum. There was no choice. I slowly walked over to the phone, I looked up the number, and I called City Boys Towing. The phone was answered by a man with a deep voice and an Israeli accent.

"Hello, City Boys."

I had to explain what the call was about; that I was in court; that I had just given the debtor permission to inspect the motorcycle for damage; that it was to be shown to the debtor, but not released, not yet, but soon, upon settlement; and that we were all coming over within a half hour.

"Hello. This is Jonah Cohen."

"Who?"

"I'm the judgment creditor from the Small Claims Court and ..."

"What?"

"You're storing a motorcycle for me? A Moto Guzzi motorcycle?"

"Oh! Mr. Can!"

He got the name wrong, but it didn't matter. He knew who I was.

"Mr. Can! How long do you expect us to store this motorcycle? You told us a couple of weeks, and now it's almost seven weeks!"

"I know, well ..."

"WELL, WE HAVEN'T BEEN PAID!"

"I know, but I've just reached a settlement with ..."

"Mr. Can! WE NEED $150.00 NOW!"

"Ok, ok. I know. I'm calling from the court and I just reached a settlement with the debtor and ..."

"Mr. Can, WE HAVE TO GET PAID NOW!!!"

"Ok, I'll pay you ..."

"When?"

"Well, I just reached a settlement agreement with the debtor and he'll be over in a little while to look at the bike and inspect ..."

"A HUNDRED AND FIFTY NOW OR NOBODY

GETS TO LOOK AT NOTHING!!"

"Will you listen to me!?"

"NO!! YOU LISTEN TO ME! THE MOTORCYCLE WAS SUPPOSED TO BE STORED FOR TWO WEEKS. IT'S NOW SEVEN WEEKS AND WE HAVEN'T BEEN PAID! NOBODY GETS TO LOOK AT THE BIKE. NOBODY GETS TO INSPECT NOTHING, OK? AND FURTHERMORE, YOU SHOULD BE AWARE THAT WE'RE PLACING A MECHANIC'S LEIN ON THE MOTORCYCLE FOR NON-PAYMENT OF MONEY YOU OWE US! UNDERSTAND?! AND IF WE DON'T RECEIVE ONE HUNDRED FIFTY DOLLARS WITHIN THE NEXT TWENTY-FOUR HOURS, WE'LL NOTIFY OUR LAWYERS AND ..."

"Click."

It was no use. I just couldn't take anymore of City Boys. Communication became impossible and I just wasn't in the mood to hear any more of it. Mr. Ahrens, the judge's assistant probably overheard both ends of this bizarre interchange and asked,

"What happened?"

"Oh, nothing," I replied, which was the truth.

Neville, Ms. Callucci, and the Solarz girlfriend - the evil triumvirate - wasting no time, had already taken a cab to the City Boys facility. I decided to walk - I was in no hurry. I didn't mind making the unholy trinity wait, and besides, I really needed the exercise and fresh air to clear my mind. I had arrived at City Boys about a half an hour after my opposition.

During my absence, Ms. Callucci had somehow managed to convince the intransigent Mr. Reuben, the City Boys manager, to show the motorcycle to Neville, who surprisingly found no damage or other faults with it. Neville was standing in a corner of the room by a file cabinet, the Solarz girlfriend was seated near the doorway, and Ms. Callucci stood in the middle of the room.

I took a seat at the far wall opposite the entrance and again read the agreement. Neville was satisfied that no damage had been done to the motorcycle, and so, we agreed to delete the part about responsibility for damages, but certain additional words were very much needed. Ms. Callucci's lawyerly writing needed some supplementation. I wrote,

"Plaintiff accepts motorcycle as is. Mr. Cohen accepts no responsibility for any damages."

Ms. Callucci took exception.

"Mr. Cohen! This is a signed document! You can't make any changes!"

"Ms. Callucci, I'm not making changes. I'm adding a necessary statement."

"Mr. Cohen, you can't do that!"

"Why not? I didn't sign it yet, and the judge didn't sign it!"

"But I signed it!"

"Are you telling me that you won't agree to this? Ok, lawyer! You fix it!"

I held the settlement papers out to Ms. Callucci for her correction in order to let her add whatever words might make her happy, but just then, the City Boys manager came in, recognized me, and flew into a rage. The argument over the telephone, began earlier that afternoon, resumed from where it left off.

"MR. CAN! YOU PISSED ME OFF THIS MORNING. I'M NOT DEALING WITH YOU! YOU OWE US $432.30 STORAGE CHARGES TO DATE!"

The storage charges had been adding up fast, but it seemed a little high. He explained, or rather demanded.

"$432.30. THAT'S $10.00 PER DAY PLUS TAX COMES TO $432.30. ACTUALLY RHONDA, THE SECRETARY, MADE A MISTAKE! It should have been $25.00 per day and that would come to ..."

Neville and Ms. Callucci stood quietly by as innocent bystanders and enjoyed the show. I wanted to get this over as soon as possible and move along. I took out my credit card to pay the $432.30 storage charge before I would be required to pay the premium rate.

"Mr. Can, I don't want your credit card! Payment has to be IN CASH!"

"What?? You don't accept credit cards?"

"NO!"

"Well, do I get a discount if I pay cash?"

"NO!"

"But I paid for the tow by credit card. When did you begin the cash only policy?"

"TODAY! FOR YOU!"

My eyes glanced over at the VISA and MasterCard emblems, flagrantly displayed on the wall behind the desk. Mr. Reuben was clearly taking advantage of me. He seemed to derive personal enjoyment in embarrassing me in front of my opponents, but the show was over.

"I don't have $432.00 in cash!"

At this point, my opposition's amusement and the free

entertainment that City Boys and I were providing came to an end. There was genuine concern on the other side, and rightfully so. The settlement agreement was in trouble, again. I looked to the lawyer for help, but it wasn't for legal advice.

"Ms. Callucci, would you like to help pay part of this?"

"No! The storage bill is your responsibility."

"Well, you know, I didn't sign the settlement agreement yet ... and maybe I won't!"

"MR. COHEN! THIS IS SETTLED! WE WON! WE WON!"

I think it was these words that pained me far more than the $432.00 storage charge - to be paid in cash. I stared down the incompetent Ms. Callucci in wide eyed fury while I attempted to explain "settlement."

"Ms. Callucci - YOU DIDN'T WIN! THIS IS A SETTLEMENT - A COMPROMISE - MUTUAL CONCESSIONS! AND AN AS YET UNSIGNED SETTLEMENT! I'm asking you to pay part of the storage charge, or maybe there won't be a settlement! I DON'T HAVE $432.00!"

The Solarz girlfriend, who had been silent throughout this ordeal, suddenly came to life.

"You mean you don't have $432.00, or you have to go to the bank?"

So now they expected me to go to my bank and drain my account to satisfy the greedy Mr. Reuben! But the question was seriously intended. In the underground world of Midnite - with a residence somewhere in the ruins of Williamsburg, Brooklyn, and with part time cash-off-the-books jobs in bars - to say that you didn't have $432.00 was a perfectly credible statement, but it also meant the end of the settlement. And at this, she broke down, her rage and frustration vented directly at me.

"DO YOU THINK THIS HASN'T COST US ANYTHING? IN COURT COSTS? EXPENSES? IN TIME? DO YOU KNOW WHAT WE'VE GONE THROUGH? DO YOU HAVE ANY IDEA? DO YOU KNOW WHAT WE HAD TO DO TO COME UP WITH $3,000.00? DO YOU KNOW? ..."

No, I didn't know. I received the young woman's abusive tirade of disgust, hardship, and hate with curious delight, for it told me that it was not Ms. Callucci and company who won, but the judgment creditor. This was my victory, not complete, not perfect, and not just; but, nevertheless, a victory. There was pain and suffering on the side of the opposition. It wasn't the great victory that Ms. Callucci had deluded herself into thinking that she had won. Nor was it a carefree frolic through the galaxies on Captain Midnite's space ship. It was an ordeal of trouble and tribulation. In her rage, she continued.

"WHO ARE YOU? WHAT KIND OF A PERSON ARE YOU? ... ECHHH!! ..."

I tried again, but I wasn't about to run to the cash machine at my bank and drain it of cash for City Boys, Ms. Callucci, Neville, or anyone else.

"Mr. Reuben, last chance! Here's my credit card. Will you accept it?"

"NO! ONLY CASH!"

"Ms. Callucci, do you have some cash?"

"NO!"

I looked again at Mr. Reuben, and then I looked at Ms. Callucci. The next move was all mine and I made it.

"DEAL'S OFF!! NO SETTLEMENT!!"

I turned, walked to the door, glanced at the red-eyed, weeping, and now even more emaciated Solarz girlfriend, and exited. I was free, I was redeemed, and I was not a traitor! Rome was saved! My judgments were intact, my case was on, and the settlement agreement papers (which I did sign, but which were not signed by or submitted to the judge) were safely with me inside my briefcase.

I turned the corner and walked downtown, back to the court. I had to tell them that I killed the deal, and that the settlement was quashed. They would ask why? What happened? What is it that you intend to do? What is your policy? And what is your aim? I will say,

> *"It is to wage war, by sea, land, and air, with all our might, and with all the strength that G-d can give us: to wage war against a monstrous tyranny ... You ask, what is our aim? I can answer in one word: Victory - victory at all costs, victory in spite of all terror, victory, however long and hard the road may be; for without victory, there is no survival ..."*

(Winston Churchill - House of Commons - 13 May 1940)

LX. Goodbye Guzzi

There were so many things to be done. My case was on
again. But first, and as soon as possible, I had to get the
motorcycle out of City Boys. Mr. Reuben and I were not on
the best terms, and the ten dollars per day storage fee, plus
tax, was killing me. It looked like it was going to be very
long term storage. Perhaps it would be for months, and who
knows, even years. And now that the debtor knew its
location, it certainly wasn't safe there anymore. I had to call
the Sheriff's Office and get the Sheriff's permission to get
the Guzzi moved to another storage facility. I'd have to pay
another towing charge, but it had to be done. It was now
after four o'clock in the afternoon, and too late to call the
Sheriff's Office. I would do that the first thing the next day.

I walked quickly back to the court, zigzagging my way
downtown through the Village, crossed Canal Street, and
reached the court in twenty minutes. I'd have to tell them
that the hard negotiated settlement agreement was dead. I'd
tell them that I wanted the hearing, but that I needed an
adjournment for the purpose of obtaining the services of an
attorney. Exactly who it was going to be, I didn't know, but
it wasn't going to be Blumfield.

And the contempt hearing with Midnite at Queens
County Civil Court was also on again. I'd have my attorney
handling that also. Expenses would be adding up - legal
fees, towing charges, storages, etc. - but it had to be done.
There was more at stake here than just money! What had

started out as lost money - lost rent money, had evolved into something on a far higher level. The physical and concrete had been transformed into something spiritual and ideal. Where was justice? The coerced settlement agreement wasn't justice. I needed a just conclusion - and I would get it whatever it took. And as Midnite had said that he would do whatever he had to do, so I too would do whatever I had to do. The just conclusion: complete satisfaction of both judgments, all interest paid, the contempt fine paid, the bond paid, all sheriff fees paid, the Guzzi sold at auction, and Midnite in jail - or better yet, on a boat back to Trinidad! Now, here was justice!

I entered the courtroom. Mr. Ahrens, the judge's clerk was surprised to see me, but he didn't look happy. It was he who spoke first.

"Do you know what happened?"

I looked at him, and I replied defiantly.

"Yeah, the settlement is dead. I killed it!"

"You mean you don't know what happened?"

"Happened? Something happened? What happened?"

Mr. Ahrens paused, looked me straight in the eye, and in a somber tone that could only have meant misfortune replied,

"The motorcycle was released! The debtor paid them cash, and they released the motorcycle!"

LXI. En Attendant Midnite

The impossible, even the unthinkable had happened. Again, disaster had struck. I stood dazed, silent, and motionless for at least several seconds. I turned white, and then red, but still found enough strength to stagger into the jury box. At this point, I had no motorcycle, no assets, and no money - but I still had the signed settlement agreement, for whatever it was worth, and I had to work with that. Mr. Ahrens continued.

"Ok, look, I don't know what happened there at the towing company - you didn't like him - he didn't like you - the guy was a jerk - but maybe we could still put this thing together. Now, what did happen?"

"Well ... eh ... the storage charges for one thing. It was more than it was supposed to be, and then there was the tax on the storage charges ... oh, and then there was the thing with the credit card ..."

"Ok, ok. If the debtor were to agree to pay say half of the storage charge, would you then agree to the settlement?"

Settlement? They still wanted to settle!? Images of Captain Midnite on the Moto Guzzi, speeding south on the New Jersey Turnpike to the tune of "Matilda, she take me money and run Venezuela" began to fade, and soon, we were back to serious negotiation. I had nothing to negotiate with, but still they wanted a settlement - a clean slate for Midnite. Reality began to set in, perhaps for both plaintiff and defendant, but who was who? I really didn't know, or for that matter, care anymore. There would be no contempt hearing, only a partial payment on the judgments, and certainly no deportation. The time of reconciliation, compromise, and mutual concessions was at hand. We were coming to the end. Mr. Ahrens repeated the question.

"Well, would you agree to the settlement?"

"What?"

"The SETTLEMENT! Do you agree to the settlement?"

"Yes, I agree to the settlement."

I reluctantly took the settlement papers out of my briefcase and handed them to Mr. Ahrens, who held them in his left hand while he dialed City Boys with his right. Amazingly, Neville, Ms. Callucci, and the girlfriend were all still at City Boys waiting for a deal - waiting for a deal from me.

Yes, the debtor agreed to pay half the storage charge. But since the debtor had already paid the full storage charge, it was I who now had to pay the debtor - in cash! I had to convince myself that I was actually making another $216.00 on the settlement. The judge's clerk annotated the settlement agreement papers. Ms. Callucci did not object to the additional wording.

"Mr. Cohen to reimburse debtor $216.15 upon receipt of certified check for $3,000.00."

It was now twenty minutes to five in the afternoon. The court would close at 5:00 P.M. We agreed that the debtor would meet the creditor at the court building at 5:00 P.M. The final details and logistics of the settlement agreement still had to be worked out.

"Mr. Cohen, do you have the cash on you?"

"No, I'll have to go to my bank."

"They're closed!"

"I'll use the cash machine. Where's the closest Chemical

Bank?"

The law clerk tried to be helpful, but the detailed instructions of how to get to my bank for the purpose of draining it of $220.00 in twenty-dollar bills, in order to give it to Midnite on a street corner in Manhattan, to effect a settlement that I didn't want in the first place, was like a kick in the *baytsim*.

So, this was the transaction: I would give Neville a signed copy of the Settlement Agreement, a copy of the Sheriff's Waiver, and $216.15 in cash; and Neville would give me a certified check in the amount of $3,000.00. I would meet Neville in front of the court building at 60 Centre Street at 5:00 P.M. and hand over the cash – TWO HUNDRD SIXTEEN DOLLARS in cold cash to Midnite! Was this a victory? Was this justice? I could have puked! But out of politeness, I forced myself to thank Mr. Ahrens for his "help." His response was a simple, but well intentioned,

"Good luck!"

And so, finally, I was at the end of my seven year crusade - not the end that I wanted, but an end. I kept telling myself that I did well. I had gotten blood out of a stone, accomplished the impossible, and in effect, achieved a sort of victory where anybody else, that is, anybody of normal disposition, ability, and endurance, would have failed. But the truth was that I had been duped and cheated by the system, by the judge, by the lawyer, and by the still slick and streetwise Captain Midnite - and I was sick to my stomach. There was nothing left to do but to get the final transaction over with.

I reached the courthouse at about ten minutes to five and raced up to the courtroom where it had all happened. Neville wasn't there yet, and Judge Grossinger and Mr. Ahrens had already gone home. The young black woman at the desk, a lower level clerk, was taking care of last minute duties, and getting ready to close up. I had to explain to her why I was there.

"I have to meet someone here - the defendant ... I mean the plaintiff. I have to settle up. We have a settlement."

The young woman shrugged and responded,

"Well, I don't know anything about that. You can wait outside the room on one of the benches, if you like."

The law clerk cleaned off her desk and took her keys. I followed her out and she locked the door. I had noticed the calendar sheet, listing the scheduled cases to be called for that day, and found on it my own case: Michaels vs. Cohen.

I asked her if I could have the calendar sheet for a souvenir. The day was over - they wouldn't be needing it anymore.

"Souvenir? Why would anyone ...?"

I was going to tell her that it was sort of a special case, and then, continuing with a curious smile she replied,

"Sure, take it ... Good night."

"Thanks ... and good night."

I waited for a few minutes seated on the bench and realized the pointlessness if this. It was clear that no one was there, or would be coming. But then I realized that the settlement agreement was to meet him in front of the courthouse. I went back downstairs. I waited in front of the court building to see if my former adversary had arrived. No, not yet. It was exactly 5:00 P.M.

I waited in nervous anticipation for Neville and his lawyer. They would be here any minute now. I looked over the court papers again to make sure that they were all signed and properly completed. And, although not a very smart thing to do in a public area, I counted out the $216.00 in cash, and then the $ .15 in change. Everything was in order. We were now almost in the sabbatical year, the year of remission of debts. I recalled how it all began nearly seven years ago, when I was waiting at the steps of the Queens County Courthouse for Midnite to come to the first Small Claims trial. But now it was already past 5:30 P.M., and here I was, now on the steps of Supreme Court in Manhattan, and again waiting for Midnite. Where was he? And again, while nervously waiting and observing both lawyer and litigant, and the occasional pro se idiot, I had to ask myself,

"Would Midnite show?"

I watched the traffic while I scanned the streets in front of the court building for any sign of a motorcycle. Would he come on the Guzzi? Would he come with Ms. Callucci riding with him in back, her short fleshy arms tightly clutching Midnite's waist? And I watched the people. Would the Spirit of Captain Midnite suddenly and mysteriously emerge from the crowd, holding in his hand a certified check for $3,000.00! And I watched the clock. It was now nearly 6:00 P.M. And again, where was he? And now 6:00 P.M. quickly turned into 6:30 P.M., but no Midnite. The old Harry Bellefonte calypso song happened to come into my head again, and there was no way to get rid of it.

"MATILDA .... MATILDA, SHE TAKE ME MONEY AND RUN VENEZUELA ..."

Surely Midnite had reached Trenton by now! I started to think. Had I been duped again? And my thoughts had begun to degenerate, like a whirlwind into the abyss, into a self-destructive self-dialogue, at a time when self-control and cool-headedness was most needed for the transaction. And yes, I still naively believed that there was going to be a transaction.

"Transaction? What TRANSACTION? FOOL! There is no TRANSACTION! You still think he'll show? The court's been closed for an hour and a half. There's no one here! He's got the bike, and you have worthless settlement papers. The judge went home, the judge's assistant went home, and the assistant janitor has already gone home! There's no one here left at the court, and Midnite's riding around on YOUR MOTORCYCLE! You've been had! Had by a corrupt legal system and a slick streetwise alien! Seven wasted years! Time wasted! Money wasted! All the waiting, frustrations, phone calls, faxes, certified mail, process servers, court trials, sheriffs, sheriff's deputies, marshals ... Do something! Do something now! OH! You thought you were smart. You thought you could be your own lawyer. YOU CANNOT GO TO COURT AND BE YOUR OWN LAWYER! Now look at yourself! This was all for nothing! NOTHING! THIS IS THE END!"

"How art thou fallen from heaven, O day-star, son of the morning! How art thou cut down to the ground, that didst lay low the nations! And thou saidst in thy heart, 'I will ascend into heaven, I will exalt my throne above the stars of G-d; and I will sit upon the mount of congregation, in the uttermost

parts of the north; I will ascend above the heights of the clouds; I will make myself like the Most High.' Yet thou shalt be brought down to Sheol, to the uttermost parts of the pit."

(Isaiah 14:12)

"It's all over. You should have gotten a LAWYER! He won! You lost! Do something! DO SOMETHING NOW!! Throw yourself in front of a truck! Do it now! COWARD! DO IT!!"

I viewed the big cement truck barreling down Lafayette to a nearby construction site, and I reconsidered. It wasn't over. I still had my judgments. They were still good for another thirteen years or so, and earning nine percent. They weren't exactly U.S. Government bonds, but the rate was good. I would find him! Again! I would find some assets, a job … something! It would take a little longer, but,

"I WILL FIND HIM!"

"Le loi, c'est le loi."

(Les Miserables - Victor Hugo)

But now, once back in control, my eyes welled up with tears, and amidst several deep sighs, and maybe even a quiet sob or two, I seemed to recall the end of the movie classic, "The Maltese Falcon." It was the part where Sydney Greenstreet as the Fat Man discovers that the famous bird is a phony. The years of effort and frustration had proved

414

fruitless and futile, and finally, to have come so close, only to fail. In a rage, the fake is destroyed, but then self-control is restored – the mission will be completed.

"... shall we go to Istanbul? ... seventeen years ... we must spend another year on the quest... "

I thought some more. Perhaps Neville was waiting for me upstairs. Was it possible that he'd wait for me for an hour and a half - with every office, every courtroom, and everything else locked up? Perhaps he had come up on another elevator at precisely the same time that I came down? The odds weren't just against it; it was almost impossible! And the clerk that I had spoken to would have mentioned it.

Or was it that I simply had to take one last look at the courtroom where it all happened, one last look back as if looking back at the destroyed plain cities of Sodom and Gomorrah. And so, for whatever reason, or no reason, and although it was pointless, I had to do it, and like Lot's wife, risk being turned into a pillar of salt. I turned, ascended the stairs of Supreme Court for one last time, about to enter the building.

LXII. The Transaction

I didn't hear it at first. The noise blended in with the rest of the traffic of the City. Nor did I hear the call of its rider, but the sound of a motorcycle grew louder, and the call came again. It was now unmistakable.

"MISTER COHEN!"

I turned. It was Midnite on the Guzzi. I had to recover quickly - the settlement was alive, the transaction was on. Conversation should be kept to a minimum, and the transaction completed as soon as possible. I motioned towards the doors of the court building.

"Let's go inside."

"I, eh ... I can't."

He waved his arm in one motion from the north corner of the court building, to the south corner. Parking was for official vehicles only, and every parking spot was taken. He pointed to the north corner, and I met him there. The Guzzi had survived well the six weeks or so at City Boys, despite having been "stored" in an open area exposed to rain and debris in what was little more than a junk yard. It really was a shame, but it was beyond my control, and I hadn't planned it that way. Nevertheless, it still looked new, exactly as I saw it at the Ace Bar. It shined with a mirror finish, and its chromium was blinding. It was big, beautiful, and powerful - a masterpiece of fine engineering - and it would never be mine!

"Do you have the check?"

Still straddling the motorcycle, he took out the certified check and held it up with both hands for me to see.

"Do you have the cash?"

I didn't answer Neville. It was obvious that our transaction was going to be extremely awkward at best. I turned to my left and noticed a police officer nearby. He was a black traffic cop patrolling in front of the court building.

"Officer! ... Excuse me, Officer!"

He turned and hesitatingly moved in our direction. "Officer, we have to do a cash transaction. Can you just stand by here and witness this?"

The officer continued walking towards us, now more with curiosity than caution.

"A what kind of transaction?"

It might have sounded like a drug deal in the works, but it was Neville who explained.

"We have a paper from the court. I have to give him a check, and he has to give me $216.00."

The officer now stood between us and agreed to witness the transaction.

"I'd like to see that check again."

Neville displayed it again. It was a certified check for $3,000.00, payable to me, and drawn on the Bank of New York. I counted out the $216.15 and held the cash in my left hand.

"Let me have the check."

"No, you first."

The feeling of mutual mistrust was still very much present, but I was giving him cash, and he was giving me a check - and nobody was giving receipts.

"No, you!"

Neville relented and passed the check on to the officer, who held it up to me for a closer look. It was made payable to me and it looked real. I examined the certified stamp, the authorized signature, and the payor's signature. It wasn't Neville's. I didn't know the name, but it had to be the Solarz girlfriend. I guess Neville never really did have any money. I nodded approval and held out the cash to the Officer to pass over to Neville.

"I, eh ... I can't take the cash - it's like a bribe."

"Oh,"

I answered, slightly embarrassed. I would have to hand it directly to Midnite, and I did. And at the precise instant that my hand loosened its grip on the wad of bills containing $216.00, Midnite's big black hand tightened on it. It was as if some great cataclysmic cosmic event would take place. But here the heavens were quiet and peace prevailed.

"Ok, you guys are on your way."

And with that, the officer handed me the check, departed, and returned to his post.

Midnite took the money and counted it out quickly, as one who was experienced in handling large amounts of cash. He folded the bills in thirds and tucked them into his shirt pocket. He didn't ask for the fifteen cents.

"All r i g h t !"

He was ready to leave.

"Wait!"

I reached into by briefcase and took out the Stipulation of Settlement, and the Sheriff's Affidavit, and not with minimized animation, tore off the debtor's copy of each. I held it out to Neville with a straight arm and he took it. The transaction was complete.

And now, what was there to do? Should I have extended my hand to my former foe in friendship? Should I have wished him goodbye and good luck? Should I have said something like, *"I enjoyed the adventure - you were a worthy opponent?"* Or perhaps I should have given him some big brotherly parting words of advice? They might have gone something like,

> *"Neville, I don't understand you. Why do you choose to live like this? You're not stupid. If you had put all this energy into getting an education, getting a real job, making a life for yourself - you would have money, a career, a purpose and a place in society, and respect from your fellow man."*

Or perhaps I secretly did harbor a bizarre kind of respect for Neville and his loose, carefree, underground lifestyle. It was a life of cash-off-the-books jobs in bars, tips, rock bands, night life, deals, and motorcycles. It was life on the edge, it was exciting, it was adventurous, and it was dangerous. It held a certain romantic quality about it that almost might make one envy it. But like the Guzzi was never mine, that lifestyle was not mine, and it was one that I would never, nor could ever live or accept. We were truly of different worlds.

> *"Do not regard anyone with contempt, and do not reject anything, for there is no man who does not have his hour, and nothing which does not have its place."*

> *(Ethics of our Fathers, Chap. IV)*

I said nothing and turned to walk south on Lafayette. The Guzzi engine was fired up again with one final thunderous roar. Neville headed north with the Guzzi. I listened as the sound of its powerful engine became more and more faint, until finally becoming absorbed, and in unison with the rest of the City, and until I could hear it no more. I did not look back. I was all over. Midnite paid his rent.

LXIII. Cohen vs. City Boys Towing

And so, the seemingly endless crusade for justice had come to a close, finally ending in the seventh year, the sabbatical year. It was a victory of sorts, but it wasn't complete. Midnite had gotten off cheap. The hard earned judgments were only partially satisfied. Was the objective after all to recover some lost money, or was it to get the motorcycle sold at auction? If the latter, then I had failed! The scales of justice needed some fine tuning. I needed a new debtor, a new target, and one with assets. It would be City Boys Towing.

I could not adjust emotionally to the entire episode at City Boys - the rude treatment, the abusive language, and the refusal to accept my credit card as payment. It was as if I were the deadbeat! It was an ego crushing experience. It was an embarrassment. The sadistic performance was carried out with joy to the great delight of my enemies - Midnite and Ms. Callucci. The scales of justice still needed to be balanced.

I decided to sue City Boys Towing for breach of contract - for releasing the motorcycle to the debtor without the authorization of the Sheriff. City Boys had made their contract with me, not the debtor. And like the powerful engine of the Moto Guzzi revving up again after its long storage at the junk yard at City Boys, so was I on my new case.

First, I needed the signed copy of the Sheriff's Agreement. My copy didn't have the City Boys authorized signature on it. The signed copy was faxed directly to the

421

Sheriff by City Boys. I wrote a letter to the Sheriff's Office requesting a copy of their signed agreement. The signed copy of the agreement came back to me by fax. It was signed by Rhoda as City Boys manager.

I would also need to prove loss. What was the Guzzi really worth? I would be able to sue up to the value of the motorcycle subject to the Small Claims limit, now $3,000.00. I'd get the proof regarding the value of the motorcycle later.

It was about this time that I signed up with "The Legal Plan." For only $11.99 a month, you would have a lawyer to talk to, make calls on your behalf, write threatening letters to deadbeats, etc. For only $11.99, you would have someone to be on your side - someone to be your friend! There would be no more screw-ups and no more mistakes. There would be no more judges, lawyers, or law clerks to intimidate or take advantage of the poor, frightened pro se litigant helplessly pursuing what he thinks will be justice. I would now have a friend - I would have a lawyer!

I liked Greg. He was easy to talk to, he'd always listen, and sometimes, he'd even return my calls. Maybe he wasn't the greatest of lawyers, but for $11.99 a month, it was a bargain. One didn't need a good lawyer - one just needed a lawyer. Midnite taught me that. The incompetent little Ms. Callucci was able to work out the settlement deal. I always thought that a stuffed dummy dressed appropriately in a suit and tie would work fine. In order to dispel any doubts as to its credentials, I could hang a sign around its neck that would read,

"LAWYER."

For added effect, a low tech sound chip could be added. It would say,

"APPLICATION! ... OBJECTION! ... YES, YOUR HONOR! ...REQUEST ADJOURNMENT!"

Oh, I nearly forgot. It would also scream out loud,

"BULLSHIT!"

Greg wasn't really a bad lawyer. I had him write a letter to City Boys demanding payment for the unauthorized release of the Moto Guzzi motorcycle before settlement. It was before settlement because at the time of release, the settlement agreement was not yet submitted to the judge, nor did I intend to submit it. This of course made City Boys responsible for the unpaid part of the judgments plus interest and expenses. The letter was typed up on expensive legal stationery with a bold and impressive lawyer's letterhead. It sounded ominous and threatening. It ended with,

"... My client has given us the authority to execute on said judgment using all legal remedies available to judgment creditors.

GOVERN YOURSELF ACCORDINGLY."

It looked good. I discussed the letter with Greg over the phone and had him read it to me. Greg ended the conversation with an air of confidence.

"THAT SHOULD SCARE 'EM!!"

Unfortunately, it didn't. As usual, the mighty forces behind the lawyer's powerful letter was still just little me. The five day time limit that he gave them came and went without incident. It was two weeks later that I began my suit. I sent Mr. Abramovitch, the City Boys owner, my own demand letter by certified mail, return-receipt-requested. It was honest, detailed, factual, and to the point - and it received no response. City Boys would not be coaxed, cajoled, or intimidated. I had them served with a Notice of Claim from the Small Claims Court. It was going to trial.

I worked on my case and collected the needed evidence. There happened to be a Moto Guzzi dealer in my area, Super Moto Italia. I decided to pay them a visit. The surrealistic, déjà vu image appearing before me as I entered the showroom nearly floored me, but the thing was really there. On display was the motorcycle - it looked like the same Guzzi - the "California" model - black with cream color gas tank. It differed only as to the absence of its rider and the Illinois license plate - but it really could have been the Guzzi!

"Hi, can I help you?"

"Eh, well … yeah. What year is that motorcycle?"

"'96."

"What's it selling for?"

"I'll look it up for you … $8,490.00. Interested?"

"Well, uh … I need a written estimate."

I learned that I always couldn't tell the truth. I couldn't say that I was a judgment creditor, and that I was going to sue someone in Small Claims Court. Nobody likes judgment creditors. We're automatically the "bad guys." I didn't know where it was going, but he asked the question first.

"Oh, you were in an accident?"

Well, Midnite did have an accident, but it wasn't with the Guzzi. And subletting the apartment to Midnite in the first place certainly happened by accident, but that wasn't what he meant.

"Well, no ..."

The Moto Guzzi guy tried again.

"It was stolen!"

Stolen? Well, sort of. City Boys released the motorcycle to Midnite and his lawyer, and it wasn't authorized by the Sheriff. To take without authorization is stealing. Right? Here was the answer.

"Yeah ... that's it, uh ... it was stolen."

"Gee, that's a shame. Did you report it to the police?"

Did I report it to the police? Well, no, not exactly. I reported it to the Sheriff, but of course I couldn't tell him that.

"To the police? Uh, no ... not yet."

The Super Moto guy gave me a strange look. It was obvious that something was wrong here. I didn't meet his eyes directly, but turned to view the display of motorcycles, as if I were ready to buy. The man from Super Moto continued.

"Well, I'd get going on that right away. When was it stolen?"

It must have been at least a few weeks since the release at City Boys, but that would have sounded ridiculous, and then he'd know for sure that something was definitely wrong. I answered quickly.

"Yesterday."

I'm sure Super Moto sensed something strange here, but they wrote up the estimate for me. The bike went for $10,490.00 new; it Blue-Booked for $7,930.00; and the floor model with 2,000 miles on the clock was selling for $8,490.00. All the prices were easily over the unsatisfied part of the judgments, and well over the Small Claims limit.

"By the way, I'm a retired cop."

"Oh," I gulped.

"Mention my name when you report it to the police."

He handed me the estimate.

"There you go."

"Do I owe you anything for this?"

"No, but come back soon. We'll deal."

"Ok, and thanks! Thanks a lot!"

"Good luck!"

Everything is work and deception in this business, but now I had my written estimate, the first piece of evidence for my case. A trip to the local library gave me the N.A.D.A. appraisal guide prices: $9,690.00 to $10,490.00 suggested list. So now, in addition to the signed contract that I had with City Boys, I had two proofs of the motorcycle's value. What I needed next was a statement from the Sheriff with regard to the unauthorized release.

This last item, needed to prove breach of contract, was crucial to my case, but turned out to be a problem. Several phone calls to the Sheriff's Office were seemingly delayed or ignored. I finally was able to get through, and spoke directly with the Deputy. I had to be firm. I explained what I needed and why.

"Deputy Schatzer, what I need is a simple statement from the Sheriff's Office stating that the motorcycle was released without the authorization of the Sheriff. I have to have it to prove breach of contract. I have no other proof."

"Ok, ok, let me talk to Stan. Write up the statement you want us to sign and send it to us. We'll get back to you.

You have my word on it."

There was definitely a problem, but I wasn't sure what it was. Anyway, I wrote up the statement following the Deputy's instructions. It was short, simple, and to the point.

"This will serve to indicate that the Moto Guzzi motorcycle was released by City Boys Towing to the debtor in the above referenced case, without the authorization of the Sheriff, and was in violation of their contract."

Sheriff's offices are notoriously always understaffed and backlogged. Debt collection in our society is the lowest of low priorities. Civil debt collection brings in only modest revenue in sheriff fees for our municipalities. And taxpayer money spent on Sheriff Offices for debt collection doesn't feed the hungry, house the homeless, clothe the naked, or provide for the general welfare of the state. Indeed, it might actually do all of the opposite. Nor does it help politicians get elected. Has any candidate for political office ever said,

"And I stand for creditor rights! I stand for the rights of the judgment creditor! I promise to clean up the shameful backlog of unpaid judgments awarded in the courts of our state. I will work to pass legislation to increase the percentage of wage garnishments to 75 percent, bring back debtor's prison, deport illegal aliens, and confiscate their assets, ... I WILL MAKE THE DEADBEATS PAY!?"

Of course not! Nobody really cares about the judgment creditor. We're the "bad guys."

Nevertheless, my signed statement came back several weeks later, but it had been severely edited to the point of uselessness.

"This will serve to indicate that the motorcycle was released to the debtor without the authorization of the Sheriff after settlement."

The "after settlement" addition killed my case. If the release occurred after settlement, there would be no loss. I was furious. I hit the ceiling. THE IDIOTS! The statement was useless ... and it was also false! I called the Deputy. I was still in control, but now spoke more firmly to him than I had ever spoken to him before.

"Deputy Schatzer, I received your statement. Thank you very much. Unfortunately, it is inaccurate and useless. I am therefore returning it to you for correction. The motorcycle was released before settlement - BEFORE! This is precisely the point. You added the words 'after settlement.'"

The Deputy didn't want to hear it. His only response was,

"Talk to Stan!"

I did talk to the Sheriff, but the discussion became overly heated and deteriorated into a shouting match.

"Look Stan, it was released before settlement. It was not released after settlement! Before! Before!"

"Well ... WE DON'T KNOW WHEN IT WAS RELEASED!"

"IF YOU DON'T KNOW - THEN YOU CAN'T SAY AFTER!!!"

"If this is going to continue like this, I'm going to have to hang up!"

"Stan, please … just take out those two words, 'after settlement.' That's not the way it was. Just take them out, and it'll be fine, ok?"

"Let me think about it."

Weeks went by and nothing was done. It was obvious that they had a problem with it and weren't going to take any action. I called the Deputy again.

"Steve, what's happening with my statement? I need it to go to court!"

"Well, we have a problem. We can't say when. Who knows? Before - after - at - during - who knows?"

"Look, if you don't know, then say, 'The motorcycle was released without authorization, but we don't know when.'"

"Ha, ha … we can't do it that way …"

In my exhaustion and frustration, the phone went silent for a few awkward seconds, but then the Deputy offered a startling suggestion.

"Look Jon, get us down there. We'll help you."

"What!? You mean subpoena you as witnesses?"

"Yeah!"

I certainly didn't want to impose upon the Sheriff and the Deputy, or cause any inconvenience. And surely there were many far more important things that had to be done at the Sheriff's Office. On the other hand, Sheriffs and their Deputies probably do spend a good part of their time in court. Anyway, I had to ask.

"You don't mind? Really? I won't do this unless you're willing to do it."

"We'll bat for you. Subpoena us. We can't do written statements, but get us into court. We'll testify."

"Ok, Steve. You're on! And thanks! Thanks for everything."

I went down to Small Claims and got the subpoena signed. Hoping to avoid further delay, as well as the expense of a process server, I faxed the subpoena over to the Sheriff's Office with a short note.

"Personal service between agreeing parties should not be necessary. If you need it, let me know."

The service of process by fax worked fine. And so it was that I had a copy of the signed contract, two proofs of the value of the motorcycle, and featured star witness for the plaintiff, Sheriff's Deputy Steve Schatzer. Trial date was set, and placed on the court calendar.

LXIV. Witness for the Plaintiff

The case was prepared well, the evidence complete and collected, and its presentation and probable outcome well thought out; but I knew that things could still go wrong. It wasn't airtight, and even Greg said that it wasn't a sure win. The case could fall apart on the matter of whether or not there was a settlement, or the intent of a settlement. Why were we all gathered at City Boys if there were no settlement? But I had to fight it. Ultimate justice was at stake! I would fight, litigate, argue, debate, and advocate! It would be a victory for the sake of justice! I had to win!

I got to the City at a ridiculously early hour, 2:30 P.M. for my 6:30 P.M. trial. I studied my notes and evidence for at least a full three hours, but I know that for a good part of that time, my eyes were just fixated on the snapshot of the Guzzi, with my mind blindly wandering off into space.

I was the first one to arrive at the doors to the Small Claims courtroom. I sat down on one of the wooden benches outside the courtroom. I was still dry mouthed, nervous, and fidgety in spite of all my experience. This was big. I watched all the people as they began to arrive for their trials. There were all kinds of people, and they were all coming to seek justice. They were black, white, Chinese, Indian, Latino - everybody came. And they were dressed in jeans and T-shirts, shorts and sandals, ties and jackets, slacks and blouses, and a few in business suits (probably the lawyers). While seated on the bench, I continually scanned the lobby for signs of my new adversary - City Boys Towing. Perhaps they had brought along Ms. Callucci as a witness ... or even Midnite! It was almost 6:30 P.M., the time of the first calendar call. The lobby and the corridors were filling up fast, but there was no sign of anybody that had anything to do with my case. Did I get the date wrong?! Oh, you idiot! In a panic, I ran and checked the calendar list of scheduled cases to be tried on that day. It was there: Cohen vs. City Boys Towing, Inc. But where was Schatzer? Just then, two officers happened to pass by. Were they court officers? Police officers? I couldn't tell. One was short and in full blue uniform. He wore a belt of bullets and handcuffs around his waist. The other was plainclothed and towered over his partner. He had a good, strong neck, with a chain and a badge around it. I struggled to make out the names, but I could not. Anyway, I had subpoenaed only one, the Deputy, and now here there were two - they had to be there for someone else as witnesses for another trial. And besides, every Schatzer that I ever knew was short, so I knew that it couldn't be the tall one, but what about the other one? I dismissed it. No, they weren't mine. I continued looking. Where was Deputy Schatzer? He was supposed to be here. Where the hell was he!?

6:30 P.M. came and the doors to the Small Claims calendar call room opened. Still I didn't see any sign of City Boys or Deputy Schatzer. It was then that I remembered my process service by fax, which went so smoothly and seemed so brilliant at the time.

"IDIOT! YOU SHOULD HAVE USED THE ROADRUNNER!!"

And as the calendar call proceeded, I searched the room

again. There was no sign of City Boys, but I stared at the two officers who were seated at the front of the room, and I wondered for what purpose they were there. Eventually, I heard my case being called.

"Jonah Cohen."

"Cohen, ready."

Ready, right ... without my star witness! It looked like I'd be going it alone.

"City Boys Towing."

"City Boys Towing, application."

A man with thick, bushy, slightly graying black hair, and an Israeli accent, stood up to answer the calendar call. I hadn't seen him before. He must have been the City Boys owner. He looked over in my direction with a curious look which seemed to inquire,

"Who is this man who dares to sue my company in Small Claims Court?"

We were both called over to the clerk. I later discovered that the clerk's main job is to get rid of the cases before they come to trial - either by settlement, or legal technicality - and to do so as quickly and efficiently as possible. The pace was fast.

"Who are you?"

"Cohen, plaintiff."

"Abramovitch, City Boys Towing."

"Who subpoenaed the Marshals?"

Marshals? Marshals were subpoenaed? Where? Why? Marshals, yes! It was then that it hit me. They were mine!"

"Sheriffs!" I corrected. "I did!"

So they came! Glorious Sheriffs! Princes of Peace!

Guardians of Justice! Defenders of Judgments! Both of them came! But which one was Schatzer?

It was time for fast introductions. I walked over to the two officers, and I could now see the name tags and the badges clearly. The short, uniformed one was Stan. Schatzer was the tall, plainclothed one. It was he who would join us at the clerk's desk.

"Plaintiff, state your case."

"This is a case involving breach of contract ..."

"You have the contract?"

"Yes, it's a written contract."

I showed the clerk the contract.

"This is not a contract."

"Why not?! Of course it is!"

"Your motorcycle?"

"No."

"Then why are we here?"

"I'm the judgment creditor in an unrelated case ... I mean, a related case."

"And?"

"And I had the Sheriff seize the motorcycle ..."

"Whose motorcycle?"

"The debtor's."

"Is he here?"

"No."

"Why not?"

"Because we settled."

"Then why are you here?"

"I'm the judgment creditor, and I was storing the motorcycle ..."

"The debtor's?"

"Yes ... at City Boys."

"Did you sign the contract?"

"Yes. I signed and City Boys signed. It was signed by a manager at City Boys, Rhoda Berkowitz."

Another City Boys employee, the individual with whom I had had the argument about payment, walked proudly up to the bench and spoke on behalf of the City Boys defense. I recognized him immediately. It was Yitzchak, one of the managers. He was short, balding, and wore a pony tail.

"Oh, she's not a manager. She's only a secretary."

"MANAGER! It says right here, 'Manager!'"

The issue as to whether or not the contract was signed by a manager shouldn't have had anything to do with anything. The fact was, here was a signed contract. I handed the contract to the clerk who now examined it more closely, but now there was another problem.

"Did the Sheriff sign this?"

"Well, no, but ..."

"Then it's not a contract!"

"OF COURSE IT IS!"

I attempted to explain contract law to the seemingly ignorant law clerk, but it was no use.

"A contract is an agreement between or among two or more parties to perform a certain act for consideration."

"This would be a contract between City Boys and the Sheriff, not between you and City Boys."

I thought that I was doing well, but at this, my frustration tolerance threshold had been breached. If I couldn't make this idiot clerk understand, my case would die a premature death right here. In my desperation, my response was perhaps excessively emphatic.

"But it's between them and me - ME! I'M THE ONE WHO PAID THE DAMNED COSIDERATION!!"

We weren't getting anywhere. But, at this point, it was the Deputy who came to the rescue. And now, I was able to study him more carefully, for the first time. He was well over six feet tall, maybe 6 feet, 3 inches; or 6 feet, 4 inches; and thin for his height, but still a solid 220 pounds or better. The neck was strong and muscular - he must have worked out regularly with weights. And the eyes were sort of squinty, as if shutting out all danger, and as if to say,

"STAY OUT OF MY WAY!"

or,

"COME ON, MAKE MY DAY!"

He walked in a slow and determined manner, but still covered great distances quickly with what might have been a three or more foot stride. He was all of Clint Eastwood, lacking only the hat, poncho, spurs, and biddy cigarette. He was Sheriff's Deputy Schatzer - witness for the plaintiff.

"Deputy Schatzer, New York City Sheriff's Office. Perhaps I can explain. The judgment creditor contracts with a private, independent towing company. The towing company signs an agreement with the Sheriff's Office to seize and store property under the direction of the Sheriff until such time as release is authorized ..."

He spoke slowly and clearly, and only just loud enough to be heard above the noise in the calendar call room. The first stage was completed. We passed the hurdle of the calendar clerk. There were just a few more questions to be asked.

"What were the total amounts of the judgments?"

I recalled the results of all my legal work. I answered quickly, but I didn't mention the $3,000.00 that I had already received at the settlement.

"Over $7,000.00 with costs and interest."

"Why don't you take it to regular Civil Court?"

"I can do that?"

"Sure, enter a Pro Se claim …"

Here we go again! Regular Civil Court without a lawyer! No thanks! We'll keep it Small Claims, my league. The clerk was trying to be helpful, but I wanted to get on with it.

"Well, we're here now, and I'd like to have the trial."

"Ok, step over and see the calendar judge."

The plaintiff, the defendant, and the witness, now all stepped over to the judge.

"Plaintiff, are you ready?"

"Ready, Your Honor."

"Defendant, you requested application?"

"Right."

"Why?"

"I don't have my papers."

"What?"

"I don't have my papers. I need more time. I don't know what this is all about."

"Your Honor, I'm ready to put this to trial right now!"

Yitzchak had been to court before. He knew all the tricks and what to say.

"But Your Honor, I need more time. I don't have my papers."

"Your Honor, the defendant was properly served. There were several letters written, there were phone calls made, the defendant had months to prepare …"

I went on pleading for a trial right then and there - my

witnesses were there and perhaps I wouldn't be able to get them back again. And I had made the long commute from eastern Long Island, and I had to take a half day off from work for this; but in the end, the judge's compassion fell upon the defendant, as it always does.

"TWO WEEKS! And I'm marking it 'FINAL!'"

The trial would not take place that night. Afterward, I talked briefly with the Sheriff (who I later found out was really the Under-Sheriff), and his Deputy. The Sheriff began with some pointed questions that still seemed to bother him.

"I'm not trying your case, but you had a settlement. Didn't you settle? What did you mean by 'the settlement wasn't consummated'?"

I thought, paused, and then tried to explain again.

"Stan ... you had to see what happened there in Supreme Court. Look ... isn't it up to me, the judgment creditor, who decides whether he wants to settle ... or not? They coerced me into it. I had the settlement agreement with me, in my hand, and then I placed it in my briefcase. If I chose not to give it to the judge, and the judge didn't sign it, then, at that point, there was no settlement. Right?"

"Well ... maybe."

"And if City Boys released the motorcycle without the Sheriff's authorization, which would have been at the instruction of the judgment creditor; and without the judge's signature on the settlement agreement, then that's breach of contract. Right?"

"Yup, I guess so. Then you might have them. You just might have them."

"Well ... thanks guys, thanks for showing up. See you in a couple of weeks, ok?"

"Right!"

LXV. More Small Claims

It was the day of the trial. I waited at the same wooden bench in the hallway that was outside the Small Claims courtroom that had now become all too familiar. Would my witnesses show?   At 6:25 P.M., the Deputy exited the elevator, alone.   He was again plainclothed, and he was wearing the badge around his neck. He was holding a can of soda tightly in his left hand between his thumb and index finger. He brought the can up to his lips, emptying it with one huge final gulp, and then tossed the empty can into the recycling bin.

And the Sheriff's Deputy walked through the saloon doors. He proceeded to walk straight up to the bar. The sound of his boot heals and spurs on the hard wooden floor quickly silenced the room. He had presence! He commanded respect! No one would talk when the Deputy was around. No one would even dare to rise from his seat.

"Whisky!" he demanded. He took the glass in his left hand between his thumb and forefinger, brought it up to his mouth, and emptied it in one huge gulp.

He left the bar quickly. All was peaceful here, but there was other work to be done. Justice had to be served!

The Deputy acknowledged me with only a slight nod. Any conversation between the witness and the plaintiff had best be kept to a minimum. We took our usual places - I amongst the throngs of litigants, and he in the front, in that special place reserved for officialdom. I spotted Yitzchak from City Boys seated across the aisle. We were on for that night. The judge had marked the case "Final." There would be no more adjournments. The clerk went through the calendar call, and soon …

"Jonah Cohen vs. City Boys Towing Inc."

"Cohen, ready."

"City Boys, ready."

"Room 107."

And so, plaintiff, defendant, and witness all marched on to room 107, a march to justice, at last! Room 107 was an arbitrator's room. I liked room 107. It was clean, quiet, and private - no observers or litigants waiting for their cases to be heard. It would be a simple hearing with an arbitrator seated at his desk. I sat down on the chair at the left, the plaintiff's place, and proceeded to open my legal folder. It was finally happening. Win or lose, up or down, it would be the end, and the end of the whole subletting misadventure. It would be the end of Midnite, the end of Sheriffs, the end of courts and judges … and the end of motorcycles. Deputy Schatzer took the seat in the middle, the place of the witness. Yitzchak from City Boys took three steps into the room, then hesitated, then stopped dead in his tracks. What was wrong? What was happening? What other tricks was this City Boys Towing guy planning? The case was marked "Final."

"I'm Yitzchak Reuben, City Boys Towing. I would like to have this trial heard before a judge."

The seemingly absurd request took us all by surprise. The arbitrator responded.

"A trial before an arbitrator has the same legal force as a trial before a judge."

440

"I know … I know …"

"Why do you want this to be heard before a judge?"

"Well … if … if I should lose … I want to be able to appeal. I want to have the right to appeal."

"Why didn't you request so before?"

"Well, eh … well, I didn't know."

Didn't know! Of course he knew! He knew Small Claims better than I did! He must have been there a hundred times before, but both of us knew that a defendant's request for a hearing before a judge could not be denied! It was all a delay tactic, perfectly executed! I protested, of course, but I knew it was pointless. We went back to the calendar call room to begin the hopeless and futile wait for a judge. After nearly two hours of waiting, I was called up to the clerk, and then returned to relay my instructions to my witness.

"What's going on?"

"No trial tonight - they can't find a judge. We have to come back in two weeks, in the morning, at 9:00 A.M."

The Deputy forced a smile, but looked tired and disgusted. He had to come back again.

"Don't they pay you overtime for this?"

He nodded.

"Stay with me, Steve. I and the City of New York will make you a rich man."

"I don't need it, believe me."

"I know, but I need you."

LXVI. Negotiations

City Boys was running out of tricks. It seemed clear that we were headed for a trial, but a couple of days later, the call came. They were ready to deal. They wanted to settle.

"Hello, Mr. Cohen. Abramovitch, City Boys Towing."

I had five rules for successful negotiation: Rule #1 - Be cool, Rule #2 - Be business like, Rule #3 - Don't say too much, Rule #4 - Present a strong front, Rule #5 - Don't settle cheap. I had learned something from my negotiations with Midnite. A settlement here would be better than a trial. The matter of the settlement with Midnite and Ms. Callucci, and the difficulty of proving a case as to when the signing of the settlement took place verses the actual release bothered me more that it did the Sheriff. If City Boys would argue that there was a settlement, the intent of a settlement, or the signing of a settlement, or even the signing of the Stipulation of Settlement by the judge before the release, then City Boys might not be liable for any loss, regardless of whether or not the release was authorized by the Sheriff. If they would even raise any question, or cast any doubt as to the sequence of the signing of the settlement, and the release of the motorcycle, then my case might be lost. Yes, a settlement here would certainly be better.

"Hello, Mr. Abramovitch."

"Hey … uh … I'd like to settle this matter."

"Ok. Go ahead."

"Well, what are you looking for to settle?"

"How much are you willing to offer?"

"You first. What do you want?"

"You called me. Make me an offer."

"… Well, ok … $500.00."

It was a start, but it was a ridiculous offer. I didn't come this far for $500.00, and yet it would be a victory of sorts, but it really wasn't enough. Besides, it violated Rule #5 - Don't settle cheap.

"No Eli … No good."

"Well, how much?"

"I'll need something closer to the value of the motorcycle."

"Well?"

"Well, the claim is $3,000.00. I'll settle for half, $1,500.00."

"Ha! No, no, no. $500.00 - top offer."

"No good, Eli. See you in court."

"Wait, wait! I'll tell you what. Do you have a car?"

"Do I have a car? Of course I have a car."

"I'll tell you what. $500.00 plus I'll fix your car for you anytime you need it."

"What?!"

"Right. One free repair, plus, if you ever get stuck, we'll give you a free tow."

"What?!! I don't believe you guys. You think that I'm going to let you work on my car? Then you guys can really screw me!"

"Now, now … Jonah … look, we're not enemies … Think about it."

"Eli, $1,500.00, ok? That's it, or we'll have it out in court."

The negotiations weren't quite over. Mr. Abramovitch threw up his ace on the table.

"Hey … uh, I'm having the owner of the motorcycle

come … as a witness … with Ms. Callucci, his lawyer."

"Oh? Really?"

"Yeah!"

"Which one? Midnite or the other one. You know, there are two owners."

"I know. The black guy … Midnite."

"Well, I spent seven years trying to find Midnite. If you can find him and bring him to court in two weeks, you're a better man than I am. Good luck! See you in court."

LXVII. The Guzzi Trial

I thought of the strange conversation that I had had with Mr. Abramovitch regarding the offer of settlement from City Boys. He had to be bluffing about the witnesses, but I couldn't be sure. I certainly didn't need Midnite or Callucci there to testify for them. But would Midnite actually be willing to testify? Could Captain Midnite even be found? And if found, perhaps he would be "paid off" for favorable testimony. Could the alien spirit actually be resurrected? I just didn't know. I really didn't want to take a chance on going to court, and having the two witnesses for City Boys testifying.

I waited for another call from City Boys - I'd take $1,000.00. Should I take less - $900.00? Should I call them? No! That would show weakness, and a plaintiff must never be weak! I would be in violation of Rules #4 and #5! But another call from City Boys didn't come.

The day before the trial, I called Deputy Schatzer. I knew that he would be there for the trial, but I had to make sure and a call wouldn't hurt.

"Don't worry - I'll be there."

It was reassuring, but the prospect of seeing Midnite and has lawyer again was horrifying. I didn't sleep well that night. They would destroy my case. I didn't need them there. Certainly they had more important things to do than come to court to testify for City Boys. Could Midnite even be found? Probably not, but what about Callucci? Would she come? Would the plump, sweaty, little Ms. Callucci show? Oh Ms. Callucci ... Ms. Callucci ...

Judge: "Ms. Callucci, call your witness."

Ms. Callucci: "I call Neville Michaels, owner of the Moto Guzzi bicycle."

Mr. Michaels took the stand. His appearance was immaculate. He wore an all white suit, perfectly cleaned and pressed. The shirt was jet black, and opened at the collar. He still wore a gold medallion, a 24 carat piece of pure gold, about the size of a Mexican 50 Peso gold coin, attached with a chain around his neck. He looked dashing, and in a way that I had never seen him before. He seemed to be irradiated with a supernal light, and from his lips, there emanated only truth. He was sworn in and took the witness stand.

Ms. Callucci: "Mr. Michaels, are you the owner of the Moto Guzzi bicycle?"

Midnite: "I'm the owner of the Moto Guzzi motorcycle - not bicycle, Ms. Callucci!"

Ms. Callucci: "I stand corrected. Thank you Mr. Michaels. Now ... did you settle the case at hand with Mr. Cohen?"

Midnite: "Yes. We settled in Supreme Court for $3,000.00. It was for an ILLEGAL SUBLET!"

Ms. Callucci: "A judgment on an ILLEGAL SUBLET! That's BULLSHIT! Imagine! And then what happened, Mr. Michaels."

Midnite: *"We all met at City Boys Towing. Mister Cohen, he told us where to go."*

Ms. Callucci: *"... to get the motorcycle ... to have it released."*

Midnite: *"Yes. He agreed to release it."*

Mr. Cohen: *"OBJECTION! HE'S LYING!! TO INSPECT IT!!"*

Judge: *"Mr. Cohen - Please be quiet! One more outburst and I'll have you placed in contempt of court! You'll have your chance to cross examine."*

Ms. Callucci: *"And it was released?"*

Midnite: *"No. Mister Cohen, he didn't want to pay him. He agreed to the release, and then didn't want to pay."*

Mr. Cohen: *"NO! They didn't want my credit card. I was going to pay, but..."*

Judge: *"MR. COHEN! PLEASE BE QUIET!"*

Ms. Callucci: *"So he settled ... Mr. Cohen settled, and then the motorcycle was released."*

Midnite: *"Right. City Boys didn't do nothing wrong. We settled. We had to pay because Mister Cohen, he didn't pay, and then the Guzzi was released."*

Ms. Callucci: *"And you always pay your debts, don't you Mr. Michaels."*

Midnite: *"Right. I paid 'cause Mister Cohen didn't want to. Mister Cohen - he no never pay nobody!"*

Mr. Cohen: *"OBJECTION! HE'S LYING! THAT'S NOT HOW IT WAS!"*

Judge: *"MR. COHEN! YOU ARE NOW IN CONTEMPT OF COURT! I AM FINING YOU $250.OO AND ONE DAY IN JAIL! BAILIFF - REMOVE THIS MAN FROM MY COURT IMMEDIATELY!"*

Mr. Cohen: *"But I'm innocent! I'm innocent! I'M INNOCENT!!! ..."*

I tried hard to clear my head of my imagined witnesses, but wasn't completely successful. I reported to the assigned courtroom on the day of the trial, and arrived at about 8:30 A.M. The Deputy, faithful to his word, came again. Mr. Reuben, representing City Boys Towing, also came. I nervously scanned the room for any sign of the short, plump, little Ms. Callucci and her client, the tall, thin black man with the gold medallion. There was none. Things seemed to move along now with lightning speed. It was happening.

"Jonah Cohen vs. City Boys Towing."

"Cohen, ready."

"City Boys, application."

Here we go again, I thought. They were doing it again. Mr. Reuben reported to the clerk, but there would be no more adjournments. This was it. I took the plaintiff's seat on the left; City Boys took the defendant's seat on the right. It was a trial before a judge, in a regular courtroom filled with lawyers, litigants, witnesses, and observers. A court stenographer was seated below the judge at his right, and a uniformed court officer stood on each side of the judge's bench. The trial began.

"Judge Raymond Goldberg presiding. All rise!"

The judge explained the rules. This was his Court. He would conduct it his way, and while this was still Small Claims, we would follow standard courtroom procedure. The plaintiff would begin first, presenting his case; the defendant would present his case; the plaintiff would question the defendant; the defendant would question the plaintiff; the plaintiff would call his witnesses; the defendant would cross examine; the defendant would call his witnesses; the plaintiff would cross examine; the plaintiff and the defendant would present their summations.

I got lost in all the rules, and so played it one step at a time. We were sworn in. It was really happening.

"Plaintiff, begin."

I looked up to the judge for assurance, way up to the bench, into the eyes of His Honor. He nodded. It was time to begin. I spoke loudly, slowly, and clearly.

"This is a case involving breach of contract. On June 24, 1997, I contracted with City Boys Towing, Inc. to tow and store at their facilities, assets seized by the New York City Sheriff, namely a 1996 Moto Guzzi Motorcycle."

My presentation was interrupted. The stenographer needed the correct spelling of the name of the motorcycle. I was delighted to help.

"Moto Guzzi, two words: Moto, M ... O ... T ...O, Guzzi, G ... U ... Z ... Z ... I."

"Thank you."

"I have here a written, signed contract. It was signed by the City Boy's manager, Rhoda Berkowitz."

I looked up at the judge, who was now completely absorbed in my case. I proceeded to read the contract with his apparent approval, and without interruption.

"It is hereby agreed that City Boys Towing will transport and or store property seized by the Sheriff and hold said property pending further direction by the Sheriff; and it is further agreed that the property stored will be released at the Sheriff's direction ..."

I handed the copy of the contract to the court officer, who handed it to the defendant, who handed it back to the court officer, who handed it to the judge in evidence. I continued.

"On August 6, 1997, City Boys released the motorcycle directly to the debtor. This release was without the authorization, and not under the direction of the New York City Sheriff, and was in violation of their contract. I have Deputy Schatzer here to testify to this."

It wasn't time for witnesses. I was instructed by the judge to continue.

"The total amount of the judgments with expenses and interest was $7,133.92."

I had the itemized list of the breakdown in front of me, but wasn't asked to read it or submit it in evidence. I went on.

"After the UNAUTHORIZED release of the motorcycle by City Boys, settlement was reached with the debtor in the amount of $3,000.00, an amount far below the value of the motorcycle."

I had a copy of the certified check that Midnite handed me after the settlement, but I wasn't asked to present it. The case continued smoothly, and without interruption. We were coming to the motorcycle. The question as to what the motorcycle might have sold for at a Sheriff's auction did not arise. I read off the selling price and appraised values from the evidence before me.

"The value of a 1996 Moto Guzzi Motorcycle, California Model is $7,930.00 per Kelly Blue Book; $8,490.00 per Super Moto Italia, St. James, New York; and $9,690.00 per N.A.D.A. Appraisal Guide."

I submitted the appraisals and written estimate in evidence. I wasn't sure if I should have submitted the snapshot of the Guzzi. The picture was taken in the City Boys junk yard during a particularly severe summer thunder storm, with a disposable type camera with a flash. Conditions were absolutely awful. The camera was soaking wet. The lens was spotted with droplets of rain, and although still daytime, it was as if it were night. Despite it all, the quality of the picture was remarkable. Nothing would put that Guzzi to shame! The chromium was still blinding, the paint finish shined, and clearly across the cream-colored gas tank, one could easily read in bright gold lettering, *MOTO GUZZI*. There was no mistaking that this was the motorcycle in question. I decided to present it in evidence.

"… and I have here a photograph of the motorcycle."

It was Yitzchak himself who showed me the motorcycle at a time when we were on better terms. The judge wanted to see the photo. His interest in the case could now be described as gripping. The picture went from me, to the defendant, to the court officer, and then to the judge. His Honor studied it, glanced over at the representative from City Boys, and then looked straight at me. His Honor spoke.

"THAT'S A BIG BIKE, ISN'T IT?!"

The case was going too well, magnificently well! His Honor knew bikes! He was a biker!

"Yes, Your Honor! It certainly is!"

"Plaintiff, please continue."

"I am claiming $3,000.00, which is the difference between the amount of the judgments, and the settlement amount, subject to the Small Claims limit. Defendant was notified of the claim by my demand letter sent by certified mail, return-receipt-requested."

I wanted to present the demand letter in evidence. I thought it summarized the events of the case well and might help, but it wasn't accepted, or needed. City Boys' awareness of the claim was not an issue. My initial presentation was now complete. Does the plaintiff rest? It was now my opposition's turn.

Mr. Reuben began his story from the beginning. He told of how I called him for a pick-up and storage of the motorcycle, and how it was supposed to be for only ten to fifteen days. I took notes and wrote down, *"NO!"* I didn't know how long - maybe a couple of weeks, maybe more - until the Sheriff's auction. He argued that the $10.00 per day fee was below the regular price, that he called me about the release, that he was bound by rules and regulations preventing him from storage in excess of fifteen days, and that I was present at the release and agreed to it.

Again, I wrote it all down in my notes, and followed each of his statements with a bold, *"NO! NO! NO!"* And then he argued that I didn't want to pay him, that I was "yelling and screaming, and carrying on like a madman," and that I demanded a discount. I did ask that if I paid by cash instead of credit card, would I receive a discount. It was not an unreasonable request, but "yelling and screaming," no. I think it was my right to yell and scream if I so chose, but anyway, it had nothing to do with anything. At this point, I put my pen down, and continued to listen to Mr. Reuben's ridiculous and false tirade of accusation without interrupting him. There was something about the credit card, and something about certified amounts (whatever that was) and a lot more about me not wanting to pay him, but there was nothing, absolutely nothing at all about the settlement with Midnite - did it take place, or when did it take place? His entire argument was basically that I didn't want to pay him. It was beautiful, just perfectly beautiful, and the longer that he went on, the better it was.

There was a slight pause in his presentation. Mr. Reuben was about to present his bombshell. He took out a letter from an envelope and unfolded it.

"I have here a letter from Ms. Callucci, the motorcycle owner's attorney ..."

He was about to read it when the judge abruptly cut him off.

"PUT THAT AWAY!"

"But Your Honor ..."

"I said put it away, NOW!"

"Your Honor, Ms. Callucci is out of town. She's in Washington, D.C. and she couldn't be here today. She gave me this signed, notarized affidavit ..."

"PUT ... IT ... AWAY, NOW!!!"

I braced myself during this exchange. I didn't know what it was that Ms. Callucci had said in her letter, but none of it could have been very good. There might have very well been something about the settlement that supposedly took place before the release. Anyway, it was good that she wasn't there, as a witness or otherwise. Mr. Reuben tried again.

"But Your Honor, this affidavit …"

"Mr. Reuben, did you hear me? I don't want to see it. PUT IT AWAY!"

He slowly and reluctantly folded it up in accordance with the judge's wishes. The problem with a written affidavit is that it can't be cross examined, as a live witness can. But what about Midnite? Was he there?

It could have been that City Boys really didn't understand the importance of a contract, or the argument that took place over the settlement. What seemed important to them was that I didn't pay them … in cash! Mr. Reuben concluded his presentation for City Boys. He was asked if he had any questions to ask me. He did not. I was asked if I had any questions to ask him. No. I was then given the opportunity to respond to Mr. Reuben's remarks and presentation. I looked down at my notes, but what was important? What needed a response? What was needed to win?

"Your Honor, the defendant has made many inaccurate statements. There is nothing in the contract that says anything about ten to fifteen days - the contract says, "… until the motorcycle is released." The defendant says that he is bound by certain rules and regulations, but he has neglected to say what rules and regulations. And it is not true that I didn't want to pay. I wanted to pay by credit card. I paid for the tow by credit card."

I took out the faxed credit card receipt for the tow showing the charge on my MasterCard and presented it in evidence. City Boys did in fact accept credit cards.

"It is the policy of City Boys to accept credit cards as payment. To demand cash in excess of $400.00 is unreasonable, and to refuse payment by credit card when the VISA and MasterCard emblems are clearly displayed on the wall is just plain ridiculous, and in violation of good business practices. I asked Mr. Reuben when City Boys started the cash only policy. His response was, 'Today. For you.'"

I concluded my rebuttal. It was time for witnesses. His Honor repeated the witness procedure. The matter of the settlement was still troublesome. I wondered if somehow word of the possible settlement agreement that took place at Supreme Court had found its way to the Sheriff's Office. Was the Sheriff's Office notified? Did somebody at the Sheriff's Office actually authorize the release, possibly without the Deputy's knowledge? Wouldn't Mr. Reuben have said something? Was there a witness? And so it was not without some anxiety that I called Deputy Schatzer to the stand.

"Plaintiff, call your witness."

I stood up and looked toward the back of the courtroom. He was there.

"I call Sheriff's Deputy Steven Schatzer."

I never called or questioned a witness before. It was my moment of glory. He was sworn in and took the seat between Mr. Reuben and me. I continued standing, faced the Deputy, and again spoke loudly, slowly, and clearly. The entire courtroom had gone completely silent in anticipation of the Deputy's account of the events. The Deputy was about to give his testimony. His Honor was not the only one who was interested in this case. I had just three simple questions. I began.

"Deputy Schatzer, were you the Deputy assigned to the case in question, Sheriff's Case #M583279 and #M783279?"

"Excuse me. What case? Could you repeat that?"

It was the court stenographer. I was going too fast! It was beautiful! Just too beautiful! I spoke even slower - very slowly and repeated the question.

"Deputy Schatzer, were you ... the Deputy Sheriff ...assigned ... to Case #M ... 5 ... 8 ... 3 ... 2 ... 7 ... 9 ... and Case #M ... 7 ... 8 ... 3 ... 2 ... 7 ... 9?"

"Yes."

"And, Deputy Schatzer, did you ... authorize ... or direct ... the release of ... the Moto ... Guzzi ... motorcycle?"

"No."

I was up to the last question, and could not be completely sure of the answer. I proceeded to ask it.

"And, Deputy Schatzer, did <u>anyone</u> ... at the New York City Sheriff's Office ... authorize ... or direct ... the release ... or give any instructions to anyone ... regarding the release ... of the Moto Guzzi motorcycle?"

"No."

"Thank you Deputy Schatzer. No further questions, Your Honor."

"Defendant, you may now cross examine the witness."

It was now Mr. Reuben's turn for the cross examination, but the bizarre interchange that followed was confusing and pointless. City Boys had no questions, but instead engaged the Deputy in a dialogue which seemed to have nothing to do with the case and the facts thereof. The Deputy responded with a very blunt,

"That's irrelevant."

The judge broke in and instructed the defendant to ask questions. Mr. Reuben tried again.

"Deputy Schatzer, how is it that City Boys Towing was chosen to be the towing and storage company?"

They still didn't get it.

"Mr. Rueben, please ask relevant questions of the witness."

"Deputy Schatzer, you know, we at City Boys have been in business over fifteen years and we are hardworking people. We give the public top quality service, and we expect to get paid for our service. Now, you service the public also. How long have you been a Deputy Sheriff?"

It was hopeless. The judge ended it. City Boys really needed a lawyer.

"The witness is excused. Does City Boys have any witnesses?"

I braced. Were there any witnesses? At least I wouldn't be dealing with the sweaty, little Ms. Callucci, but what about Midnite? Would the alien spirit suddenly emerge from the crowd at the back of the courtroom? I looked up at the ceiling, almost as if I had expected to find him swinging from a chandelier, or would he re-molecularize upon the witness stand like an alien from Star Trek. Mr. Rueben responded to the question regarding witnesses.

"No witnesses, Your Honor."

It was almost over. It was now time for summations. I was brief and to the point.

"What we have here is a signed, written contract. City Boys Towing violated the contract in releasing the motorcycle without the authorization of the New York City Sheriff, as Deputy Schatzer has testified. This business of not wanting to pay City Boys is just plain ridiculous. I wanted to pay by credit card. It is unreasonable for a merchant, whose policy it is to accept credit cards, who flagrantly displays the VISA and MasterCard emblems throughout the walls of his establishment, to suddenly decide to demand cash, and in an amount in excess of $400.00.

After Mr. Reuben refused my credit card, I cancelled the settlement agreement that I had with the debtor, and declared very audibly and unmistakably, that the settlement was off. I believe that perhaps this is what the defendant was referring to when he said I was "yelling and screaming like a madman." When I returned to Supreme Court for a new court date, I had learned that City Boys had accepted a cash payment from the debtor, and had released the motorcycle without the authorization of the Sheriff, and in direct violation of their contract. Therefore, based upon all the evidence, the provisions of the contract, and the testimony of Deputy Schatzer, payment is requested in the amount of $3,000.00 plus costs and interest."

I lowered my eyes humbly, partly out of respect for the court, but also to turn away from the wrath of His Honor, which was not directed toward me, but toward my opposition.

It was City Boys' turn. Mr. Reuben argued again that I didn't want to pay him, and also argued that the contract was invalid because it was signed by a secretary, and not by an officer of the company. Nevertheless, she signed as "manager," and besides, who signed was irrelevant because the events themselves led to the obvious conclusion that there was indeed a contract. The judge was unimpressed.

Contrary to normal Small Claims procedure, the judge gave his own summation and announced his decision on the spot, in open court.

"The court recognizes that there is a contract between plaintiff and defendant, that the contract was violated by the defendant, that the plaintiff has suffered financial loss due to the negligence of the defendant in not following the terms and conditions of the contract, that the defendant was in effect acting as agent for the Sheriff and violated their fiduciary responsibility in releasing the asset, the Moto Guzzi motorcycle, without the Sheriff's knowledge, and certainly without their authorization. In the event of non-payment, a merchant always has the right to place a mechanic's lien on property held, a procedure not followed in the case at hand.

The court therefore awards to the plaintiff the sum of $3,000.00, the Small Claims limit, plus costs and interest as applicable."

The judge let down the gavel with a loud knock. The trial was ended.

I sat motionless for several very long seconds, while I tried to digest my complete, absolute, and total victory. Do I thank the judge for his decision? No, probably not. I looked around me. People were moving. It was time to get up, and as I did, I looked over at my opponent. His eyes were transfixed on the judge's bench. He was completely motionless. He gazed with wide open, red, swollen, watery eyes into the great abyss, the nothingness of a failed defense. His face was flushed bright red. He had the look of defeat, shameful and ignominious defeat - the depths of degradation - the horrors of humiliation. City Boys had lost.

"When your enemy falls do not rejoice, and when he stumbles, let your heart not be glad, lest the L-rd see and it will not be pleasing to Him, and He will divert his wrath from him (to you)."

(Ethics of Our Fathers, Chapter IV)

It was like the end of a great Perry Mason trial. The

plaintiff, wronged and cheated, receives his just judgment. It was time for congratulations and celebrations. I searched the back of the courtroom for Deputy Schatzer, but he had already gone. He had a job to do in the pursuit of justice - there were bank accounts to be levied on, vehicles to be seized, businesses to be padlocked, tenants to be evicted, and arrests to be made. And so, the end of the great victory was strangely quiet. But it was a victory! A sweet, total, absolute, and complete victory! A victory pure, clean, and whole. A victory, hard fought, and valiantly won.

LXVIII. The End

Like all deadbeats, City Boys didn't pay either. We had to play the collection game. First, I went to the County Clerk's Office in the Municipal Building in order to find out who the owner of City Boys Towing really was, but I was unsuccessful. Next I wrote to the New York State Department of State in Albany. This time, I received an answer. It was Eliezer Abramovitch. I had him served with an Information Subpoena and Restraining Notice, and of course, it was ignored. Another problem had presented itself - a corporation cannot be put in contempt of court. It has to be an officer of the corporation, preferably an owner, but the judgment was against the corporation, not the owner. I asked the Special Term clerk about putting the owner in contempt, but he wasn't sure. It would be up to the judge.

I asked Greg, my plan attorney. He thought that it could be done. And so, I got The Roadrunner to serve Mr. Abramovitch with an Order to Show Cause for Contempt. I explained to The Roadrunner exactly what had to be done, that it was the owner that had to be served, personally and in-hand. He wanted the easy way out.

"Can't I just leave it with the secretary?"

"No! It must be in-hand! The judge wants in-hand service."

We got the owner of City Boys served with the Order to Show Cause, but I was the only one to show up at the hearing. So, the next step was to have a judge sign a fining order. However, and as usual, there were problems with getting the fining order signed. I was told that they didn't have a judge available to do it.

"The judge is away on Official Business. Come back in two weeks."

It took three trips into the City to get a judge to sign my Fining Order. Eventually, the order was signed with a $250.00 fine imposed upon the defendant, plus an additional $10.00 in court costs. I called City Boys to demand payment of the judgment, plus interest, costs, and now, the fine. I asked to speak directly with the owner, Mr. Abramovitch, but the news was not good. Eli skipped.

"He's not here. He left the country. We don't know when he'll be back. Can I help you?"

"Who are you?"

"I'm Yitzchak Reuben. I'm running the company now. Who are you!?"

"Jonah Cohen. Remember me?"

It was amazing. Yitzchak screws up, loses in court, and now he's running the company! Abramovitch wasn't really important anyway. The judgment was against the corporation.

The important thing now was to locate assets. On one of my many trips into the City, I went spying on City Boys for the purpose of finding seizable assets. Did they own the building? Some motorcycles? And then my eyes fell on City Boys' most prized assets. It was so obvious. Of course! THE TOW TRUCKS!!!

I decided that I would have Deputy Schatzer seize the tow trucks, or maybe just one. First, I'd have to find another towing company. Let's see, who tows tow trucks? I quickly jotted down the license plate numbers of three trucks, and got the title record from the DMV. Yes, they owned them, all three!

Before I could act on the trucks, my information services company got back to me with the results of the bank search. It turned out that City Boys had a business account at the Chase Manhattan Bank with a current balance of $14,000.00. The tow trucks would have been nice, but a little messy. The bank account was clean. A Restraining Notice to the bank froze the account solid. I had City Boys at my mercy. They were momentarily out of business.

Yitzchak called me and I felt sorry for them. I had taken out seven years of pent up frustration and revenge on City Boys, when it should have been on Midnite. They had taken the rap, so to speak, or part of it anyway. I had their bank account frozen, and their towing business halted, but there was no anger, bitterness, or vengeance sought. He was in complete submission, and only wanted to cooperate and get on with the towing business. "Mr. Cohen, what do I have to do to end this?" I itemized the list for him.

"Well, Yitzchak, you have to pay the judgment, costs, interest ... I have the list right here. It comes to $3,000.00 for the judgment, $234.71 in interest, $250.00 for the contempt fine, $10.00 for court costs, $142.90 for City Boys Johnson vs. Towing ..." WHAT?! ... What's this $142.90 for?"

"Oh, somebody else has a judgment against you."

"So, what does that have to do with you?"

"I bought it from them. Johnson vs. City Boys is now mine. It's been assigned to me. ... $37.23 interest on Johnson vs. City Boys, and $30.00 in sheriff fees for a total of $3,704.84"

"Tell me Jonah. Do you do this for a living?"

"Well, no. I try to stay out of the courts. Believe me! I really do try!"

"Ok, I'll need a letter from you stating that the judgments are paid off ..."

"I'll give you two notarized Satisfactions of Judgment on Blumberg forms."

"Would you like to come and pick up the checks? I'll have two certified checks waiting for you - one for each judgment."

"Well, Yitzchak ... you know, it's a long trip into the City. Can you mail it?

"I'd rather not ... I'll have a driver come out to you tomorrow. Where do you live?"

I told him where, but there was a small problem.

"Yitzchak, tomorrow isn't really a good day. It's the day of the Rabbi's son's *bris*, and I may not be here at home when you come."

"I can't do it during the week. Can't we do it tomorrow? Tell me when."

"Ok, tomorrow at 9:00 A.M. Oh, I'll need another $4.44 in interest for the additional day."

"No problem, boss. You got it. Sammy will be over at 9:00 A.M."

The driver pulled into my driveway at exactly 9:00 A.M. and exited the car. I called out to him.

"Sammy? City Boys Towing?"

"Right. Mr. Cohen?"

"Yeah. Let me get the papers for you."

We made the exchange. He gave me the two certified checks, and I gave him the two Satisfactions of Judgment. The $4.44 was paid in cash. I changed a $20.00 bill and gave him a receipt. City Boys was back in the towing business.

There was now one small thing that had to be done. I viewed the emblems on display at the shop. There was an emblem for the Fire Department, the Police Department, two hands shaking ... but there was nothing for the Sheriff's Office. And then I spotted the blindfolded, female image holding the scales of justice. It was perfect. I told the man at the Awards Shoppe to make the plaque up for me, and I mailed it to Deputy Schatzer at the Sheriff's Office. They had done an absolutely superb job on it, too good.

The Deputy called me to thank me, but he said that there might be a problem with it.

"Hey! Did you run out of paper?"

It was a little more than your typical thank you note. It was on a polished block of wood and it must have weighed like a brick.

"Well ... you earned it."

"Look, I had to run that thing by our lawyers, just to make sure that it doesn't go beyond the usual cup of coffee. It's up there right now. They're laughing like hell over it. ... Hey ... gotta go. We'll be in touch, ok. Be good. Take care."

"Thanks for everything, Steve. I enjoyed working with you."

It turned out that there was a problem. It violated a City regulation about the giving of valuable gifts to public officers. And while it was little more than a worthless piece of wood with a thank you note, the Deputy could not be corrupted. The "award" came back with a politely written letter of explanation and apology, but it didn't matter. The plaque was presented, and "served" on the Deputy by the United States Postal Service. Despite the obstacles, the message of appreciation got through. The plaque read:

THIS AWARD IS PRESENTED TO SHERIFF'S DEPUTY STEPHEN SCHATZER FOR COURAGE, DILIGENCE, PROFESSIONALISM, AND OUTSTANDING SERVICE BEYOND THE CALL OF DUTY, RESULTING IN THE SUCCESSFUL SEIZURE OF THE MOTO GUZZI MOTORCYCLE ON JUNE 24, 1997 IN THE CASE OF

COHEN VS. NEVILLE MICHAELS A/K/A MIDNITE

AND FOR HIS TRUTHFUL TESTIMONY AND COOPERATION IN THE RELATED CASE OF

COHEN VS. CITY BOYS TOWING INC.

"JUDGE RIGHTEOUSLY BETWEEN A MAN AND HIS BROTHER." DEUT. 1:16

SPECIAL THANKS & APPRECIATION